Approaches to Ancient Judaism
Volume II

Number 9

Approaches to Ancient Judaism
Volume II

by William Scott Green

Approaches to Ancient Judaism

Volume II

by
William Scott Green

Scholars Press

Distributed by
SCHOLARS PRESS
101 Salem Street
Chico, CA 95926

Approaches to Ancient Judaism
Volume II

by
William Scott Green

Library of Congress Cataloging in Publication Data
(Revised)
    Main entry under title:

    Approaches to ancient Judaism.

    (Brown Judaic studies ; no. 1, 9)
    Vol. 2 has special title: Essays in religion and history.
    Includes bibliographical references and indexes.
    1.   Judaism--History--Post-exilic period, 586 B. C.-
210 A. D.--Addresses, essays, lectures.   2. Rabbinical
literature--History and criticism--Addresses, essays, lectures.
3.   Judaism--History--Post-exilic period, 586 B. C. -210
A. D. --Historiography--Addresses, essays, lectures. I.
Green, William Scott. II.   Series: Brown Judaic
studies ; no. 1 [etc.]
BM173.A66   296'.09'01   76-57656
ISBN 0-89130-130-5 (v.1)
ISBN 0-89130-447-9 (v.2)
ISBN 0-89130-448-7 (v.2) (pbk.)

Printed in the United States of America
        1   2   3   4   5
McNaughton & Gunn
Ann Arbor, Michigan 48106

For Nancy, Gene, and Julia

TABLE OF CONTENTS

PREFACE

My thanks go to my teacher, Jacob Neusner, whose assistance, both scholarly and material, helped to make the appearance of this book possible.

The Jewish Community Federation of Rochester, New York, supported the publication of *Approaches to Ancient Judaism I* and thereby also assisted in the publication of the present work. I am pleased to acknowledge the interest and support of a superior and enlightened community institution, its President, Mr. Merwyn Kroll, and its Executive Director, Mr. Henry Rosenbaum.

Mrs. Claire Sundeen, Dean's Office, College of Arts and Science, University of Rochester, prepared this volume for publication with extraordinary skill and intelligence; I owe her much. Miriam B. Rock, Associate Dean of the College of Arts and Science, and Miss Dana Rittenhouse, Secretary of the College, offered assistance at every step and placed many resources at my disposal. I thank them both. Mr. Paul Flesher, University of Oxford, with his usual dedication, helped in the proofreading and preparation of the indices. He also has my gratitude.

I have tried to maintain uniformity in the transliteration of unvocalized Hebrew and Aramaic terms. The transliteration of vocalized terms, the spelling of proper names, and other matters of style and notation reflect the preferences of the various authors.

Jacob Neusner's paper, "The Use of the Later Rabbinic Evidence for the Study of Paul," in a slightly revised and edited form, is reprinted from "Comparing Judaisms," from *History of Religions*, Vol. 18, No. 2, November 1978, pp. 177-191, by permission of The University of Chicago Press, © 1978 by The University of Chicago.

This book is dedicated to my sister and brother-in-law in celebration of the birth of their daughter, Julia Green Fleming.

W. S. G.

Program of Religious Studies
Center for Special Degree Programs
University of Rochester

ABBREVIATIONS

AGAJU	Arbeiten zur Geschichte des Antiken Judentums und des Urchristentums
AJP	*American Journal of Philology*
ANRW	*Aufstieg und Niedergang der Römischen Welt*
Ant	Josephus, *Antiquities*
ARN	Avot de Rabbi Nathan
ARNA	Avot de Rabbi Nathan, version A
A.Z.	'Avodah Zarah
b.	Babylonian Talmud
BA	*Biblical Archaeologist*
BASOR	*Bulletin of the American Schools of Oriental Research*
Ber.	Berakot
BerR	Genesis (Bereshit) Rabbah
Bert.	Mishnah commentary of Obadiah of Bertinoro, ca. 1450-1516, from reprint of Mishnah, ed. Meoroth (Jerusalem, 1968)
Bes.	Besah
BGU	*Berliner Griechische Urkunden*
BS	M. Schwabe and B. Lifshitz, *Beth She'arim*, vol. 2, *The Greek Inscriptions* (New Brunswick, N.J., 1974)
BS^a	N. Avigad, *Beth She'arim* vol. 3, *The Excavations 1953-1958* (New Brunswick, N.J., 1964)
C. Apion	Josephus, *Contra Apian*
CCL	*Corpus Christianorum. serie Latina*
Chron.	Chronicles
CIJ	J. B. Frey, *Corpus Inscriptionum Judaicarum* (Rome, 1936)
CIL	*Corpus Inscriptionum Latinarum*
Col.	Colossians
Cor.	Corinthians
ConB	Coniectanea biblica
CPJ	V. Tcherikover, A. Fuks, and M. Stern, *Corpus Papyrorum Judaicarum* (Cambridge, Mass., 1964), vol. 3, pp. 138-166
Dig.	*Digesta*
Deut.	Deuteronomy
DevR	Deuteronomy (Devarim) Rabbah

DSSE	Geza Vermes, *The Dead Sea Scrolls in English*[2] (Harmondsworth, 1975)
Ed.	^cEduyyot
EJ	*Encyclopaedia Judaica*
EkhaR	Lamentations (Ekha) Rabbah
Eliezer	Jacob Neusner, *Eliezer ben Hyrcanus: The Tradition and the Man*, I–II (Leiden, 1973)
Eruv.	^cEruvin
EvT	*Evangelishe Theologie*
Ex.	Exodus
Gal.	Galatians
GCS	*Die griechischen christlichen Schriftsteller*, herausgegeben von der Berliner Akademie der Wissenschaften
Gen.	Genesis
HA	*Historia Augusta*
Hab.	Habakkuk
Hag.	Haggai
Ḥag.	Ḥagigah
Harv. Stud. Class. Phil.	*Harvard Studies in Classical Philology*
HE	Eusebius, *Historia Ecclesiastica*
Hor.	Horayot
HTR	*Harvard Theological Review*
Hul.	Ḥullin
IEJ	*Israel Exploration Journal*
JAC	*Jahrbuch für Antike und Christentum*
Jastrow	M. Jastrow, *A Dictionary of the Targumim, the Talmud Babli and Yerushalmi and the Midrashic Literature* (Reprint, New York, 1950)
JBL	*Journal of Biblical Literature*
JE	*Jewish Encyclopaedia*
Jer.	Jeremiah
JQR	*Jewish Quarterly Review*
JRelHist	*Journal of Religious History*
JRH	See above
JRS	*Journal of Roman Studies*
JSJ	*Journal for the Study of Judaism*
K	Georg Beer, *Faksimile-Ausgabe des Mischnakodex Kaufman A50* (Reprint Jerusalem, 1968)
L	W. H. Lowe, *The Mishnah on which the Palestinian Talmud Rests* (Reprint Jerusalem, 1967)

M	*Babylonian Talmud Codex Munich* (95) (Reprint Jerusalem, 1971)
M.	Mishnah
Macc.	Maccabees
Migne, *PG*	Migne, *Patrologiae Cursus, Series Graeca*
Miq.	Miqva'ot
M.S.	Ma^caser Sheni
Novt	*Novum Testamentum*
Orac-Sib.	Oracula Sibyllina
PAAJR	*Proceedings of the American Academy of Jewish Research*
PEQ	*Palestine Exploration Quarterly*
Pes.	Pesaḥim
PesR	Pesiqta Rabbati
Phil.	'Philippians
Purities	Jacob Neusner, *A History of the Mishnaic Law of Purities*, I-XXII (Leiden, 1974-1977)
P-W	A. Pauly, G. Wissowa, and W. Kroll, *Real Encyclopädie d. klassischen Altertumwissenschaft*
QohR	Ecclesiastes (Qohelet) Rabbah
RB	*Revue Biblique*
RelSRev	*Religious Studies Review*
REJ	*Revue des Etudes Juives*
Rm.	Romans
Rom.	See Rm.
RQ	*Revue de Qumran*
RutR	Ruth Rabbah
Sanh.	Sanhedrin
SBLSBS	Society of Biblical Literature Sources for Biblical Study
Shab.	Shabbat
ShemR	Exodus (Shemot) Rabbah
Shev.	Shevi^cit
Sif.Dev.	Sifré Devarim (Deuteronomy)
SJLA	Studies in Judaism in Late Antiquity
SNTSMS	Society for New Testament Studies Monograph Series
Spec. Leg.	Philo, *De Specialibus Legibus*
StUNT	Studien zur Umwelt des Neuen Testaments
Suk.	Sukkah
Ta.	Ta^canit

T.	Tosefta
Tan.	Tanḥuma
Thess.	Thessalonians
TKZ	Saul Lieberman, *Tosefta kifshuṭah: Order Zera^cim*, Parts I, II (New York, 1955)
Toh.	Tohorot
Tos.	See T.
TYY	*Tife'ret Yiśra'el: Yakin.* Israel ben Gedaliah Lipschutz, 1782-1860, from reprint of Mishnah, ed. Meoroth (Jerusalem, 1968)
U	*Mishnah: Sedarim Zeraim, Moed, Nashim. Unknown Edition* (Jerusalem, 1970)
UTB	Uni-Taschenbücher
WUNT	Wissenschaftliche Untersuchungen zum Neuen Testament
y.	Palestinian Talmud
Yalq. Jes.	*Yalqut*, Isaiah
Yalq. *naso'*	*Yalqut*, *naso'*
Yalq. Prov.	*Yalqut*, Proverbs
Yev.	Yevamot
ZNW	*Zeitschrift für die neutestamentliche Wissenschaft*
ZPE	*Zeitschrift für Papyrologie und Epigraphik*

TRANSLITERATION OF HEBREW

א	=	'	מ ם	=	*m*
ב	=	*b*	נ ן	=	*n*
ג	=	*g*	ס	=	*s*
ד	=	*d*	ע	=	*ᶜ*
ה	=	*h*	פ ף	=	*p*
ו	=	*w*	צ ץ	=	*ṣ*
ז	=	*z*	ק	=	*q*
ח	=	*ḥ*	ר	=	*r*
ט	=	*ṭ*	שׁ	=	*š̌*
י	=	*y*	שׂ	=	*ś*
ך כ	=	*k*	ת	=	*t*
ל	=	*l*			

INTRODUCTION
William Scott Green

It is perhaps no exaggeration to suggest that the study of
ancient Judaism has reached a methodological watershed. The
past several years have witnessed the steady passing away of conventional methods of investigation and the dissolution of long-
accepted axioms of explanation and interpretation. Close and
critical scrutiny of the nature of rabbinic documents has under-
mined the epistemological certainty that marks the classic works
of rabbinic or Talmudic history, and fresh approaches to the analysis of religion have made the sharply theological focus of
such writers as Schechter, Moore, and Urbach seem at best incomplete. The expiration of older methods of study, however, has
not led to an impasse. Rather, as the papers collected here suggest, it has catalyzed persistent scholarly efforts to devise
more adequate methods for the critical description, analysis,
explanation, and interpretation of the data of ancient Judaism.
The purpose of *Approaches to Ancient Judaism*, which with this
volume becomes a sub-series of *Brown Judaic Studies*, is to call
attention to important methodological and procedural developments
in the study of ancient Judaism, to provide a forum for the presentation, analysis, and discussion of varied theoretical perspectives, and thereby to help secure a central place within the
field for sustained and serious attention to issues of method and
theory.

That such attention is an urgent desideratum in scholarship
on ancient Judaism is one important implication of Jonathan Z.
Smith's "Fences and Neighbors: Some Contours of Early Judaism,"
with which this volume begins. Observing that the problems confronting students of ancient Judaism are those of theory and
method rather than of data, Smith takes up a problem central to
any intellectual endeavor, but especially acute in the study of
religion: the problem of definition and classification. He observes that most classifications of religion have followed the
model of monothetic classification, which seeks to achieve definition through the "progressive, orderly reduction of characteristics to a single, decisive trait." These efforts, however, have
been marred by apologetics and exhibit staggering and ubiquitous
ineptitude. 'Phenomenological' taxonomies of religion, for example, have transformed the single differentia of monothetic

classification into a kind of metaphysical "essence," held to
contain and reveal the fundamental, definitive characteristic of
a given religion. Such taxonomies invariably cast Christianity
as the "religion of love" and Judaism as the religion of "obedience to the Law," as if these were neutral, objective traits.

To counter such undisciplined and apologetic thinking and
to restrain the tendency toward totalization, integration, and
unification, Smith proposes the application to religion of polythetic classification, a procedure that abandons "the notion of
a perfect, unique, single differentia" and defines a class as
"consisting of a set of properties, each individual member of
the class to possess a 'large (but unspecified) number' of these
properties, with each property to be possessed by a 'large number' of the individuals in the class, but no single property
to be possessed by every member of the class." His essay offers
a propaedeutic to such a classification of ancient Judaism.
Smith's immediate purpose is to begin the process of listing all
the characteristics of the taxon, ancient Judaism. At some future point, these characteristics and those on other comparable
lists can be made part of a "ranked but diverse and motely catalogue of traits," which, "with comparative materials. . .will
have to be grouped according to some quantatative technique of
multidimensional scaling in the service of some theory."

To accomplish his goal, Smith adopts two techniques. The
first consists of the mapping of a single taxic indicator, in
this case circumcision, through a variety of ancient Jewish literary materials to test the extent of its application. For the
second, Smith examines a limited body of materials, funerary inscriptions, in order to map all its taxic indicators. This
shrewd strategy reflects sound psychological insight, for matters
of definition loom large at the times of birth and death. The
results of these surveys, while not probative, are interesting and
suggestive. No normative Jewish understanding of circumcision is
evident in the texts Smith examines, and the funerary inscriptions
yield a cluster of characteristics that center on the synagogue.

Smith's essay serves as an important corrective to conventional methods of analysing and understanding ancient Judaism,
and it also shows how students of religion can adopt and adapt
methods used in other disciplines. Although his results are preliminary and subject to various refinements and problems of interpretation, Smith demonstrates the viability of his approach.

His essay exposes the error of construing ancient Judaism as a monolith, everywhere distinguished by a single, invariant trait, and of depicting ancient Jews as a "community constituted by a systematic set of beliefs." Instead of searching for the "essence" of ancient Judaism, he suggests, "we need to map the variety of Judaisms, each a shifting cluster of characteristics which vary over time."

Wayne Meeks shares Smith's conviction that the characterization of religion in terms of essentials or theological catchwords skews its description and tells little of how it "works," but he supplies an alternative methodological strategy. Meeks lays the foundation for the social description of ancient religion, and takes Pauline Christianity as his test case. The goal of social description is to describe both "the environment of the early Christian groups" and "the world as they perceive it and give form and significance to it through their special language and other meaningful actions." In Meeks's words, "the one is the 'world' that they share with other people who live in the Roman empire; the other, the 'world' that they have 'constructed.'"

In a disciplined and judicious essay, drawing selectively on the insights of social theory and social anthropology, Meeks identifies the topics essential to any social description of religion. He considers in turn the geography of the Pauline mission, the social constituency of the Pauline groups, the form of Pauline congregations, the group's perception of its social boundaries, the exercise of authority and discipline, the major rituals, and, finally, the social functions of major beliefs. The picture he draws is more nuanced and far richer than anything produced by works on Pauline theology, and his essay therefore signals an important conceptual and methodological advance. Meeks points out that the character of sources for Pauline Christianity make social description possible, and it is useful to observe that not all the data about ancient Judaism are equally susceptible to this sort of analysis. Nevertheless, Meeks demonstrates that a 'sociological hermeneutic' can be effectively applied to the materials of an ancient religion, and his essay demonstrates not only that such work can be done, but that it can be done very well indeed.

The exchange between Jacob Neusner and E. P. Sanders takes up several issues raised in the first two essays, and serves to refine and define the parameters of an important current discussion. In his *Paul and Palestinian Judaism: A Comparison of Patterns of Religion*, Sanders sought to make a methodological advance over the comparisons of reduced essences or individual motifs that characterize so much work on ancient Judaism and early Christianity. His goal was to compare an "entire religion, parts and all, with an entire religion, parts and all." His endeavor resulted in the identification of a pattern of "covenantal nomism" in Palestinian Judaism and a pattern of "participationist eschatology" in Pauline Christianity. Neusner's criticism of Sanders's book hardly can be replicated here in detail, but three of its salient points can be listed. First, Neusner agrees in principle that Sanders has asked the right question, but he argues that it has been answered wrongly. Second, he suggests that Sanders has homogenized different forms of Palestinian Judaism, ignoring important distinctive traits. Third, he contends that description must precede comparison and that the religions to be compared must be described in their own terms. His complaint is that Sanders has described rabbinic materials, particularly Mishnah, in terms of a Pauline agenda, ignoring what the texts actually say and bypassing their "generative problematic." The result is an artificial dialogue between Palestinian Judaism and Paul.

In reply, Sanders acknowledges that his treatment of Palestinian Judaism focussed on what he perceived as common elements and overlooked important differentiating characteristics. He argues, however, that the pattern of "covenantal nomism" existed in Palestinian Judaism, and that even if not discussed outright, is presupposed by Mishnah and other ancient Jewish texts. On the basis of a reading of Mishnah-tractate Yoma, Sanders concludes that "the concept of atonement for transgression. . .was alive and well among the rabbis." He argues that atonement for transgression "seems to presuppose the conception of sin as disobedience to law." Further, this presupposes a relationship between God and Israel susceptible to damage "by disobedience," and it is not "unreasonable" to call this relationship "the conception of the covenant," whether the rabbis labelled it as such or not.

At issue here is a fundamental question about the use of literary evidence for the description and analysis of religion. Neusner operates on the not unreasonable assumption that the contents of a text reflect the interests of its authors and compilers,

and that these contents ought to constitute the principal components in any description of religion drawn from that text. He
furthermore insists that Mishnah represents a "system," a coherent
set of ideas, and that this "system" must be described and interpreted in its own terms. For his part, Sanders is less interested in the nuts and bolts of Mishnah than he is in the
"pattern of religion" that allegedly stands behind it. For
Sanders, the religion of Mishnah lies unspoken beneath its surface; for Neusner, it is manifest in Mishnah's own language and
preoccupations.

This is not the place to resolve this important question,
but since the issue in important ways is a matter of strategic
reading of the literature, one observation may be in order. If
two bodies of literature are taken to represent two different
religions that are to be compared, it seems reasonable to require
that the two texts be read in equivalent ways. That is, to focus
on the explicit, discursive themes of one text and the allegedly
subsurface, recondite themes in another is bound to produce an
imbalance, a skewed comparison. Sanders's argument rests heavily on the unstated assumptions he perceives in Mishnah, but
these then are compared to the more articulated concerns of
Paul. It is not clear, then, that he has read the two bodies
of material in the same way, and this may help to account for
some of the objections raised against his ambitious project.

A methodological alternative to Sanders's proposal is provided by Richard Sarason, who demonstrates how the theory of a
document can be extracted from what it does say, from its detailed
and sometimes arcane propositions. Sarason's focus is on the
tithing laws in the Mishnaic Order of Seeds, and to discern the
distinctive theoretical context within which those laws operate,
he adroitly compares the scriptural legacy on tithing with Mishnah's use of that legacy. He argues that "if we wish to analyze
Mishnah as a system of ideas and rules -- as a document with a
particular point of view -- then we must ask not only where Mishnah depends on Scripture and where it does not, but also which
parts of Scripture interest Mishnah and which do not. . . ." That
is, a distinction must be drawn between "Scripture's topics" and
"Mishnah's interests." Following this line of reasoning, Sarason
concisely and convincingly limns the "transactional" theory of
holiness that gives coherence to the discrete tithing laws in the
Order of Seeds. Sarason's contribution to the foregoing discussion

consists in part in his manner of reading his texts. In the present instance he not only has asked the same questions of two texts, he also has asked them to answer those questions in the same way. His essay, in other words, shows the salutary results of an exceedingly disciplined reading.

With the conclusion of Sarason's essay the focus of the papers shifts from religion to history. To the debate about the proper use of rabbinic materials for the writing of history, both my paper and Peter Schäfer's contribute a single methodological observation. In Schäfer's words, "a condition of any historical evaluation of rabbinic texts is the consistent and rigorous application of literary criticism. Historical reality is not revealed by adding together isolated pieces of information from which all contradictions have been painstakingly removed. It is only after careful analysis of the context and all versions of a tradition that the historical value of each individual item of information can be ascertained." My essay attempts to show how the redaction of rabbinic documents can manipulate the saying of an individual rabbi so as to obscure its meaning or to make the lemma's intelligibility wholly dependent on the redactor's context. It suggests that the redacted character of rabbinic documents complicates all forms of rabbinic biography, even the modest attempt to determine the range and foci of a rabbi's interests. Peter Schäfer takes up a more interesting and dramatic historical problem, the role of Aqiba in the Bar Kokhba rebellion. By applying literary critical techniques to the relevant sources, he shows that the information about Aqiba's participation in the rebellion is meagre and cryptic, affected by a host of literary conventions and *topoi*, and of remarkably little historical value. Schäfer's conclusions are supported by Glen Bowersock's essay, which surveys the Roman evidence for the rebellion. Bowersock's meticulous research contradicts the conventional historical accounts of the revolt at virtually every point. His conclusion is arresting: "The imposition of a second legion in Judaea and the province's elevation to consular rank belong to the circumstances of the Trajanic, rather than the Hadrianic revolt. There is no evidence for any tensions in the 120's or underground preparation for war. The foundation of Aelia Capitolina was a natural part of Hadrian's tour of Palestine and not the cause of revolt. . . There is no evidence for the loss of a Roman legion, none for a rebel capture of Jerusalem, and none for a Roman

temple on the site of the Jewish temple." One could hardly ask
for a better reason to be cautious about reading rabbinic documents as historical records.

While Peter Schäfer demonstrates the importance of literary
criticism as a tool of historical research on rabbinic sources,
Lawrence Schiffman suggests that philology can play a similar
role in the study of ancient Judaism. He argues that "literary
and philological characteristics may. . . serve as a clue to
the affinity of ideologies among the authors of various texts,"
and he applies this insight, with great effect, to an examination
of the Temple Scroll. On the basis of a careful review of its
philological and literary features, Schiffman concludes, against
the view of Yigael Yadin, that the Temple Scroll "does not correspond to what we would have expected from a Qumran sectarian
text composed in the Hasmonean period. Neither its linguistic
topography nor its literary structure justify Yadin's assumption
that this scroll represents a text composed by the so-called
Dead Sea sect." Observing linguistic affinities between the
Temple Scroll and some rabbinic texts, Schiffman speculates that
it might have been "composed by a group that was ideologically
aligned between Qumran sectarianism and the Pharisaic tradition,
tending towards Pharisaism." Schiffman acknowledges that definitive conclusions about the origin of the Temple Scroll depend
on a substantive analysis as well, but his essay nevertheless
demonstrates the importance and potential of philological criticism to the historical enterprise.

The Temple Scroll also figures prominently in Hermann
Lichtenberger's survey of the theology of atonement at Qumran.
His goal is to chart and explain theological diversity and development within the Dead Sea community, as it is reflected in
the documents found in the sect's library. In the Manual of
Discipline, for instance, atonement through sacrifice is rejected,
and "purity, sanctification, and atonement depend on the fulfillment of God's will through the perfect life. The temple, represented by the community itself, is founded on the holy spirit,
which enables man to fulfill God's will." In addition, atonement
is achieved through hymns of praise, a surrogate for animal sacrifice, and construed as service with the angels. In the Temple
Scroll, by contrast, "the community is not the temple," and
atonement is effected by real sacrifice offered at a real temple.
Lichtenberger suggests, however, that the Temple Scroll depicts

an idealized temple, and that it also contains the belief, present in other Qumran documents as well, of an eschatological temple to be built by God at the end of time. In his view, these different versions of temple and atonement constitute theological strategies for dealing with the incongruity of an existing but illegitimate locus of atonement and the non-existence of the precisely described legitimate place of atonement. By living the "perfect life" and offering sacrificial hymns of praise, the members of the Qumran community simultaneously claimed to represent the discredited Jerusalem temple and the idealized institution depicted in the Temple Scroll. By construing their worship as service with the angels, they also anticiapted, and to some degree participated in, the life promised for the eschaton.

Jacob Neusner's concluding essay, which celebrates the twentieth anniversary of Geza Vermes' *Scripture and Tradition in Judaism*, explores the various relationships between Scripture and Mishnah. Neusner traces the strengths and weaknesses of traditions-history as a vehicle for understanding the relationship between Scripture and tradition, and sharply distinguishes its mode of inquiry from his own. The question about Scripture and tradition is properly phrased, in his view, only when "tradition" is treated as an entity roughly comparable to Scripture. Mishnah satisfies this condition, permitting the question about Mishnah and Scripture to be correctly framed. But when Mishnah is deemed to be "the Tradition," its relationships to Scripture appear ambiguous. On the one hand, Mishnah's language and formal traits make it seem autonomous of Scripture, a source of revelation in its own right. On the other hand, the rabbinic tradition that follows Mishnah treats it as contingent, as dependent on Scripture. The answer to the question about the relationship of Scripture and Mishnah can only come from a reversal of the question; in Neusner's words, "What statement does Mishnah make about Scripture?" The answer comes in three parts. Some tractates of Mishnah simply repeat Scripture, others take up Scriptural facts but work them out in an utterly fresh way. Still others "either take up problems in no way suggested by Scripture, or begin from facts at best merely relevant to facts of Scripture." Neusner concludes that "the philosophers of the Mishnah concede to Scripture the highest authority. At the same time what they will choose to hear among the authoritative statements of Scripture, will, in the end, form a statement of its own. To state matters

simply: all of Scripture is authoritative. But only some of
Scripture is deemed relevant." Mishnah, then, can be construed
as an exegesis of Scripture only after the fact, because the
framers of Mishnah come to Scripture with an established agenda
of concerns, and those concerns define for them how Scripture
is to be read, what it is to mean, and the degree to which its
words will be authoritative. Neusner's essay not only helps
to clarify the relationship of Mishnah to Scripture, it also
provokes serious reflection about two categories fundamental to
the study of religion.

The essays collected in this volume give palpable evidence
of the importance of theory and method in the study of ancient
Judaism. No claim is made that these papers provide any answers.
But if they have served to generate interesting questions, this
book will have served its purpose.

FENCES AND NEIGHBORS:

SOME CONTOURS OF EARLY JUDAISM

Jonathan Z. Smith

University of Chicago

I

In February, 1948, that remarkable French poet, Francis
Ponge, noted in his journal, later to be published under the
title, *Méthodes*:

> Analogies are interesting, but less so than
> differences. What is important is to grasp, through
> analogies, the differential quality. When I say that
> the inside of a walnut is similar to a praline, it is
> interesting. But even more interesting is their
> difference. To make one feel analogies, that is
> something. To name the differential quality of the
> walnut, that is purpose, that is progress.[1]

My task in this essay is to inquire whether we have made some
"progress" in "naming the differential quality" of what has been
termed early Judaism. To do so will require us to take what may
appear to be a long detour. This is necessary because our problem is not one of data. We have more than enough materials, more
indeed than are available for most religious traditions, gathered,
for the most part, in convenient and accessible collections. Our
central problems are those of theory and method.

The quotation from Ponge with which I began not only serves
as the motto for our endeavor, it signals the difficulties as
well. In what respects is it interesting to compare and contrast
the walnut and the praline? Shall we compare with respect to
color, texture, taste? Is the difference best stated as being
between a walnut and a pecan (from which latter nut most pralines
are fashioned, although both the walnut and the pecan are members
of the same botanical family, the *Juglandaceae*, a complex group
which contains three sub-families, eight genera and fifty-seven
species), or is the difference best stated as being between a
natural, raw nut and a manufactured, cooked product? Is the
difference a factor of the oils in each nut, our chemistry of
taste, or a factor of the large quantities of sugar added to the
praline during its manufacture? Is the taxon, praline, well
determined? Individual specimens of pralines differ widely from
one another as arduous research in New Orleans' French Quarter has
established. The proportion of brown to white sugar, those
manufacturers who do or do not use vinegar and/or lemon juice,

those who do or do not use quantities of cream and/or butter,
represent a far wider range of possibilities and variations than
exists within the taxon, walnut. One may need to confront the
issue of internal comparison between pralines before moving on to
external comparisons with walnuts.

The problems raised above are only surface, obvious issues.
There are much deeper and more difficult questions which strike
at the heart of the enterprise.

There are several types of ordering systems which seek to
define categories, thereby yielding entities which may be compared.

The most frequent, and the least useful, is some artificial,
unscientific system of classification which makes no pretense of
revealing anything about its subject matter, whose major justification is the relative ease with which information may be located
and recalled. The most familiar example of this sort of classification is that employed in our libraries, whether they use the
Dewey Decimal or the Library of Congress systems, or simply the
sequential assignment of accession numbers or arbitrary computer
codes.[2] Another would be the equally artificial, alphabetical
arrangement employed by directories, encyclopaedia and lexica.
Indeed, in the new, fifteenth edition of *The Encyclopaedia Britannica*, in the "Macropaedia," the article, "Judaism, History of"
comes immediately before the article, "Juglandales," the botanical
order to which both the walnut and the pecan belong. Yet there is
no implication (to the ordinary reader) that these two topics are
related or comparable in any other sense than that the combination
of their initial consonants and vowels 'happen' to be sequential.

The botanical article in the *Britannica* depends upon the most
widely used scientific system of ordering, the taxonomy.[3] The
central feature of a taxonomy, when properly constructed, is hier-
archy. Taxa at the same level differ from and exclude one another;
taxa at a higher level include the lower categories as being similar. The lowest division, the *infima species*, is thus the most
different; the highest, the *summum genus*, the most inclusive.
Biological taxonomies enumerate a graded series of hierarchical
categories--e.g., kingdom, phylum, class, order, family, genus,
species--which are related and distinguished on the basis of mor-
phological and/or genetic features. Thus, on the species level,
the white walnut (*J. cinerea*) and the black walnut (*J. nigra*)
differ from each other, but are included in the same genus. The
walnuts differ from the willows and birches at the level of genus,
but are included in the same class (*Dicotyledonae*). The walnuts
and the algae differ at every level, save for their inclusion in

the plant kingdom.

In theory as well as in practice, taxonomies are determined by monothetic procedures and presuppositions, the quest for a single item of discrimination, the *sine qua non*, the 'that without which' a taxon would not be itself but some other. Formally and strategically, a taxonomy closely resembles the "logical tree" of Porphyry which focusses on features and attributes and asks a set of binary questions (yes/no? present/absent?) with respect to a graded series of singular features. For example:

Does it have chlorophyll or not?

If it has chlorophyll, does it have true flowers or not?

If it has true flowers, are its ovules in a closed ovary or not?

If its ovules are in a closed ovary, does its embryo have two cotyledons or not?

If it has two cotyledons, are the flowers bisexual or not?

If the flowers are bisexual, are they in spike form or not?

If the flowers are in spike form, are there secondary, sterile catkins in addition to the fertile flowers or not?

If there are secondary, sterile catkins, do the fertile flowers have a corolla or not?

If not, is there a four toothed calyx or not?

At this point we have reached the unique walnut family and have excluded all other possibilities. We now can ask the question of ultimate, least discrimination.

If there is a four toothed calyx, does it have petals or not? If it has petals, it *must* be a walnut; if it lacks petals, it *must* be a pecan.[4]

In giving this example, I have remained faithful to the pre-occupations of Linnaeus in that the binary questions were posed exclusively in terms of the plant's reproductive organs. A quite different, but no less definitive agenda can and has been generated by ordering the questions according to their differentia such as wood anatomy or the morphology of pollen grains.[5] The intention remains the same: the definition of a walnut by means of the progressive, orderly reduction of its characteristics to a single, decisive trait--in the Linnaean system, the possession of a four toothed calyx with petals. This is a specification of the walnut's absolute uniqueness with respect to a wider, but closely similar, set and lacks ambiguity. The same cannot be said for the more familiar lexical definition such as that given for the walnut in a popular dictionary: "a tree which yields both valuable timber and a distinctively flavored nut."[6] This statement could be applied with equal accuracy to both other related species (e.g. the hickory) and unrelated species (e.g. the chestnut).

The classical system of taxonomy was a monothetic, definitional enterprise which held, simultaneously, that all members of a given taxon invariably shared common features while differing from other, closely adjacent taxa by a single, definitive feature. This system had its roots in classical Greek theories of definition and is for-ever associated with the works of the mid-eighteenth century *savant*, Linnaeus.[7] By the last quarter of the nineteenth century, this system was perturbed by evolutionary theories which seemed to hold forth the possibility of a more "natural" system of classification. Time was factored into the system, and the logical definition of class by the possession of common attributes was replaced by an historical definition of class as descended from a common ancestor. The *logical prior* gave way to the *historical primordium*. While the notion of "common" was maintained, it became something of a mirage as there was neither a theoretical basis nor an empirical warrant for the assumption that any given ancestral trait would persist in any given descendant. Variability, especially as related to geo-graphic populations, has introduced further complications at the levels of species and subspecies. Successive textbooks on taxonomy have wrestled with these dilemmas.[8]

Perhaps the most promising development in recent years has been the return to the suggestion made by Michel Adanson in 1763 in controversy with Linnaeus over the question of the mutability of species.[9] Adanson argued that the members of a given taxon need *not* possess all of the defining characteristics of that taxon and that there was no *a priori* justification for deciding what charac-teristics were most definitive.[10] Although the state of the art was not such that Adanson could have put it this way, he was sug-gesting something like a statistical approach to classification.

This possibility lay dormant until 1959 when it was revived in a theoretical proposal by Morton Beckner and was formulated in a pragmatic and definitive statement in 1963 in Robert Sokol and Peter Sneath's major work, *Principles of Numerical Taxonomy*.[11]

What was proposed was a new, self-consciously *polythetic* mode of classification, which surrendered the notion of perfect, unique, single differentia, which retained the notion of necessary but abandoned the notion of sufficient criteria for admission to a class. In this new mode, a class is defined as consisting of a set of properties, each individual member of the class to possess "a large (but unspecified) number" of these properties, with each

property to be possessed by a "large number" of the individuals in
the class, but no single property to be possessed by every member
of the class. If the class contained a large population, it would
be possible to arrange them according to the properties they possessed in common in such a way that each individual would most
closely resemble its nearest neighbor and least closely its farthest
neighbor. The probability would be high that the individuals at
either extreme would scarcely resemble one another, i.e. they may
have none of the properties of the set in common. There will always
be borderline cases, indeed this is welcomed as a stimulus to
further research.[12]

    To state this more concretely. Imagine a group of six indivi-
duals, each possessing three characteristics of a set, A-H.
Individual 1 has characteristics A, B, C; Individual 2 has B, C, D;
Individual 3 has A, B, D; Individual 4 has A, C, D; and Individuals
5 and 6 have characteristics F, G, H in common. Individuals 1-4
would be formed into a polythetic group sharing a number of characteristics, although no one characteristic is definitive. Individuals 5-6 form a classic, monothetic class, with the only question
remaining the determination, by comparison, as to whether F or G or
H is definitive.[13]

    Much depends on the precision with which one can define what
was left deliberately vague in the above presentation. What constitutes a "large (but unspecified) number of properties? What
constitutes a "large number" of individuals? There are complex
procedural questions of scaling, weighting and measurements of
degrees of affinity which may be addressed by a variety of statistical devices. There are also pragmatic difficulties in cluster-
type analyses of large populations for a large number of characteristics, but statistical methods and computer technology have
largely overcome these difficulties.[14] One can point to an impressive body of scholarship within and without the biological sciences
in which polythetic classification has been successfully employed.[15]
Within our own fields of study, we surely do not lack data. For
example, the computer generated *Cross-Cultural Summary*, edited by
R. B. Textor in 1967, heavily weighted toward religious data,
yields more than twenty-thousand statistically significant correlations from a sample of some sixty societies.[16]

II

All of the issues raised about biological classification return with particular force when we confront the various levels of analysis implied in the subject of this paper: the attempt to distinguish religion from other taxa of human experience and expression; the attempt to distinguish various taxa within religion; the attempt to distinguish various taxa within a particular religion. Each of these issues must be faced before we can begin to address the task of "naming the differential quality" of early Judaism.[17]

Analysis at the first level, that of the distinction of religion, most usually has been attempted in a monothetic fashion. Scholars have engaged in the quest for the unique and definitive *sine qua non*, the 'that without which' religion would not be religion but rather an instance of something else. The results of this enterprise are unconvincing, are poorly formulated, and violate the ordinary canons of definition,[18] but this disturbs me less than that the presuppositions of the monothetic enterprise have been deliberately tampered with for dubious, apologetic reasons.

Central to the monothetic procedure is the goal of achieving the unique and definitive, and the necessary corollary is that this uniqueness be both ordinary and reciprocal. In terms of the previous botanical example: the walnut is unique in possessing bisexual flowers in spiked form with four toothed calyxes, lacking corolla, and with petals; the walnut is unique with respect to the closely adjacent pecan as well as to every other species; the pecan is unique with respect to the closely related walnut as well as to every other species. None of this is admitted by scholars of religion. Some special uniqueness is claimed for religion and particular religious traditions; this uniqueness is unilateral and non-reciprocal. Thus, if religion is unique with respect to other cultural activities, it is rarely conceded that these activities are unique with respect to religion; if Israel is unique with respect to Canaan, then Canaan is unique with respect to Israel. Uniqueness is an ordinary presupposition of the definition-taxonomic procedure; it is not some odd point of pride. To the degree that it has become the latter in circles of religious scholarship, it must be set aside. As William James reminds us:

> The first thing the intellect does with an object
> is to class it along with something else. But any
> object that is infinitely important to us and
> awakens our devotion feels to us also as if it
> must be *sui generis* and unique. Probably a crab
> would be filled with a sense of personal outrage
> if it could hear us class it without ado or apo-
> logy as a crustacean, and thus dispose of it.

'I am no such thing,' it would say, 'I am *myself*, *myself* alone'.[19]

In the classification of religions a dichotomous agenda of division, bearing some resemblance to the logical tree which lies behind the monothetic taxonomic endeavor, is most frequently employed.[20] However, unlike the biological there usually are normative implications or the assignment of positive or negative valences, with the perceived positive pole identified with US and the negative with THEM. Thus the most frequent divisions, each of which may be further subdivided:

true/false	cosmic/historical
natural/revealed	free/dependent
with books/without books	healthy/sick
natural/ethical	affirming/denying
collective/individual	magical/religious
ethnic/universal	habitual/spontaneous

Perhaps the most common division could be properly formulated in the following way:

Are there gods or not?

It gods, are they personal or not?

If personal, are they in nature or above nature?

If above nature, is there one or more than one?

and so on through the history of the study of religion in the past two centuries. But such divisions beg the question of definition at every step, an irony considering that the function of such divisions is to achieve the definitive.

An allegedly alternative system, represented by long catalogues in so-called 'phenomenological' works by scholars such as G. van der Leeuw and G. Mensching, supplies a taxonomy for religious traditions by identifying a single trait which, in a dazzling semantic shift, is held to reveal the "essence," the "*Geist*" of a particular tradition. In fact, these traits are arbitrary, ill-defined, and determined by extrinsic apologetics. For example, combining van der Leeuw and Mensching's lists:[21]

Primitive: religion(s) of "magical coherence."

China: religion of "restlessness and flight" or
    religion of "cosmic harmony."

Shinto: religion of the "sacral state and family community."

Greece: religion of "stress [or impulse] and form."

Rome: religion of "expediency."

Teutonic: religion of the "numinous tribe."

India: religion(s) of "infinity and asceticism" or
    of "peaceful unity and unifying peace."

Ancient Near East: religion(s) of "astral relationships."
Egypt: religion of "immortalized life."
Israel: religion of "will and obedience."
Zoroastrianism: religion of "[ethical] struggle."
Buddhism: religion of "nothingness and compassion" or of
           "the annulment of suffering."
Islam: religion of "majesty and humility" or religion of
           "perfect submission."
Christianity: religion of "love."

None of the above can claim to be correctly drawn, mutually exclusive principles of division. They are merely slogans. But already,
at this crude, jingoistic level, we encounter those differentia
which will be claimed with greater or lesser sophistication to be
definitive of the taxon, Judaism. It is a "true," "revealed" religion, "with books," "ethical," "collective," "ethnic," "historical,"
"free," "healthy," "affirming" with its decisive and unique differentia, "obedience to the Law" as opposed to "love." Or, to give
the pedigree of this taxonomy, "law or gospel."

I find no value in our discipline continuing the effort of
making such lists of improperly constructed dichotomous, definitional divisions. I do believe it would be possible, in theory, to
construct a proper taxonomy at the cost of abandoning the inappro-
priate notion of essence. I believe as well that it would be possible, in theory, to construct a satisfying evolutionary classification of religions. This would have to eschew the impossible
model of a common ancestor, replacing it, as has already been done
in the biological sciences, with a model of multilinear evolution
that takes advantage of post-Darwinian populational theory. But I
know of no such attempt. What have been proposed as evolutionary
classifications, from Tylor and Frazer to Parsons and Bellah, are
the ordering by some quasi-chronological scheme of the previously
cited "essential" or dichotomous characteristics, the ranking of
slogans. This closely conforms to the older methods of evolutionary classification and comparison that I elsewhere have argued represent an ahistorical, self-contradictory construct that must be
overcome if progress is to be made.[22]

Finally, I know of no examples of polythetic classifications
of religions or religious phenomena.[23] It is in this area that I
believe the most fruitful work will be done.

We have now reached the end of our long way around. It seemed
at the outset to be of some value to discern in a most general
fashion how those concerned professionally with classification
approach our enterprise. For if we cannot determine how to

classify a walnut and distinguish it from a pecan, *qal ve homer*
Judaism! I think there is much about method that we can learn from
our colleagues in the biological sciences, more, indeed, than we
can appropriate from our more usual model for the sciences, experi-
mental physics.[24] I find neither aid nor comfort in previous practice within religious studies.

It would be premature to propose in this paper a proper, polythetic classification of Judaism, but we need to be clear on what
it would entail. We should want to identify a set of characteris-
tics--our colleagues in the biological sciences use from fifty to
one hundred, the possession of any one of which is sufficient for
admission to the taxon--and begin to trace the configurations that
emerge. There is no necessity, in advance, to integrate the list,
and there is an imperative against attempting to reduce it monothe-
tically. Because the notion of strict division has been abandoned,
and with it the notion of the unique and sufficient cause, it will
not matter if many of the characteristics are found to be equally
characteristic of other religious taxa. If we could generate such
a list, a Philo might possess a majority of such characteristics;
his nephew, Tiberius Julius Alexander, might possess only one;
Philo's brother might have as many characteristics as Philo, but a
significant proportion of them might be different from Philo's.

Classification is but a stage in natural history; it is not
yet science. *Mutatus mutandio* in religious studies. After the
characteristics have been determined and the clusters scaled, we
shall still have the problems of explanation. But these must be
reserved for another essay.

III

As a most preliminary beginning, I propose in this paper two
operations that might serve to free us from our usual preoccupations with political and literary history and the temptation to
reduce our phenomena to some 'essence'. I understand these to be a
propaedeutic to the later task, after much additional research, of
constructing a polythetic classification of the taxon early Judaism.

The first operation would be to select a single taxic indicator, an item that appears to function as an internal agent of discrimination, and map it through the variety of materials at our
disposal in order to gain some appreciation of the range of its
application. For the purposes of this paper, I have chosen circumcision. The second operation would be to take a limited body of
material and attempt to map out all of its taxonomic indicators.
These would be later compared with other, quite different, bodies

of material. For the purposes of this paper, I have chosen a set
of funerary inscriptions. In neither case is the intention of the
analysis a monothetic one. We are not seeking integration and definition, rather we are attempting to take the first steps toward
a listing of all characteristics. The final results, well beyond
the confines of this paper, will be in the form of a ranked but
diverse and motley catalogue of traits. At some later date, and
with comparative materials, they will have to be grouped according
to some quantitative technique of multidimensional scaling in the
service of some theory.

One of the most important indicators for the taxon, Jew, is
the practice of male circumcision. It plays, in many contexts, the
same sort of definitive role for both the birthright and the converted Jew that the absence of a corolla but the possession of a
four toothed calyx with petals did for the walnut. Spinoza's oft
quoted dictum is representative: "So great is the importance that
I attach to the sign of circumcision...that I am persuaded that it
is sufficient *by itself* to maintain the separate existence of the
[Jewish] nation forever."[25] In the full range of early Jewish
materials, circumcision, as a taxic indicator, is unevenly distributed. Many documents make no mention of the practice, others are
concerned with non-classificatory aspects of circumcision. While
these must be plotted in the workroom, they need not detain us here.

Within the bulk of the Hebrew Scriptures (as in the *Qur'an*,
where it is nowhere mentioned), circumcision is assumed to be characteristic of the Israelite rather than enjoined. There is no in-
junction concerning circumcision in any of the Biblical legal codes
or in Deuteronomy. What early narratives we possess reflect some
concern with the uncircumcised outsider (Gen. 34:13; 1 Sam. 18:20--
in both of these a ploy is involved and circumcision is scarcely
the issue) or with the phenomenon of the uncircumcised Israelite
(Joshua 5:2-9; the murky narrative in Ex. 4:24-26--in each case the
'problem' is 'solved' by circumcision).

It is not until the Priestly tradition, itself an early witness
to early Judaism, that we find most of the mentions of circumcision,
including the central text, Gen. 17:9-14, where circumcision is
established as the definitive characteristic of the Israelitic male.
Understood as a covenant in the flesh, it is required of every male
Israelite and bondsman; the failure to circumcise means being cut
off from the people, excluded from the taxon. This establishes a
dichotomous, definitive division within the horizon of this tradition. Is he male? If male, is he circumcised? The affirmative
answer to both these questions is a necessary, and in some

interpretations, a sufficient reason to classify the individual as
an Israelite or Jew (compare the late addition to P in Ex. 12:43-49).

Within Israelitic tradition, circumcision and the lack of circumcision can serve as general ethnic classifiers. For example, in
early narrative strands, the Philistines are consistently referred
to as "uncircumcised" (Judges, Samuel); $^c rl$ becomes the term for
gentile from its massive use in Ezekiel on. But there is a well
known problem with this taxic indicator. Circumcision was not a
distinctive mark of the Israelite within the wider Near Eastern and
Mediterranean world. Nor, for that matter, is it exclusive from a
broader comparative perspective; circumcision is the most common
form of male initiation in non-literate societies.[26] Herodotus, in
Book Two of his Histories, chapter 104, gives a catalogue of seven
peoples who practice circumcision and offers his usual theory that
each of them, with the possible exception of the Ethiopians, bor-
rowed the custom from the Egyptians.[27] The question of borrowing
and diffusion will be raised within the ancient world, returned to
in the Deist debates, and will become a major plank in Freud's reconstruction of the Egyptian Moses.

While there are few signs of an Israelitic ethnographic
endeavor analogous to Ionian traditions--although Deut. 2:9-3:11
and, from another perspective, Gen. 10 are sufficient to demonstrate
that such traditions did exist--it is inconceivable that this problem would not have been raised in learned circles. Jeremiah 9:25
gives both an ethnographic catalogue and attempts a solution: "I
will punish all those who are circumcised but yet uncircumcised,
Egypt, Judah, Edom, the sons of Ammon, Moab and all who dwell in
the desert." In later centuries, the same polemic, "circumcised
but yet uncircumcised" will be applied by the Samaritans (literally)
and the Christians (figuratively) against the Jews.[28]

In the Greco-Roman period, circumcision, along with Sabbath
observance and abstinence from pork, serves as an equally common
indicator employed by non-Jews in classifying an individual as
Jewish, particularly within the Latin literary tradition. The
Greek tradition, in addition, appears fascinated by the Maccabean
practice of forcible circumcision, particularly of the Idumeneans.
It was thus seen by outsiders to be the *sine qua non* of Judaism, at
times, as in the case of the Idumeneans, regardless of beliefs. If
polemicized against, it is largely because it is perceived to be an
act of bodily mutilation which takes its place in a series from
tattooing and branding to loss of limb and castration--shameful
operations performed on the body, most frequently in the case of
criminals and slaves. The oft-cited interdiction by Hadrian seems

to have had this sense in mind. The law was an extension of the
prohibitions of Sulla, Domitian and Nerva against castration to include circumcision and was not limited to prohibiting the practice
by Jews. A similar notion animates the bitter invective by Paul
in Gal. 5:12 and Phil. 3:2b and is the major charge in the Mandaean
critique of Jewish circumcision.

The strongest, most persistent use of circumcision as a taxic
indicator is in Paul and the deutero-Pauline literature. His self-
description is framed in terms of the two most fundamental halakic
definitions of the Jewish male: circumcision and birth from a
Jewish mother--

> circumcised on the eighth day [by virtue of which
> I am] of the people of Israel/ of the tribe of
> Benjamin, a Hebrew born of Hebrews... (Phil. 3:5).

"Circumcised" is consistently used as a technical term for the Jew;
"uncircumcised," for the gentile.

However, Paul is a boundary-crossing figure. He is one of the
circumcised, preaching the gospel of Christ, "the servant of the
circumcised" (Rm. 15:8) to the uncircumcised. What is at issue is
the attempt to establish a new taxon: "where there cannot be Greek
and Jew, circumcised and uncircumcised, barbarian and Scythian"
(Col. 3:11), "for neither circumcision counts for anything nor
uncircumcision, but a *new creation*"(Gal. 6:15). Taking this last
phrase in a taxonomic sense, the Christian is no longer to be
classified by the old, dichotomous principles of division. In contemporary technical taxonomic language, he is a member of a "third
race" (τρίτον γένος), a term developed in Pythagorean circles to
explain the unique position of Pythagoras and other kings and sages
as neither gods nor men. This description of the Christian is
shouted by Roman opponents (Tertullian, *Scorpiace*, 10) and affirmed
by early Christians, perhaps most concisely in the *Epistle to
Diognetus* where Christianity is described as neither Hellenic nor
Jewish, it is a "new race" (I) which, in order to understand, one
must become a "new man" and listen to a "new story" (II.1). The
fifth chapter, with considerable rhetorical skill, heaps paradox
upon paradox in an ethnography of this "new race." Christianity
is neither this nor that, it is some "third thing."

Paul's theological arguments about circumcision, which have
their own internal logic and situation--that, in the case of
Abraham, it was posterior to faith (Rm. 4:9-12); that spiritual
things are superior to physical things (Col. 3:11-14); that the
Christian is the "true circumcision" as opposed to the Jew
(Phil. 3:3); that the time is short, therefore "every man must

remain in the state in which he was called," the circumcised and
the uncircumcised (1 Cor. 7:18-24)--all seem to me to be secondary
to this fundamental taxonomic premise. The "circumcision party"
(Gal. 2:11) fails to perceive this and seeks to enforce the old
taxonomy rather than recognize a new taxon whose characteristic
principles of division are described by the key words in Paul's
theology, and into which baptism, the new rite of initiation,
called "the circumcision that belongs to Christ," (Col. 2:11b)
provides entry.

In contradistinction to the situation faced by Paul and his
disciples, the events of 175-167 B.C. raised the possibility of a
Jewish 'uncircumcision party' (but see 1 Cor. 7:18)!

One of the few significant mentions of circumcision in that
collection of early Jewish writings unfortunately lumped together
by modern editors under the artificial title, pseudepigrapha, is
the expansion of the Priestly narrative of Genesis 17:9-14 in
Jubilees 15.11-34. In a manner quite characteristic of this work,
the practice is given a cosmic setting. The ordinance to circumcise on the eighth day is "an eternal ordinance [fore] ordained and
written on the heavenly tablets" (vs. 25). The angels of the presence and of the sanctification were created circumcised (vs. 27).
The text concludes with a dark warning that there will be:

> children of Israel...who will not circumcise their
> children according to all this law...they will omit
> this circumcision of their sons and all of them...
> will leave their sons uncircumcised as they are born
> ...they have treated their genitals as gentiles...
> (vss. 33f.).

This event seems to be the same as that referred to in the
Maccabaean literature. In several widely discussed passages, the
Maccabaean tradition portrays what must be understood as two separate, though not unrelated acts. The first is the reference in
1 Macc. 1:15 to the voluntary action by some Jews, who quite clearly
perceived themselves as remaining Jews, perhaps even as being
superior to Jews, in removing the mark of circumcision. For this
group, epispasm was part of a positive political and religious
program in which this taxonomic marker could be abandoned.[29]

The second act is portrayed as being at the initiative of
Antiochus IV. In a decree, he forbade the practice of infant circumcision; the Jews were to leave their sons uncircumcised (1 Macc.
1:48, 60, 2 Macc. 6:10, cf. Josephus, *Ant.* 12.254).

There would appear to be two borderline, anomic conditions:
a group of Jews, who considered themselves to be Jews, who voluntarily reversed circumcision and a group of children of pious Jews

who were forced to leave their children uncircumcised. I am
tempted to conjecture that these two groups were, in fact, the same;
that the 'hellenistic reform party' might voluntarily reverse their
own circumcision if adult and leave their children uncircumcised
when newly born. This is the only sense I can make of the difficult passage in 1 Macc. 2:46 that Mattathias and his friends
"*forcibly* circumcised all the uncircumcised babies they found within the borders of Israel. They drove out the men of arrogance" who
"fled to the gentiles" (vs. 44b). Against whose objections was
force necessary? The "uncircumcised babies" are clearly Jewish.
The opponents in this passage ("sinners," "lawless men," "men of
arrogance") are all Jews. It would appear that by forcible circumcision, the children of the 'reform party' were reclaimed to one
definition of the taxon; the adults were expelled from the taxon,
being forced to flee "to the gentiles" and being barred from re-
entry.[30]

Josephus is far more complex in the range of instances and
understandings of circumcision that he displays. Indeed, he is
worth a separate study.[31] Space will only allow a bald summary
of the six, quite different sorts of statements that he makes.
(1) Jews are circumcised as a part of their "ancestral ways" which
are constitutive of being a Jew (e.g. *Ant*. 1. 192, 214). (2) Jews
remain classified as Jews if they are circumcised, regardless of
their adherence to "ancestral ways" (e.g. *Ant*. 20.200). (3) One
may be considered a Jew, or a "half Jew" if one is forcibly circumcised (*Ant*. 14.403 *et passim*), but no one ought to be forcibly
circumcised (*Vita* 113). (4) A convert to Judaism need not be
circumcised, but may elect to do so (*Ant*. 20. 41, 46). (5) Egyptians and others are circumcised. Circumcision is not uniquely
definitive of the taxon Jew (*Ant*. 1.214; *C. Apion* 2.141). (6) Circumcision can occur for strictly medical reasons (e.g. in the case
of an ulcer of the penis) with neither religious nor ethnic significance (*C. Apion* 2.144).

Josephus states on two occasions that he will treat the reasons
for circumcision more extensively in a later work. Perhaps the
reference is to *Customs and Causes*, which is alluded to throughout
Antiquities and appears never to have been written. If it had, it
probably would closely resemble Philo's treatment of the subject,
in which Josephus' fifth and sixth understandings of circumcision
appear surprisingly dominant.

Writing in Egypt where, sanctioned by Rome, circumcision remained an elaborate, official procedure for male members of Egyptian priestly families well into the second century A.D.,[32] Philo

might be supposed to be the one who would be most concerned with a
taxic understanding of circumcision and a desire to differentiate
Egyptian from Jewish praxis. Not in the least! He seems chiefly
preoccupied with refuting a charge that the practice is foolish.
In answering this polemic, he deliberately disturbs the careful
order of his treatise on Special Laws in order to insert a preface
dealing with circumcision. He offers three arguments of his own.
The first, the most extensive, is an appeal to the Egyptian prece-
dent. They are "a race regarded as preëminent for...its antiquity
and its dedication to philosophy" (*Spec. Leg.* 1.2f.)---a unique
passage in the Philonic corpus in its praise of Egypt in terms usually reserved to Israel. Therefore, if the Egyptians circumcise,
the Jewish practice is legitimated. It cannot, by definition, be
foolish. The second and third arguments are extremely compressed
allegories to the effect that the removal of the foreskin is symbolic of the excision of pleasure or conceit.

What is of more interest is that the bulk of this section is
an anthology of defenses made by his predecessors, "from the ancient
studies of divinely gifted men who made deep researches into the
writings of Moses" (*Spec. Leg.* 1.8). Four reasons are given:
(1) It prevents contracting an ulcerated penis. (2) It promotes
cleanliness; indeed, the Egyptians go further and shave the pubic
hair as well. (4) It increases fertility by enabling the semen to
travel in a straight line. The third argument is of a different
order; it symbolically relates the genitals to the heart and seems
to call up the phrase "circumcised heart" that appears in Scripture
(Deut. 10:16, 30:6; Jer. 4:4; cf. "uncircumcised heart" in
Lev. 26:41 cited in his extensive commentary on Gen. 17 in *Quest.
in Gen.* 3.46-47). Philo rejects none of these reasons, although
each seems dependent upon exegetical traditions that he elsewhere
criticizes. Neither in *Special Laws*, nor in the more extensive
parallel passage in *Questions in Genesis* 3.46-52 is there any taxonomic interpretation. The practice, for Philo, seems to have little
to do with either ethnic or religious identity. It is largely
understood as practiced by intelligent peoples for hygenic reasons.

This concludes our brief survey. While other passages can be
added from other strata of early Jewish literature, they will not
alter its conclusions. The incredibly wide range of uses and understandings of circumcision as a taxic indicator suggests that, even
with respect to this most fundamental division, we cannot sustain
the impossible construct of *a* normative, Jewish understanding. We
must conceive of a variety of early Juadisms, which cluster in
varying configurations.[33]

As the second operation in our investigation, I have adopted
the stratagem of describing systems of Jewish identity as gleaned
from a set of funerary inscriptions. I have chosen this body of
data for several reasons. It is possible to gain a significant
sample from widely scattered locales. There is an excellent body
of scholarship on these remains. Of greater significance to our
mapping enterprise is the fact that tombstones, by their very
nature, are labels. They identify not only the name of the deceased,
but also the way the individual wished himself, or his relatives
wished him, to be remembered. It is the one major collection of
sources we have that is rarely argumentative or proscriptive. For
all their stylized elements, I have more confidence in these texts
and in the concreteness of the communities and personalities that
lie behind them than I do in most of the other literary remains.[34]

For our present experiment, I have chosen three collections:
a group of 584 inscriptions from Rome,[35] 318 inscriptions from Beth
She'arim in Galilee,[36] and 92 inscriptions from Egypt;[37] the
collection totals 944 inscriptions, more than three-quarters of
which are in Greek. In all three cases the vast percentage of
names, the most fundamental form of self-identification, are of
Greek or Latin derivation.

Taking the total collection of Jewish inscriptions and noting
only explicit taxic indicators, the following distribution may
be observed:

> 111 inscriptions identify the deceased by one or
> more of fourteen titles, almost all of these
> relate to synagogue officials.
> 26 name the synagogue of which the deceased was a member.
> 25 call the deceased "pious".
> 23 name the individual as a rabbi (only in Beth She'arim).
> 11 make mention of priestly descent.
> 11 refer to the deity.
> 11 refer to the Law.
> 9 term the deceased a "Hebrew".
> 7 term the deceased a "Jew".
> 1 terms the deceased an "Israelite".
> 1 makes reference to "Judaism".

In addition, a number of unique descriptions may be noted, e.g.
"lover of his people" (*CIJ* 203), "lover of truth" (*CIJ* 481), "one
who plucked the fruits of *sophia*" (*BS* 127).

The iconography found *on* these inscriptions exhibits, as
Goodenough has led us to expect, an extremely limited vocabulary:

111 instances of a menorah.

 41 instances of a lulab.

 30 instances of an ethrog.

 27 instances of a "flask" (only in Rome).

 18 instances of a shofar.

  6 representations of the Ark (only in Rome).

The evidence of Jewish coins leaves little doubt that these various
iconographic figures, especially the menorah, functioned as Jewish
'trademarks', but in contradistinction to other symbols found on
coins (e.g. the palm tree), all these symbols are associated with
the Temple-synagogue cult. If these be added to the preponderance
of textual references to the synagogue in the inscriptions (some
12% of the total collection), the most basic self-definition of
these Jews is in terms of relationship to, membership in, and
service for the synagogue. I know of no other body of early Jewish
evidence that would yield such a configuration.

If one were to use this collection of inscriptions as an
index of characteristics, the two most frequent would be the use of
Greek and identification with the synagogue. But if one were to
separate out the data by provenance, scaling only for these two
characteristics, they would cluster quite differently. All three
areas would score high in the use of Greek: 70% of the inscriptions
from Rome, 60% from Beth She'arim, 97% from Egypt. One could make
further distinctions in the data, by catacomb or family, and get
quite different clusters, e.g. at Beth She'arim catacombs 6, 8, 20
[Semitic] as opposed to 1-4, 7, 11 [Greek]; despite the overwhelming use of Greek, in Rome, Appia and Monteverde appear most Roman-
ized, Nomentana, least. In Rome, some 54% of the inscriptions are
synagogue related, Beth She'arim has few inscriptions that appear
related to the synagogue, Egypt has none. In Beth She'arim, the
title *rabbi* recurs with some frequency; it is absent from the other
two areas. All three collections praise piety. Rome and Beth
She'arim make mention of priestly descent of both males and females.
There are relatively few references to the deity in any of the
collections; both the Law and the self-designation "Jew" occur in
Rome and Beth She'arim. Egypt appears to have neither distinctive
Jewish titles nor institutions.

The most common epithet is "pious" (ὅσιος or *ḥsyd*). It most
frequently occurs as a virtuous attribute of the deceased (*CIJ* 1,
72, 93, 100, 103, 111, 145, 154, 158, 321, 363; *BS* 34, 35, 38, 157,
158, 163, 193), at times in conjunction with, or apparently synony-
mous with, a set of closely related terms such as "righteous"
(δικεών or *ṣdyq*, *CIJ* 78, 110, 118, 150, 193, 201, 321, 363;

BS^a 25, 26), "irreproachable" (ἄμεμπτος, *CIJ* 100, 154, 193) and
perhaps "holy ones" (*hqdwšym*, BS^a 17) and terms suggesting inno-
cence and purity (e.g. *CIJ* 233, *filiae sanctissimae*; 466 *anima
innox* cf. 210 *anima bona*) Four times, unique to Beth She'arim, it
appears as an element in a titular name (Rabbi X, the Pious--*BS* 41,
43, 44, 126). Twice, it appears to be an individual's name (*BS* 157;
CPJ 1536). There is also the collective use in the formula "with
the righteous, his sleep" (*CIJ* 55, 340).

The problem confronting the interpreter is what meaning to
give this designation. There are several excellent studies for
both the Hebrew and Greek words,[38] but none takes our epigraphic
evidence into account. The only brief study with which I am familiar, that by Saul Lieberman in a few pages of *Greek in Jewish
Palestine*, concludes on an almost ironic note: "the epithet
[pious] was readily and easily conferred on a person who more or
less deserved it."[39]

It was, of course, an epigraphic convention throughout the
Greek and Roman world to enumerate the virtues of the deceased,
with piety preëminent among the list. Some laudations were bare
catalogues; others wove the elements into a rich, usually domestic,
narrative description.[40] In light of this, but conscious of the
synagogal self-definition in the majority of the Jewish inscriptions, it is tempting to interpret the epithet as piety in relation to the Law, to Jewish practice and the synagogue. In its
nominative forms, I do not doubt that such a case might be made.
Likewise in the very few instances where the content of the piety
is made explicit, such as the Roman inscription, "pious observer of
the Law" (*CIJ* 72). But other cases scarcely fit such an understanding. For example, of the Roman tombstones which give the
individual's age at the time of death, three occurrences of the
epithet "pious" are on young children's graves. One, a boy, lived
only two years, two months and five days (*CIJ* 1)! What might piety
mean here? In a goodly number of cases, "pious" seems to me to be
readily interchangeable with more 'secular' virtues such as "sweet"
(*CIJ* 1, 84, 96, 119, 126, 141, 155, 169, 222, 225, 267, 273, 457)
or with the uniquely Egyptian epithet, χρηστή, which recurs forty-
four times.[41] It does not seem possible to give further content to
the term on the basis of the available evidence, but the matter deserves further research.

I shall conclude my observations with some brief remarks on
the most explicit taxic indicators, the use of the terms "Hebrew,"
"Jew," and "Israelite." "Hebrew" does not occur in the Egyptian
or Beth She'arim inscriptions. It occurs, as a self-designation,

five times in Rome, in each case for a male (*CIJ* 354, 370, 379, 502, 505) and four times in the title, "Synagogue of the Hebrews" (*CIJ* 291, 317, 510, 535). I would suggest that *CIJ* 370, "Macedonius, the Hebrew, a Caesarean of Palestine" delimits the term. It is not a linguistic designation, but rather an ethno-geographical one. It indicates that one's place of birth was in Syro-Palestine from which the individual emigrated to Rome.[42] As the linguistic understanding appears dominant in the scholarly literature, each occurrence merits re-examination.

The term, "Jew," occurs six times in the Roman epitaphs (*CIJ* 21, 41, 68, 202, 250, 296--possibly 367 as well) and once from Beth She'arim (*BS* 158); four times on women's tombs; three times on prosyltes'. To this list the important Roman inscription of the daughter of Menophilus should be added: "she lived a good life in Judaism" (*CIJ* 537). In none of these cases is there a hint of the older ethno-geographical sense of Judaean; the term is entirely confined to the religious sphere into which one can be born and to which one can convert. There is a unique and puzzling compound formula on one of the Roman inscriptions: "Irene, foster child, proselyte, her father and mother Jewish, an Israelite, lived three years, seven months and one day" (*CIJ* 21). "Jew" in this text would appear to refer to birthright Jews, but what sense the term, "Israelite," has for a proselyte remains uncertain. This is the only occurrence of the designation "Israelite" in the entire corpus; "Israel" occurs several times, but never as a self-designation (e.g. *CIJ* 349, 526 as well as in the formula $šlwm$ $^c l$ $yšr'l$).

The data considered in this survey are skewed to some degree by the nature and conventions of sepulchral inscriptions, by socio-economic factors of who gets buried with whom and in what manner, and by the accidents of discovery and preservation. But we ought not to become preoccupied with this. The same limitations obtain for every other form of evidence for early Judaism.

The picture that has emerged is not neat, and there remain specific problems of interpretation. Nevertheless, it has been possible to rough out a preliminary map, a set of characteristics largely centered on the synagogue which may be used as one cluster toward the eventual polythetic classification of early Judaism. What has animated these reflections and explorations has been the conviction that we need to abandon the notion of 'essence', of a *sine qua non*, of a unique definitive for early Judaism, as well as the socially impossible correlative of a community constituted by a systematic set of beliefs. The cartography appears far messier. We need to map the variety of Judaisms, each a shifting cluster of characteristics which vary over time.

As the anthropologist has begun to abandon a functionalist view of culture as a well-articulated, highly integrated mechanism and has slowly turned to accepting the sort of image set forth by F. E. Williams of culture as a "heap of rubbish," a "tangle," a "hotch-potch,"[43] but partially organized, so we in religious studies must set about a similar dismantling of the old theological and imperialistic impulse toward totalization, unification, and integration. The labor toward achieving the as yet unrealized goal of a polythetic classification of Judaisms, rather than a mono-thetic definition of early Judaism, is but a beginning step toward this end.[44]

NOTES

FENCES AND NEIGHBORS

[1]F. Ponge, *Le Grand Recueil*, vol. 2, *Méthodes* (Paris, 1961), pp. 41f.

[2]For a good introduction to the theoretical issues inherent in library classification, see A. Broadfield, *The Principles of Classification* (London, 1946).

[3]For an initial orientation to taxonomy, see J. Z. Smith, "Animals and Plants in Myths and Legends," *The Encyclopaedia Brittanica*, 15 ed. (Chicago, 1974), *Macropaedia*, vol. 1, esp. pp. 916-918.

[4]This is, of course, a gross oversimplification for purposes of illustration. What I have provided is more of a "key" than a "taxonomy." On this distinction, see G. G. Simpson, *Principles of Animal Taxonomy* (New York, 1961), pp. 13-17. For a properly complex discussion of the taxonomy of the *Juglandales*, see J. F. Levy, *Étude sur les Juglandaceae* (Paris, 1955) in the series, *Mémoires du Muséum National d'Histoire Naturelle*, n.s. B, Botanique, vol. 6.

[5]E.g. C. Heimsch, Jr. and R. H. Wetmore, "The Significance of Wood Anatomy in the Taxonomy of the Juglandaceae," *American Journal of Botany* 26 (1939), 651-660; D. R. Whitehead, "Pollen Morphology in the Juglandaceae," *Journal of the Arnold Arboretum*, 46 (1965), 369-410.

[6]*The American College Dictionary* (New York, 1950), p. 1371, s. v., walnut (2).

[7]I am aware that I am raising a controversial matter in equating logical definition with taxonomic classification. This equivalence has been asserted on a variety of grounds by scholars such as H. Daudin, *De Linné à Jussieu: Méthodes de la classification et idée de série en botanique et an zoologie* (Paris, 1926), esp. pp. 6-19; J. Piaget, "La pensée biologique," in *Introduction à l'epistémologie génétique* (Paris, 1950), vol. 3, pp. 14f.; A. J. Cain, "Logic and Meaning in Linnaeus's System of Taxonomy," *Proceedings of the Linnaean Society, London*, 169 (1958), 144-163 and, most convincingly, E. Cassirer, *The Problem of Knowledge* (New Haven, 1950), pp. 124-128. The most searching refutation that I am familiar with is that by J. L. Larson, *Reason and Experience: The Representation of Natural Order in the Work of Carl von Linné* (Berkeley, 1971), esp. pp. 2f., 22-24 and note 43, 100f., 143-151. For a quite different perspective, see R. Bambrough, "Universals and Family Resemblances," *Proceedings of the Aristotelian Society*, 60 (1961), 207-222.

[8]This observation scarcely requires documentation. A useful, brief overview is given by J. S. L. Gilmour, "The Development of Taxonomic Theory since 1851," *Nature* [London], 168 (1951), 400-402. The most lucid theoretician remains E. Mayr, "The Evolutionary Significance of the Systematic Enterprise," *Uppsala Universitets Årsskrift*, 1958:6, 13-20 and *Animal Species and Evolution* (Cambridge, Mass., 1963).

[9]M. Adanson, "Préface Istorike sur l'état ancien et actual de la Botanike, et une Téorie de cette science," *Familles des Plantes* (Paris, 1763), vol. 1, pp. i-cccxxv, esp. pp. cliv-clxv, cccxiii. On Adanson, in addition to the works cited in note 11, below, see A. J. Cain, "Post-Linnaean Development of Taxonomy," *Proceedings of the Linnaean Society, London,* 170 (1959), 234-244; D. Floodgate, "Some Comments on the Adansonian Taxonomic Method," *International Bulletin of Bacteriological Nomenclature and Taxonomy,* 12 (1962), 171-179.

[10]For the logical point, here, see W. S. Jevons, *The Principles of Science,* 2 ed. (London, 1877), pp. 682-698.

[11]M. Beckner, *The Biological Way of Thought* (New York, 1959), esp. pp. 21-25, 55-80; R. R. Sokol and P. H. A. Sneath, *Principles of Numerical Taxonomy* (San Francisco, 1963), pp. 11-20 *et passim,* cf. Sneath, "The Construction of Taxonomic Groups," in G. C. Ainsworth and Sneath, eds., *Microbial Classification* (Cambridge, 1962), pp. 289-332. See the comments on these works in G. G. Simpson, *Principles of Animal Taxonomy,* pp. 41-57 and E. Mayr, *Principles of Systematic Zoology* (New York, 1969), pp. 82-88.

[12]Beckner, *Biological Way of Thought,* pp. 22-25.

[13]Sokol and Sneath, *Numerical Taxonomy,* p. 15; Simpson, *Principles of Animal Taxonomy,* pp. 42f.

[14]See Sokol and Sneath, *Numerical Taxonomy,* chs. 4-7 and appendix. The best introduction to techniques, with rich bibliography, is N. Jardine and R. Simpson, *Mathematical Taxonomy* (New York, 1971).

[15]In addition to the fulsome bibliography in Sokol and Sneath, two important works are D. Harvey, *Explanation in Geography* (London, 1964), esp. pp. 331-348 and R. Needham, "Polythetic Classification: Convergence and Consequences," *Man,* n.s. 10 (1975), 349-369.

[16]R. B. Textor, *Cross-Cultural Summary* (New Haven, 1967).

[17]I do not intend any false analogy between cultural artifacts and biological species, the latter's capacity for reproduction guarantees the taxonomic enterprise in a manner impossible for the cultural. See C. Lévi-Strauss, *Structural Anthropology* (New York, 1963), vol. 1, pp. 4f.

[18]See H. Penner and E. Yonan, "Is a Science of Religion Possible?," *Journal of Religion,* 51 (1972), 107-133.

[19]W. James, *The Varieties of Religious Experience* (New York, 1929: Modern Library edition), p. 10.

[20]See the useful article and bibliography by C. J. Adams, "Religions, Classification of," in *The Encyclopaedia Britannica,* 15 ed. *Macropaedia,* vol. 15, pp. 628-634.

[21]G. van der Leeuw, *Religion in Essence and Manifestation* (New York, 1963), esp. pp. 591-649; G. Mensching, *Structures and Patterns of Religion* (Delhi, 1976), esp. pp. 4-56.

[22]J. Z. Smith, *Map Is Not Territory: Studies in the History of Religions* (Leiden, 1978), esp. pp. 259-264.

[23]Some grounds for this enterprise have been laid in this country by the work of A. L. Kroeber ranging from his early work (with H. E. Driver), "Quantitative Expressions of Cultural Relationships," *University of California Publications in American Archaeology and Ethnography*, 31 (1932), 211-256 to his more mature essay, "Statistics, Indo-European and Taxonomy," *Language*, 36 (1960), 1-21.

[24]I mean this, in part, because of the necessity of taking the historical into account in biological theory. For a preliminary account, M. Beckner, *The Biological Way of Thought* should be required reading for every humanist concerned with methodological issues. S. Toulmin, *Human Understanding* (Princeton, 1972), vol. 1, pp. 319-356 *et passim*, would be a good illustration of a fruitful application of some of the implications of biological procedures and theories discussed above.

[25]B. Spinoza, *Tractatus Theologico-Politicus*, 3 in C. Gebhard, ed., *Spinoza Opera* (Heidelberg, 1925), vol. 3, p. 56.

[26]See the excellent bibliography in A. M. di Nola, "Circoncisione," *Enciclopedia delle Religioni* (Firenze, 1970), vol. 2, pp. 253f.

[27]With most scholars, I take Herodotus' phrase Σύριοι οἱ ἐν τῇ Παλιστίνῃ to include, but not be limited to, the Israelites.

[28]A variant of this paradigm, circumcised but uncircumcised, is raised in an early debate between the two Houses in *Tosefta* and *Sifra* as to the question of a 'second circumcision' for a child born without a foreskin or a proselyte already circumcised (Tos. *Shab*. 3:18; 15:9; *Sifra Tazri'a* 1:5 [ed. Weiss, 58b]). There is later Greek evidence, in the *Chronikon Paschale*, for this problem being particularly acute in the case of the Samaritans who are, from a Jewish point of view, Israel but not Israel (Migne, *PG*, vol. 92, p. 652b).

I should note that I have deliberately excluded the Taanitic materials from this paper, although not from my larger sample. They represent a quite different horizon of concern for circumcision.

[29]In general, I have accepted V. Tcherikover, *Hellenistic Civilization and the Jews* (Philadelphia, 1959) on the political rationale and E. Bickermann, *Der Gott der Makkabäer* (Berlin, 1937) on the religious.

[30]That the babies were *voluntarily* left uncircumcised by the 'reform party' is the understanding of Jub 15:33f.; that epispasm was a *voluntary* action by the 'reform party' is the understanding of 1 Macc 1:15 (cf. Josephus, *Ant*. 12:241). In their different understanding of Jewish piety and their theory that all alterations in Jewish practice was at the command of the Syrians, 1 Macc 1:48, 60f.; 2 Macc 6:10 (cf. Josephus, *Ant*. 12:254) see the former act as being forcibly imposed on Jewish youths by Syrian officials.

The alternative understanding of 1 Macc 2:46 would be that the force was applied against Syrian officials who sought to prevent circumcision. See already, Josephus, *Ant*. 12:278.

[31]See R. Kraft, "Judaism on the World Scene," in S. Benko and J. J. O'Rourke, *The Catacombs and the Colosseum* (Valley Forge, 1971), pp. 81-98, esp. pp. 84f. Kraft's essay in many respects parallels the overall stance which has animated this essay.

[32]The classic studies of the relevant Greco-Egyptian papyri, remain R. Reitzenstein, *Zwei religionsgeschichtlichen Fragen* (Strassburg, 1901), pp. 1-46 and U. Wilcken, "Die ägyptische Beschneidungsurkunden," *Archiv für Papyrusforschung*, 2 (1903), 4-13. New material continues to be added, see, among others, M. Stracmans, "A propos d'une texte relatif à la circoncision égyptienne," *Annuaire de l'Institut de Philologie d'Histoire Orientale et Slave d'Université de Bruxelles*, 13 (1953), 631-639.

[33]It is striking that most of the scholars from G. F. Moore to E. P. Sanders who have pursued the will-o-the-wisp of "normative Judaism" have failed to cite or consider most of the passages and positions described above.

[34]This is not to make some facile argument that the inscriptions provide a "window" into popular Judaism as opposed to elite. While I reject this dichotomy as a useful tool, I should note that the majority of the inscriptions appear to me to be relentlessly elite.

[35]For Rome, I have used J-B. Frey, *Corpus Inscriptionum Judaicarum* (Rome, 1936) vol. 1, nos. 1-532 [with the important corrections by B. Lifshitz in the reprint of this volume--New York, 1975] as re-edited by H. J. Leon, *The Jews of Ancient Rome* (Philadelphia, 1960), pp. 263-346. Designated in text as *CIJ*.

[36]For Beth She'arim, I have used M. Schwabe and B. Lifshitz, *Beth She'arim*, vol. 2, *The Greek Inscriptions* (New Brunswick, N. J., 1974) designated as *BS* and the important section on the Hebrew and Aramaic inscriptions from catacombs 12-14 and 20 in N. Avigad, *Beth She'arim*, vol. 3, *The Excavations 1953-1958* New Brunswick, N. J., 1976), pp. 230-258 designated as *BS*[a].

[37]For Egypt, I have used Frey, *Corpus* (Rome, 1952), vol. 2, nos. 1424-1539 as re-edited by D. M. Lewis in V. Tcherikover, A. Fuks and M. Stern, *Corpus Papyrorum Judaicarum* (Cambridge, Mass., 1964), vol. 3, pp. 138-166. Designated in text as *CPJ*.

[38]See F. Hauck, "Hosios, Hosiōs," *Theological Dictionary of the New Testament* (Grand Rapids, 1964-), vol. 5, pp. 489-492, who gives the basic bibliography and conclusions.

[39]S. Lieberman, *Greek in Jewish Palestine* (New York, 1942), pp. 69-78, esp. p. 71. L. H. Feldman, "Jewish 'Sympathizers' in Classical Literature and Inscriptions,'" *Transactions of the American Philological Association*, 81 (1950), 200-208, esp. 204f. while not discussing epithets which use ὅσιος develops the puzzling notion of people who were "simply and literally 'pious' Jews in the general and not the technical sense." I confess to having no notion of the two senses of pious to which he alludes.

[40]There is no necessity for a full bibliography. For a brief overview, see R. Lattimore, *Themes in Greek and Latin Epitaphs* (Urbana, 1962), pp. 266-300, esp. pp. 290-299.

[41]*CPJ* 1452, 1453, 1454, 1456, 1458, 1460, 1466, 1468, 1469, 1470, 1471, 1473, 1474, 1475, 1476, 1480, 1481, 1482, 1483, 1484, 1485, 1486, 1487, [1491], 1492, 1494, 1495, 1496, 1497, 1498, 1499, 1500, 1501, 1502, 1503, 1504, 1514, 1419, 1521, 1523, 1525, 1526, 1527, 1530.

[42]This is to support Frey's contention (*Corpus*, p. lxxvi) that the Synagogue of the Hebrews belonged, at least in origin, to a community which came from Judea in contradistinction to the "Vernacular" Synagogue which he understands to have been formed by "indigenous" Jews, born in Rome. A. Momigliano, "I nomi delle prime 'sinagoghe' romane e la condizione giuridica della communità in Roma sotto Augusto," *Rassegna Mensile di Israël*, 6 (1931), 283-292, esp. 290f. forcefully argues the opposite, linguistic understanding.

[43]F. E. Williams, *"The Vailala Madness" and Other Essays* (Honolulu, 1977), pp. 404f.

[44]This paper was first delivered as a Centennial Lecture of the Society of Biblical Literature at its 1978 Annual Meeting. I have retained the necessary brevity and oral style, only adding a minimum of references.

TOWARD A SOCIAL DESCRIPTION
OF PAULINE CHRISTIANITY

Wayne A. Meeks

Yale University

The topic announced above may seem out of place in the company of essays about problems in Jewish history,[1] but two considerations may justify its presence. The first is so obvious that it is astonishing how seldom it is taken seriously: of all the sects of Judaism in the first century, Christianity is the best documented. Only from the group at Qumran and from the sophisticated Alexandrian community do we have a comparable range of datable and localizable primary sources. Second, this essay suggests an approach (to speak of "a method" would be premature) that, if it succeeds in illuminating some aspects of early Christianity, may also be serviceable in the study of other kinds of Judaism and other Greco-Roman cults.

The comparative study of the varieties of early Christianity with the varieties of early Judaism has made significant progress in our generation. Yet such study is still troubled by the fundamental question, What things ought to be compared with what? The problem confronts the reader of most commentaries on books of the New Testament, in which a phrase will often be set alongside several similar phrases drawn from various rabbinic documents, but little help is provided for understanding the context or the function of the phrase in each case. Or, at the opposite extreme of scale, we are invited to compare the "legalism" of the rabbis with the "grace" taught by Paul, or the "romanticism" of the latter with the "realism" of the former. It is against such distortions that E. P. Sanders has argued so forcefully for the "holistic comparison" of "patterns of religion."[2] Yet his own book, monumental as it is, shows how powerful are the habits of our religious and scholarly traditions. For Sanders' definition of "pattern of religion" turns out instead to be a pattern of theology, an *ordo salutis* that can be reduced--despite Sanders' own strictures in the introduction of his book--to its essentials: "covenantal nomism" on the one hand, "participationist eschatology" on the other. These may be useful catchwords to summarize some recurrent patterns of language, but they are not apt descriptions of "the way the religion works."[3]

It is at this point that the historian of Christianity or of Judaism may learn something from his colleagues in the social

sciences, for when they look at religions, it is precisely "the way
the religion works" that interests them. At the same time, we are
also learning anew how much we need to get back on speaking terms
with the classicists and especially the social historians of antiquity, in order to understand better the broad social context within which the minority groups that specially interest us lived
their lives.[4] The theoretical perspectives of sociologists and
anthropologists can help the historian to form questions he might
otherwise not have thought to ask.[5] Yet because we have to be
satisfied with kinds of evidence very different from those available to a social scientist investigating contemporary societies,
there are fewer checks on our constructions. We will therefore do
well to be wary of theory on too grand a scale. Something like
what Geertz calls "thick description," guided by theory that hovers
very close above the data, should be our model,[6] and the empiricist
habits of the social historians can be of a great help in keeping
our eyes on the evidence. It is convenient to use John Gager's
phrase, "the social world of early Christianity,"[7] to sum up both
sides of the task, for this phrase has a double meaning. It refers
to the environment of the early Christian groups and also to the
world as they perceive it and give form and significance to it
through their special language and other meaningful actions. The
one is the "world" that they share with other people who live in
the Roman empire; the other, the "world" that they have
"constructed."

Of all the identifiable varieties of early Christianity, the
circle of Paul is the best documented. We have at least seven
letters indubitably by the principal figure (which in their received form may contain fragments of yet other letters). These are
the earliest extant Christian writings--and the earliest writings
by anyone calling himself a Pharisee. Two characteristics of the
letters make them particularly useful for sociological inquiry:
(1) each is evoked by some specific issue in the life of one of the
local churches or in the public activity of Paul; (2) they
frequently quote traditional material, which provides glimpses of
rituals, rules, paraenesis, and formulated beliefs common to the
Pauline communities. In addition, the Acts of the Apostles contains an extended description of the Pauline mission, written within a few decades of Paul's death by someone who was apparently not
an immediate member of the "Pauline school." From both the letters
and Acts it is evident that Pauline Christianity was not the work
of a single individual, but of a fairly extended group of associates. Finally, there are six letters in the canon which purport to

be by Paul but whose authorship is disputed by modern scholars.
At least some of these are best understood as products of Paul's
disciples and therefore evidence that the Pauline association continued as a self-conscious movement for some time after the
apostle's death.

What follows is a programmatic but quite tentative outline of
what might constitute a social description of Pauline Christianity,
a broad map of the "social world" of Paul and the congregations
associated with him. Space permits only a sketch, not argument or
presentation of the data.[8]

1. *The Geography of the Pauline Mission*

From the middle of the nineteenth century until the middle of
the twentieth, most historians of early Christianity sought the
key to its evolution in its transplanting out of the "Palestinian
Jewish" environment into a "Hellenistic" one. Paul was regarded as
a pivotal figure in that transition, but his precise role was de-
bated. Now, however, the simplistic geocultural division presupposed by that view has been generally abandoned. We recognize that
Palestine was as much a part of the Hellenistic--and Roman--world
as were the other Eastern provinces. The major transition was
rather from the village culture inhabited by Jesus and his disciples
to the culture of cities.

That transition crossed the most fundamental division in the
society of the Roman empire: between rural people and city
dwellers.[9] Their worlds were different: the peasant's and the
villager's infinitely narrower, harsher, poorer, less hopeful.
Between the two suspicion and hostility reigned. They did not
speak the same language. The fact that virtually all extant Christian literature of the first two centuries was composed in Greek is
itself eloquent testimony how quickly Christianity became an urban
movement.

Consequently, we must locate the Pauline Christians within the
world of the provincial city. An inquiry into their social context
must have constantly in view as much as we can know of urban
society. Furthermore, this elementary fact should have an important consequence for the question, With what kinds of Judaism is it
most fruitful to compare Paulinism? As interesting and important
as comparisons with Palestinian and rabbinic Judaism may be for
apologetic or for biographical questions, for the strictly historical questions the most obvious and most neglected area is the study
of the Diaspora communities' adaptation to their urban environment.
If we look at the empire as a whole, it is clear that the dominant
forms of both Christianity and Judaism were urban movements. Even

such an endlessly overanalyzed issue as the controversy of "law versus gospel" in Galatians might receive fresh light if we asked for once about the functions of circumcision, festivals, and purity laws in the dialectic of identity and adaptation of Jewish communities in Greek cities. Further, the particular struggles and forms of adaptation in which Pauline Christians engaged need to be seen as one segment of the social history of interaction between Jewish and Christian communities from the beginning until the time of Justinian. Perhaps the best way of organizing that history would be city by city.[10]

The geographical boundaries of the Pauline mission emerge rather clearly from the New Testament sources. It was confined to the Northeastern quadrant of the Mediterranean basin, with its center in western Asia Minor and mainland Greece. It was a world in which, for urban and mobile people, Greek was the lingua franca, but upon which the overwhelming political fact of Rome was superimposed. When Paul, writing to Christians in the capital, chooses a rhetorical phrase to encompass the whole human world, it is "Greeks and barbarians, wise and ignorant" (Rom. 1:14). But when he introduces the theme of his letter a few verses later, the significant division becomes rather "Jew and Greek." Paul's mental world is (1) that of the Greek-speaking Eastern provinces, (2) specifically that of the Greek-speaking Jew. But it is a Roman world, and he is drawn magnetically to the capital as he hopes to move to the western half of the empire by journeying to Spain (Rom. 15:22-24).

Early this century Sir William Ramsay published a book, *The Cities of St. Paul*.[11] It did not fully live up to its title, for it discussed only a few of the cities, but it called attention to the important fact that the churches of the Pauline circle were founded in commercial centers, located on major roads or sea routes or both. To this date no one has undertaken to complete Ramsay's project by a systematic survey of characteristics of each of the dozen-odd cities. Ramsay also pointed to the importance of travel for the early Christians.[12] The Pauline letters were extraordinarily mobile. Whether this physical mobility was associated also with anything like what we call social mobility is a question that also needs to be addressed.

2. *The Social Constituency of the Pauline Groups*

From what social classes were the early Christians drawn? Many of the pagan opponents of Christianity in the second, third, and fourth centuries sought to stigmatize it as a lower-class superstition. But when Pliny wrote his famous letter to Trajan to inquire about proper procedure in the trial of Christians, he expressed alarm that they came from *omnis ordines*.[13] The notion of early Christianity as a proletarian movement has been a favorite with many modern scholars, too, whether for romantic or for Marxist reasons. But recent studies of several sorts tend to confirm Pliny's report. As Floyd Filson said in 1939, "The apostolic church was more nearly a cross-section of society than we have sometimes thought."[14]

From the Pauline letters and the book of Acts together, we can draw up a prosopography of nearly eighty individuals or small groups who are named or otherwise specified. For most of them, we have no more information than the name and location. For perhaps a quarter of them, though, there are some indicators of status, and in every instance these are relatively high, particularly in economic level. This has been especially emphasized in recent works by E. A. Judge, Gerd Theissen, and Abraham Malherbe.[15] Yet I think we can go one step farther. There are five identifiable categories of converts to Pauline Christianity: members of the *familia caesaris* (these would be slaves and freedmen); free artisans and merchants who are financially well off; women who have money and head households or businesses; Greek-speaking, well-to-do Jews, including leaders of synagogues; so-called God-fearers, i.e. pagans who had attached themselves to the Jewish community without taking the step of becoming full proselytes. What do these categories have in common? They all are marked by conflicting indicators of status. They have "high achieved status" and "low attributed status," i.e. money without prestige. They are "upwardly mobile." They live in what M. I. Finley calls "criss-crossing categories."[16]

The status of the anonymous majority of Pauline Christians is of course even more difficult to estimate than that of the named leaders. Some clues appear, however, in the several conflicts to which Paul's letters respond. Gerd Theissen, for example, has shown that both the dissonance experienced in the meetings for the common meal in Corinth and the disagreement over eating "meat offered to idols" indicate conflicts between wealthier and poorer Christians.[17] Other direct evidence in the letters also confirms the impression that the Pauline congregations were not socially homogeneous but drawn from multiple classes: slave and free, Jew and Greek, male and female, poor and relatively well off, dependent and independent. Many indicators point to an ethos of artisans and traders of modest means.[18]

3. *The Form of the Congregation*

The meeting places of the Pauline groups were private homes, a fact that had important implications for the internal structure of the groups as well as for their relationship to the larger society. Christianity at Corinth, for example, began when Paul baptized "Stephanus and his household," followed quickly by the household of Crispus, who was head of the synagogue, and Gaius, who was city treasurer and had a house large enough to accommodate at one time all of the individual house-units of the Corinthian church. The urban household became the basic cell of Pauline Christianity, and thus the Pauline groups were adopting what the pagan moralists regarded as the primary unit of society. It was, of course, much broader than our families: the household included not only immediate relatives, but also slaves, freedmen, hired workers, and sometimes tenants and partners in trade or craft. By baptizing this unit, the Christians adopted a hierarchical structure, which stood in tension with certain egalitarian and communal tendencies strongly represented in its beliefs, rituals, and ecstatic behavior. They also thus became involved in the networks of obligation through friendship and patronage that were so important in Greco-Roman society.[19]

The householders who became hosts of Christian house-churches incurred certain legal liabilities as a result, and evidently expected certain privileges in return--which sometimes conflicted with charismatic forms of leadership in the groups. The role of the hosts could be compared with that of patrons of the various clubs that proliferated in the early Empire. Indeed, both in antiquity and by modern scholars, the organization of the Christian congregations has been compared with these clubs--whether cultic *thiasoi* or *eranoi* burial societies or so-called crafts guilds. The legal status of Jewish communities in Greco-Roman cities has also been often identified with that of the collegia, and also for the synagogue the role of patrons seems to have been important.[20] But there were important differences as well, and much more work needs to be done here. The collegia were purely local organizations; there is nothing in Greek and Roman clubs, even cultic ones, to compare with the sense of extra-local unity of the People of God in both its Jewish and its derived Christian forms.

4. *Group Boundaries*

One important aspect of a sect's "response to the world," to use Brian Wilson's term,[21] is the degree to which the group is aware of a boundary between itself and the macrosociety, and the

ways in which it establishes that boundary. We have a number of
clues in the Pauline and deutero-Pauline letters from which we can
infer an interestingly ambivalent map of boundaries.

(1) Language emphasizing separation. Insiders are "chosen,"
"beloved," "holy," "brothers and sisters," "believers," while outsiders are "outsiders" (*hoi exō*) as well as "unbelievers," "un-
righteous," and even "those despised in the church." The pagan
world is characterized by catalogues of vices, stemming from the
primary sin of idolatry--language taken over directly from Jewish
polemic. Dualist language distinguishes children of light from
those of darkness, this world from those whose *politeuma* is in
heaven. Outsiders are expected to be hostile; new converts are
taught to expect suffering, just as Jesus suffered. Any kind of
hostility experienced later thus confirms this prediction, fits
the fundamental analogue of the belief system, and reinforces the
group's boundaries. Internally, the language of the sect is marked
especially by highly affective language: love, joy, anxiety,
longing, and the terms of fictive kinship (brothers, sisters,
father, children).

(2) Rules and rituals of purity. The Pauline school rejected
circumcision and purity rules, thus giving up one of the most
effective ways by which the Jewish community maintained its identity over against the pagan society in which it lived. This was
the practical issue at dispute between Paul and his opponents in
Galatia, which our preoccupation with Paul's theological and midrashic arguments has perhaps obscured. Would abolition of the
symbolic boundaries between Jew and Gentile *within* the sect mean
also lowering the boundaries between the sect and the world? The
Pauline Christians answered this question with significant ambi-
valence, which can be illustrated by two cases discussed in Pauline
letters: the question of idolatry (1 Cor. 8-10) and rules for marriage and sex (1 Thess. 4:1-8; 1 Cor.7). Purity and holiness of
the body, both the individual body and the metaphorical "body of
Christ," are emphasized. Yet Paul, agreeing with the higher-status
people at Corinth, does not want to draw the logical consequence
that this purity entails rigorous separation from the larger
society. The directive "not to mix" with sinners applies only
within the community, not to those "of this world," for "then you
would need to go out of the world" (1 Cor. 5:9-10). Marriages with
pagan partners are to be kept intact if possible, and the ordinary
social intercourse around meals with pagans is also to continue so
long as it does not disrupt internal harmony.

(3) Membership sanctions. As at Qumran, the severest form of discipline is exclusion from the group, especially from the common meals. Absence of Qumran's purity taboos weakens this sanction, but formal ejection could include a magical curse "delivering" the transgressor into the power of Satan, "for destruction of the flesh" (1 Cor. 5:5). The implication, as John Hurd observes, is that the Corinthian Christians conceived of their group as "an island of life in Christ surrounded by a sea of death ruled by Satan."[22]

(4) Autonomous institutions. The isolation of the group would be forwarded by creating institutions to perform services for the members for which they would ordinarily have relied upon municipal or other "outside" organizations. The communal meals would be one example. The social life of the community would effectively replace the need to belong to a burial society or other sort of club. The internal courts to settle disputes, advocated in 1 Cor. 6, are another example.

(5) Sanctioned interaction with the macrosociety. On the other hand, there are a number of measures, including maintenance of marriages with pagan spouses, accepting invitations to meals with pagans, and admonitions to modulate behavior with an eye to the way outsiders might view it, that indicate the intention of the Pauline groups to retain some openness to "the world." This is still clear in the later letters of the Pauline school, where for example the code of duties of the different members of a household serves to counter accusations that cults like the Christians (and Jews) undermine the basic unit of social order. The Pauline Christians want to maintain strong internal cohesion and consciousness of difference from "the world," but at the same time quite "permeable" boundaries.[23]

5. *The Exercise of Authority and Discipline*[24]

Perhaps the best way to see how authority worked in the Pauline groups is to observe the several instances of conflic resolution that we see in the letters. The primary means for settling differences was by face-to-face discussion, but in Paul's hands the apostolic letter became an important substitute, supplemented of course by the trusted messenger who delivered the letter.

There is some ambiguity in the modes of authority that are asserted by the apostle and by his opponents. On the one hand authority is conferred by tradition and by personal biography, on the other, there is the authority of "one who has the spirit of God." This ambiguity is perhaps analogous to the authority of the "millenial" prophet in modern cargo cults, as analyzed by Kennelm Burridge.[25] The prophet gains and secures his position by means of an innovative synthesis of traditional beliefs with a novel vision that confers meaning on a situation fraught with dissonance. If this synthesis is successful, it literally creates social power by organizing the perceptions, attitudes, and behavior of his followers, and thus he receives authority himself. This is close, I think, to what John Schütz means by calling authority the interpretation of power.[26]

The authority is thus highly personal, and the apostle serves as a model in the paraenetic letters, but reinforced by the claim that the model himself in turn imitates Christ. As a result, the description of appropriate power is in paradoxical terms: power in weakness, authority by renunciation of coercive power. This personal authority is exercised not only by Paul but also by his "fellow workers," who after his death develop the model in somewhat more schematic fashion.

The leadership of the local congregations is partly in the hands of ecstatics, but there are two countervailing types of authority: (a) the trans-local system of the apostle and his mobile associates and (b) the local householders or patrons.

Not very many specific rules for behavior are reported. The general ethos of Diaspora Judaism is more or less presupposed, and it is expressed in forms that are common in Hellenistic popular philosophy and rhetoric.[27] Decisions about specific problems have an ad hoc character and, in several instances, a studied ambiguity. We do get some glimpses of rule-making, though, particularly in the realm of sex and marriage, and these can yield insight into the social structure of the group.

6. Major Rituals

Naturally the references to baptism and the eucharist in Paul's letters have been intensively studied. But the questions put to them have had almost exclusively to do with theological implications or with questions of borrowing or influence from other religions. Astonishingly, there has been almost no attempt to describe the social functions of these two fundamental rituals. Yet the kind of analysis of the ritual process developed by anthropologists like Victor Turner[28] would seem readily adaptable for a functional and structural analysis of baptism and, to a lesser extent, because we have less information about it from the Pauline and deutero-Pauline letters, of the eucharist.

For example, the allusions to baptism in the Pauline and deutero-Pauline letters permit us to identify some of the principal

motifs in the ritual of initiation. . A great many of these motifs
sort themselves out as pairs of opposites:

death, dying / life, rising

descending / ascending

burial / enthronement

old Anthropos, body of flesh / new Anthropos, Body of Christ

oppositions / unity

taking off / putting on

vices / virtues

idols, demons, rulers of "this world" / living God, Christ Jesus as Lord.

Furthermore, if we array these oppositions according to the
temporal stages of the ritual, the result is two nearly symmetrical
movements. The first, characterized by descending movement, cli-
maxes with the "burial" in the water; it signifies the separation
of the baptizand from the "outside" world. The second, a rising
action, marks the integration of the baptized into another world:
on one plane the sect, on another the heavenly reality. This pro-
gression corresponds with the phases of every initiation or rite of
passage, separation, _limen_, and reaggregation.[29] Nudity, symbolic
death, rebirth as a child, abolition of distinctions of sex and
status--all these are typical of "liminal" phases in initiation.
But in a sect like early Christianity, the "reaggregation" phase is
different from that of a public rite of passage that serves the
whole of a stable and homogeneous society. Some of the characteristics of "liminality" carry over as attributes of the group into
which the baptized person is now initiated.

Anthropological analogues may also be helpful in sorting out
some of the other things that happened regularly in the group meetings, such as spirit-possession, claims and counterclaims about
miracles, and other "magical" procedures. At the same time, we
must pay attention to the less dramatic aspects of the meetings:
reading of scriptures and of apostolic letters, singing of songs,
advice, admonition, and correction.

7.   _Social Functions of Major Beliefs_

I place at the end of my survey, and will only mention without
developing, the matter that ordinarily counts as the primary and
usually the only topic in studies of Paulinism: the belief system.
So many things have been written on the theology of Paul that no
single scholar can gain command of the literature. Yet if I ask,
What difference did these beliefs make in the specific attitudes,
dispositions, and behavior of members of the Pauline groups? I find
very little in this literature that is helpful. Those of us who
want to develop a more sociological hermeneutic are therefore

tempted to ignore the theological questions altogether, or to treat
with disdain the whole problem of early Christian theology. That
would be a mistake. Beliefs themselves not only reflect aspects of
the social world of Paul and his followers and associates, and
therefore can give us another inferential window into that world,
they also helped to shape that world, to the extent they are not
idiosyncratic but participate in the effective constellation of
symbols through which members of the sect perceived what was what
and communicated it to one another. It is very tricky business to
draw sociographic inferences from stated beliefs. That is why I
place this important element at the end of my list, because we need
as full a collection of the clues to the structure of the Pauline
communities as we can gather before we try to draw out correlations
in something like Geertz's triangular schema of worldview, ethos,
and sacred symbols.[30] Nevertheless, it is part of the social description of the Pauline Christians which we must also not shirk.[31]
Though probably the most difficult part of the task, it holds perhaps the richest potential for understanding how the religion of
the early Christians "really worked."

TOWARD A SOCIAL DESCRIPTION OF PAULINE CHRISTIANITY

[1]This paper was presented as an informal lecture at the Fourth Annual Max Richter Conversation on Ancient Judaism, Brown University, 26 June 1978.

[2]*Paul and Palestinian Judaism: A Comparison of Patterns of Religion* (Philadelphia: Fortress, 1977), esp. pp. 12-24, and "Patterns of Religion in Paul and Rabbinic Judaism: A Holistic Method of Comparison," *HTR* 66 (1973), 455-78.

[3]See the criticisms by J. Neusner in the review essay below, pp.   , and by N. A. Dahl in *RelSRev* 4/3 (1978) 153-58. Despite their criticisms and mine, Sanders' work remains extraordinarily important.

[4]See, e.g., E. A. Judge, "St. Paul and Classical Society," *JAC* 15 (1972), 19-36, and A. J. Malherbe, *Social Aspects of Early Christianity* (Baton Rouge and London: LSU Press, 1977), both with extensive references to other literature.

[5]From the rapidly growing literature exploiting the social sciences for the historical investigation of early Christianity, suffice it to mention John G. Gager, *Kingdom and Community: The Social World of Early Christianity* (Prentice-Hall Studies in Religion; Englewood Cliffs, NJ: Prentice-Hall, 1975), and two of the numerous articles by Gerd Theissen, "Theoretische Probleme religionssoziologischerForschung und die Analyse des Urchristentums," *Neue Zeitschr. für syst. Theol. und Religionsphilosophie* 16 (1974), 35-56, and "Die soziologische Auswertung religiöser Überlieferungen," *Kairos* 17 (1975), 284-99.

[6]"Thick Description: Toward an Interpretive Theory of Culture," in *The Interpretation of Cultures; Selected Essays* (New York: Basic Books, 1973), 3-30, esp. 24f.

[7]See n.5 above.

[8]I have dealt with these matters at greater length in "The Social World of Pauline Christianity," to appear in *ANRW* 2/27.

[9]See especially Ramsay MacMullen, *Roman Social Relations* (New Haven and London: Yale, 1974), chap. 2, and cf. the remarks by G. E. M. de Ste. Croix, "Early Christian Attitudes to Property and Slavery," in D. Baker (ed.), *Church, Society, and Politics* (Oxford: Univ. Press, 1975), 8f.

[10]For preliminary efforts in that direction, see W. A. Meeks and R. L. Wilken, *Jews and Christians in Antioch in the First Four Centuries of the Common Era* (SBLSBS 13; Missoula, MT: Scholars Press, 1978); Lee I. Levine, *Caesarea Under Roman Rule* (SJLA 7; Leiden; Brill, 1975); Alf T. Kraabel, "Judaism in Western Asia Minor under the Roman Empire, with a Preliminary Study of the Jewish Community at Sardis, Lydia" (unpublished Th.D. diss., Harvard, 1968); R. Reuven Kimelman, "Rabbi Yohanan of Tiberias: Aspects of the social and Religious History of Third Century Palestine" (unpublished Ph.D. diss., Yale, 1977).

[11]*The Cities of St. Paul: Their Influence on His Life and Thought* (London: Hodder & Stoughton, 1907).

[12]"Roads and Travel," in J. Hastings (ed.), *A Dictionary of the Bible* (Edinburgh: T & T Clark, 1904) 5:375-402; cf. Malherbe, *Social Aspects*, 62-68, with further references there.

[13]*Ep.* 10.96.9.

[14]"The Significance of the Early House Churches," *JBL* 58 (1939) 111.

[15]E. A. Judge, "The Early Christians as a Scholastic Community, Part II," *JRelHist* 1 (1960-61), 125-37; Gerd Theissen, "Soziale Schichtung in der korinthischen Gemeinde; Ein Beitrag zur Soziologie des hellenistischen Urchristentums," *ZNW* 65 (1974), 232-72; Malherbe, *Social Aspects*, chap. 2.

[16]M. I. Finley, *The Ancient Economy* (Berkeley: Univ. California Press, 1973), 51.

[17]"Die Starken und Schwachen in Korinth; Soziologische Analyse eines theologischen Streites," *EvT* 35 (1975), 155-72; "Soziale Integration und sakramentales Handeln; Eine Analyse von 1 Cor. XI:17-34," *NovT* 24 (1974), 179-206.

[18]Malherbe, *Social Aspects*, chap. 2.

[19]Cf. E. A. Judge, *The Social Pattern of Christian Groups in the First Century* (London: Tyndale, 1960), chap. 3.

[20]See, e.g., E. Mary Smallwood, *The Jews under Roman Rule: From Pompey to Diocletian* (SJLA 20; Leiden: Brill, 1976), 133f.; cf. the remarks by Harry Leon on the synagogues of the Agrippesians and the Augustesians in Rome, *The Jews of Ancient Rome* (Philadelphia: Jewish Publication Society, 1960), 141f.

[21]*Magic and the Millenium: A Sociological Study of Religious Movements of Protest among Tribal and Third-World Peoples* (London: Heineman, 1973), 21.

[22]J. C. Hurd, *The Origin of I Corinthians* (New York: Seabury, 1965), 285.

[23]For a more detailed discussion, see W. A. Meeks, "'Since Then You Would Need to Go Out of the World': Group Boundaries in Pauline Christianity," in *Critical History and Biblical Faith: New Testament Perspectives* (Villanova, PA: College Theology Society, 1979), 4-29.

[24]See John H. Schütz, *Paul and the Anatomy of Apostolic Authority* (SNTSMS 26; Cambridge: University Press, 1975), and Bengt Holmberg, *Paul and Power: The Structure of Authority in the Primitive Church as Reflected in the Pauline Epistles* (ConB, NT Ser. 11; Lund: Gleerup, 1978).

[25]*New Heaven, New Earth: A Study of Millenarian Activities* (New York: Schocken, 1969), esp. 153-64.

[26]Schütz, 9-15 and chap. 9.

[27]See A. J. Malherbe, "Hellenistic Moralists and the New Testament," forthcoming in *ANRW* 2/28.

[28]*The Ritual Process: Structure and Anti-Structure* (Symbol, Myth, and Ritual Series; Ithaca: Cornell, 1977).

[29]Ibid. 94.

[30]Clifford Geertz, "Religion as a Cultural System," in Michael Banton (ed.), *Anthropological Approaches to the Study of Religion* (A.S.A. Monographs 3; London: Tavistock, 1966), 1-46.

[31]A summary of the procedures that might produce something like a "sociology of Pauline theology" would hardly be illuminating. Hence I must refer again to the essay cited in n.8 above, in which I have worked out a few examples.

THE USE OF THE LATER RABBINIC EVIDENCE
FOR THE STUDY OF PAUL

Jacob Neusner

Brown University

The critical problem in drawing upon Rabbinic documents edited
from the beginning of the third century down into medieval times is
assessing the antiquity of sayings and stories first brought to
redaction long after the times of those to whom they are attributed.
If a saying first appears in a fifth century compilation but is
placed in the mouth of a first century authority, to the mind and
imagination of what period in the history of Judaism does that
saying testify? Self-evidently, it is authoritative for the redactor in the age of the document in which it appears. Otherwise he
would not have put it there. But how do we know that the saying
also speaks for someone four hundred years earlier? Two urgent
issues follow from this first one. The first concerns the interpretation of the saying itself. If it belongs to the fifth century,
then other information we possess about that same century will help
us to make sense of it; but if it belongs to the first century,
then we have to draw upon a quite different and distinct corpus of
facts, including other sayings and ideas, to make sense of it. The
second concerns the use of the saying as historical evidence. Just
as we do not know whether or not we draw upon the resources of the
first century for the interpretation of the saying first in evidence in the fifth, so we do not know whether we draw upon that
saying itself in the description of the state of mind of people who
flourished a long time before the redaction of the document in
which that saying occurs.

In most fields of learning these statements will be accepted
as self-evident. Furthermore, they will be brought to bear upon
the use of evidence of diverse provenance. In the study of ancient
Judaism, by contrast, while many concede that what I have said is
so, not very many take seriously and respond to the implications
for the use of evidence represented by the acknowledged facts of
redaction. A few scholars attempt to explain away the fact that
a saying attributed, let us say, to Yohanan ben Zakkai, who flourished toward the end of the first century, first surfaces in a
fifth century compilation, with not a single hint in antecedent
documents that Yohanan or anyone else held the opinion first
attributed to him nearly half a millenium after he died. Some will

posit a great system of oral formulation and oral transmission of traditions. It simply does not matter that a "first century saying" occurs so much later, since, all along, it was there. True, until the compilation of the document which presents it, no one thought it important to write it down. That is because no one had to write down anything. Now that thesis would be more persuasive were it accompanied by systematic scholarly work to show that in fact there was a great mechanism of oral formulation and redaction, to demonstrate how this engine worked, and to explain why, alongside, people still wrote things down--for we do have Rabbinic writings. Even though a great many scholars may concur in the thesis just now described, or in some variation of that thesis, the fact remains that none of them has shown us just what evidence we have to compel us to agree.

Curiously, there are first century documents which can demonstrate that a given notion, first surfacing in much later Rabbinical writings, circulated and was important long before. The New Testament books, some apocryphal and pseudepigraphic books, and the Essene library of Qumran contain numerous sayings that are familiar in much later Rabbinical compilations, of the third through the tenth centuries. They therefore allow us to say that some Jews maintained opinions preserved and handed on, under other auspices and for our purposes, in later Rabbinical circles as well. But, at the outset, we have to observe that, if those sayings then are deemed to be early, they are not distinctively and quintessentially Rabbinic. If they are Rabbinic, they commonly are not demonstrably early. So, whether and how Essene writings from Qumran, Apocrypha and Pseudepigrapha, and New Testament materials may be illuminated by the later Rabbinic materials is not at all clear. What is clear is that the later Rabbinic materials may be illuminated by the Essene writings from Qumran, Apocrypha and Pseudepigrapha and New Testament materials. But, on the sea of scholarship of the past half century, that is not the prevailing wind. It is, as everyone knows, blowing from the other direction: "the Rabbis" and "Rabbinic Judaism" testify to the character and meaning of the Gospels and Paul. But the evangelists and Paul in no way help us to understand "the Rabbis" and "Rabbinic Judaism."

In the recent past a handful of younger scholars has determined to take seriously the problem of "dating," that is, the issue of the age to which Rabbinical sayings assigned to early authorities but first surfacing in later documents are made to testify. They have simply determined to deal in other than narrowly historical categories. Their position will be that the sole question of

importance is not whether or not [C]Aqiba or Yohanan ben Zakkai
"really" said what is attributed to him, in the age in which he is
supposed to live, and in the context in which, for our part, we now
wish to read and interpret that saying. What is important is the
shape of the structure yielded by the Rabbinic documents in general,
the character of the religious views presented by them as a whole,
and not the point at which some detail or other emerged. This
clearly sidesteps the issue of historical veracity in its gross
sense. But it introduces a different set of problems.

What is now at issue is the comparison of structures, for
instance, the larger and encompassing conceptions of "the Rabbis"
on a given topic compared to the larger and encompassing conceptions of Paul. So while we do not know whether Paul's ideas derive
from, or relate to, ideas held by "rabbis" of his own day (and we
have remarkably little evidence that there were Rabbis in Paul's
day), we may say something worthwhile. Whenever these sayings
occur, they do present a picture of religious ideas. It is that
set of religious ideas which may be brought into juxtaposition
with, and compared to, Paul's.

This notion has much to recommend it, as I have argued in my
Method and Meaning in Ancient Judaism, which takes a stand in favor
of systemic description and systemic analysis. Hence by implication I surely stand on the side, also, of systemic comparison.
But there seem to me two major problems to be taken very seriously.

The first is that the construct of "the Rabbis" is too vague
and general, because it takes for granted we have something which
we do not demonstrably have. We in no way have shown that all the
rabbis of the first seven centuries of the Common Era may be homogenized into a construct known as "the Rabbis" and then set into
juxtaposition with a single Christian thinker, whether Paul or
Irenaeus or Augustine. If, then, we compare comparables, that is,
"the Rabbis" to "the Church Fathers," we shall engage in a somewhat
similar project to that proposed by proponents of systemic comparison. I am not inclined to expect interesting results. So far
there is none, as Wolfson's *Church Fathers* shows. On the other
hand, if we compare the thought of Paul to the thought of someone
who lived in his own time, we find ourselves back where we started
from. If, again, we choose someone for whom ample, and probably
accurate, documentation is available, for instance, Abayye, Rabbah
or Raba, or perhaps even Samuel and Judah b. Ezekiel, we may discover that on the surface there is nothing to compare.

The second problem flows from the first. If we describe the
system of Paul, that is, his theology, and ask about theological

systems of either an individual Rabbi, or some well delineated
group of rabbis (for instance, the circle of Pumbedita or of
Tiberias), or even "the Rabbis" of the entire literature as a whole,
we come up with systems that exhibit few points of contact, let
alone rich possibilities for comparison. Different people, thinking about different things, in different ways, may be asked to con-
verse with one another. But it had better be a very thoughtful in-
vitation. In our own times we confront the task of talking together
with people with whom we have nothing whatsoever in common. It is,
indeed, a problem distinctive to an age of communication across
vast distances of time and of space. The labor of teaching us how
to listen to others who speak about different things in different
languages from ours is taken up by anthropologists, for example,
who confront the critical issue of humanity in diversity. So this
second problem is not insurmountable. Indeed, it is a perfectly
commonplace and routine one. If we wish to compare the thought-
world of Paul to the thought-world of a given system and circle of
the larger Rabbinical movement, for instance, of the first and
second century minds whose work comes to its fruition in the system
of Mishnah-Tosefta, the comparison is possible; the result--the
illumination of each world by the other--is worth the effort. But
to begin with, the two worlds must be laid forth, each in its *own*
terms and its *own* context. Of greater importance, a common agendum
of issues must be shaped and addressed to each party to the comparison. It must be congruent to each side, or, at least, incon-
gruent to neither. That means, self-evidently, that the interests
of one party to the comparison must not be permitted to predominate.
For if they do, then the character of the other party to the comparison is going to be flagrantly distorted.

So description comes first. Each side must allow its critical
issues and generative conceptions to determine the boundaries and
shape of its thought-world. The second step cannot be directly to
bring together the two sets of descriptions. It is the teasing out
of each of some range of questions common to both. Only at the
third stage will the systems be compared, because a foundation for
comparison will have been laid. Obviously, this mechanical pre-
scription is meant only to adumbrate the kind of scholarly and
theological thinking to be done. The interesting exercises lie in
front of us.

If, as I believe, everything I have said thus far is self-
evident, then the reader is apt to wonder why it is not possible to
cite a single work to illustrate how these propositions inform
contemporary research. I too ask the same question and find no

answer. It is, however, possible to point to a book which proposes to do what I believe is sensible and right in the study of Paul and the Rabbinical literature, the comparison of the system of the one with the system of the other. But, in the pages that follow, I shall have to point out the failure of a good intention, principally, I think, because of what must be called limited perspicacity. This limitation will be seen in diverse unhappy traits of the same book: its digressions, its incapacity to follow a single line of thought, its excessive reliance upon catalogues of materials, its heavy-handed mode of argument, in all its mechanical and unrefined exposition. But these are failures in execution. The basic theory, as I shall argue, is sound.

The book under discussion is E. P. Sanders, *Paul and Palestinian Judaism: A Comparison of Patterns of Religion* (SCM Press, 1977).

"Palestinian Judaism" is described through three bodies of evidence: Tannaitic literature, the Dead Sea Scrolls, and Apocrypha and Pseudepigrapha, in that order. I shall deal only with the first. To each set of sources, Sanders addresses questions of systematic theology: election and covenant, obedience and disobedience, reward and punishment and the world to come, salvation by membership in the covenant and atonement, proper religious behavior (so for Tannaitic sources); covenant and the covenant people, election and predestination, the commandments, fulfillment and transgression, atonement (Dead Sea Scrolls); election and covenant, the fate of the individual Israelite, atonement, commandments, the basis of salvation, the gentiles, repentance and atonement, the righteousness of God (Apocrypha and Pseudepigrapha, meaning, specifically: Ben Sira, I Enoch, Jubilees, Psalms of Solomon, IV Ezra). There follows a brief concluding chapter (pp. 419-28, summarizing pp. 1-418), and then the second part, on Paul, takes up about a fifth of the book. Sanders provides a very competent bibliography (pp. 557-82) and thorough indexes. So far as the book has a polemical charge, it is to demonstrate (pp. 420-21) that "the fundamental nature of the covenant conception...largely accounts for the relative scarcity of appearances of the term 'covenant' in Rabbinic literature. The covenant was presupposed, and the Rabbinic discussions were largely directed toward the question of how to fulfill the covenantal obligations." This wholly sound and to me self-evident proposition is then meant to disprove the conviction ("all but universally held") that Judaism is a degeneration of the Old Testament view: "The once noble idea of covenant as offered by God's grace and obedience as the consequence of that gracious gift degenerated into the idea of petty legalism, according to which one had to earn the mercy of God by minute observance of irrelevant ordinances."[1]

Sanders's search for patterns yields a common pattern in "covenantal nomism," which, in general, emerges as follows (p. 422):

> The "pattern" or "structure" of covenantal nomism is this: (1) God has chosen Israel and (2) given the law. The law implies both (3) God's promise to maintain the election and (4) the requirement to obey. (5) God rewards obedience and punishes transgression. (6) The law provides for means of atonement, and atonement results in (7) maintenance or re-establishment of the covenantal relationship. (8) All those who are maintained in the covenant by obedience, atonement, and God's mercy belong to the group which will be saved. An important interpretation of the first and last points is that election and ultimately salvation are considered to be by God's mercy rather than human achievement.

Anyone familiar with Jewish liturgy will be at home in that statement. Even though the evidence on the character of Palestinian Judaism derives from diverse groups and reaches us through various means, Sanders argues that covenantal nomism was "the basic type of religion known by Jesus and presumably by Paul..." And again, "covenantal nomism must have been the general type of religion prevalent in Palestine before the destruction of the Temple."[2]

The stated purposes require attention. Sanders states at the outset (p. xii) that he has six aims: (1) to consider methodologically how to compare two (or more) related but different religions; (2) to destroy the view of Rabbinic Judaism which is still prevalent in much, perhaps most, New Testament scholarship; (3) to establish a different view of Rabbinic Judaism; (4) to argue a case concerning Palestinian Judaism (that is, Judaism as reflected in material of Palestinian provenance) as a whole; (5) to argue for a certain understanding of Paul; and (6) to carry out a comparison of Paul and Palestinian Judaism. Numbers 4 and 6, he immediately adds, "constitute the general aim of the book, while I hope to accomplish the others along the way." Since more than a third of the work is devoted to Rabbinic Judaism, Sanders certainly cannot be accused of treating his second goal casually.

Sanders's very good intention is the proper comparison of religions (or of diverse expressions of one larger religion): "I am of the view...that the history of the comparison of Paul and Judaism is a particularly clear instance of the general need for methodological improvement in the comparative study of religion. What is difficult is to focus on what is to be compared. We have already seen that most comparisons are of reduced essences...or of individual motifs..." This sort of comparison Sanders rejects.

Here I wish to give Sanders's words in italics, because I believe
what he wants to do is precisely what he should have done but, as I
shall explain, has not succeeded in doing: *What is clearly desir-
able, then, is to compare an entire religion, parts and all, with
an entire religion, parts and all; to use the analogy of a building
to compare two buildings, not leaving out of account their individual bricks. The problem is how to discover two wholes, both of
which are considered and defined on their own merits and in their
own terms, to be compared with each other.* Now let us ask ourselves
whether or not Sanders has compared an entire religion, parts and
all, with other such *entire* religions. On the basis of my description of the contents of the book, we must conclude that he has not.
For the issues of election and covenant, obedience and disobedience,
and the like, while demonstrably present and taken for granted in
the diverse "Judaisms" of late antiquity, do not necessarily define
the generative problematic of any of the Judaisms before us.

To put matters in more general terms: Systemic description
must begin with the system to be described. Comparative description
follows. And to describe a system, we commence with the principal
documents which can be shown to form the center of a system. Our
task then is to uncover the exegetical processes, the dynamics of
the system, through which those documents serve to shape a conception, and to make sense, of reality. We then must locate the critical tensions and inner problematic of the system thereby revealed:
What is it about? The comparison of systems begins in their exegesis and interpretation.

But Sanders does not come to Rabbinic Judaism (to focus upon
what clearly is his principal polemical charge) to uncover the
issues of Rabbinic Judaism. He brings to the Rabbinic sources the
issues of Pauline scholarship and Paul.[3] This blatant trait of his
work, which begins, after all, with a long account of Christian
anti-Judaism ("The persistence of the view of Rabbinic religion as
one of legalistic works-righteousness," pp. 33-58), hardly requires
amplification. In fact, Sanders does not really undertake the systemic description of Rabbinic Judaism in terms of *its* critical tensions. True, he isolates those documents he thinks may testify to
the state of opinion in the late first and second centuries. But
Sanders does not describe Rabbinic Judaism through the systemic
categories yielded by its principal documents. His chief purpose
is to demonstrate that Rabbinism consitutes a system of covenantal
nomism. While I think he is wholly correct in maintaining the importance of the conceptions of covenant and of grace, the polemic
in behalf of Rabbinic legalism as covenantal does not bring to the

fore what Rabbinic sources themselves wish to take as their principal theme and generative problem. For them, as he says, covenantal
nomism is a datum. So far as Sanders proposes to demonstrate the
importance to all the kinds of ancient Judaism of covenantal nomism,
election, atonement, and the like, his work must be pronounced a
success. I am not sure why that proposition is important to Paul
or to "the Rabbis," but I do think for Sanders it does work. Still,
so far as he claims to effect systemic description of Rabbinic
Judaism ("a comparison of patterns of religion"), we have to evaluate that claim in its own terms.

Since in a moment I shall turn to the impact, upon Sanders's
topic, of work completed since his book was written in 1973 or 1974,
I wish to stress that my criticism at this point concerns how
Sanders does what he has chosen to do: systemic comparison. His
notion of comparing patterns of religion is, I believe, promising.
But what he has done, instead, is to impose the pattern of one
religious expression, Paul's, upon the description of another, that
of the Tannaitic-Rabbinical sources.[4] He therefore ignores the
context of the sayings adduced in the service of comparison, paying
little attention to the larger context in which those sayings find
meaning. In this connection I point to the observation of Mary
Boyce (*A History of Zoroastrianism* [Leiden, 1975], p. 246):
"Zoroaster's eschatological teachings, with the individual judgment, the resurrection of the body, the Last Judgment, and life
everlasting, became profoundly familiar, through borrowings, to
Jews, Christians, and Muslims, and have exerted enormous influence
on the lives and thoughts of men in many lands. Yet it was in the
framework of his own faith that they attained their fullest logical
coherence..." What Boyce stresses is that, taken out of the Zoro-
astrian context, these familiar teachings lose their "fullest logical coherence." Sanders, for his part, has not asked what is important and central in the system of Tannaitic-Rabbinic writings.
All he wants to know is what, in those writings, addresses questions of interest to Paul. In my judgment, even in 1973 he would
have been better served by paying close attention to his own statement of purpose.

But since 1973 the state of the art has shifted its focus,
from the mass of writings in which authorities of the first and
second centuries (Tannaim, hence Tannaitic literature) are cited,
to the character of the documents, one by one, which contain and
express Rabbinic Judaism. Future work of comparison, then, will
have to take up the results of something less encompassing than
"the Tannaitic view of...," all the more so, "*the* rabbinic idea

of..." The work of description, first for its own purposes, then
for systemic comparison, begins with Mishnah.

Mishnah certainly is the first document of Rabbinic Judaism.
Formally, it stands at the center of the system, since the principal subsequent Rabbinic documents, the Talmuds, lay themselves out
as if they were exegeses of Mishnah (or, more accurately, of Mishnah-Tosefta).[5] It follows that an account of what Mishnah is
about, of the system expressed by Mishnah and of the world view
created and sustained therein, should be required for systemic comparison such as Sanders proposes. Now if we come to Mishnah with
questions of Pauline-Lutheran theology, important to Sanders and
New Testament scholarship, we find ourselves on the peripheries of
Mishnaic literature and its chief foci. True, Mishnah contains a
very few relevant, accessible sayings, for example, on election
and covenant. But on our hands is a huge document which does not
wish to tell us much about election and covenant and which does
wish to speak about other things. Description of the Mishnaic system is not easy. It has taken me twenty-two volumes to deal with
the sixth of Mishnah's six divisions,[6] and while I think I can
describe the Mishnaic system of uncleanness, I still have no clear
notion about the relationship between that Mishnaic subsystem and
the other five divisions of Mishnah and their, as yet undescribed,
subsystems.[7] We cannot therefore blame Sanders for not doing what
has only just now been undertaken. But we have to wonder whether
Sanders has asked of himself the generative and unifying questions
of the core of Mishnah at all: Has he actually sat down and
studied (not merely "read") one document, even one tractate, beginning to end, and analyzed its inner structure, heart, and center?
By this question I do not mean to ask whether Sanders has mastered
Rabbinic writings. The evidence in his book is affirmative. He
knows Hebrew and is competent throughout. The question is, Does
Sanders so grasp the problematic of a Rabbinic compilation that he
can accurately state what it is that said compilation wishes to
express--its generative problematic? Or does he come to the Rabbinic literature with a quite separate and distinct set of questions, issues in no way natural to, and originating in, the Rabbinic writings themselves? Just now we noticed that Sanders's
theological agendum accords quite felicitously with the issues of
Pauline theology. To show that that agendum has *not* been shaped
out of the issues of Rabbinic theology, I shall now adduce negative evidence on whether Sanders with equal care analyzes the
inner structure of a document of Rabbinic Judaism.

First, throughout his "constructive" discussions of Rabbinic

ideas about theology, Sanders quotes all documents equally with no
effort at differentiation among them. He seems to have culled sayings from the diverse sources he has chosen and written them down
on cards, which he proceeded to organize around his critical categories. Then he has constructed his paragraphs and sections by
flipping through those cards and commenting on this and that. So
there is no context in which a given saying is important in its
own setting, in its own document.

Of greater importance, the diverse documents of Rabbinism are
accorded no attention on their own. Let me explain what I mean.
Anyone who sits down and actually studies Sifra, in a large unit of
its materials, for example, can hardly miss what the redactor of
the document wants to say. The reason is that the polemic of that
document is so powerfully stated and so interminably repeated as
to be inescapable. What Sifra wishes to say is this: Mishnah requires an exegetical foundation. But Mishnah notoriously avoids
scriptural proof texts. To Sifra none of its major propositions
is acceptable solely upon the basis of reason or logic. All of
them require proper grounding in exegesis--of a peculiarly formal
sort--of Scripture. One stratum of the Talmuds, moreover,
addresses the same devastating critique to Mishnah. For once a
Mishnaic proposition will be cited at the head of a Talmudic pericope, a recurrent question is, What is the source of this statement? And the natural and right answer (from the perspective of
the redactor of this sort of pericope) will be, *As it is said...,*
followed by a citation of Scripture.

Now if it is so that Sifra and at least one stratum of Talmud
so shape their materials as to make a powerful polemical point
against Mishnah's autonomous authority ("logic"), indifferent as
Mishnah is to scriptural authority for its laws, then we must ask
how we can ignore or neglect that polemic. Surely we cannot cite
isolated pericopae of these documents with no attention whatsoever
to the intention of the documents which provide said pericopae.
Even the most conservative New Testament scholars will concur that
we must pay attention to the larger purposes of the several evangelists in citing sayings assigned to Jesus in the various Gospels.
Everyone knows that if we ignore Matthew's theory of the law and
simply extract Matthew's versions of Jesus' sayings about the law
and set them up side by side with the sayings about the law given
to Jesus by other of the evangelists and attitudes imputed to him
by Paul, we create a mess of contradictions. Why then should the
context of diverse Rabbinic sayings, for example, on the law, be
ignored? In this setting it is gratuitous to ask for an

explanation of Sanders's constant reference to "the Rabbis," as though the century and a half which he claims to discuss produced no evidence of individuals' and ideas' having distinct histories.

Still more telling evidence that Sanders does not succeed in his systemic description comes when he gives one concrete example (in the entire 238 pages of discussion of "Tannaitic" Judaism) of what a document wishes to tell us. I shall focus on the matter because Sanders raises it. He states (p. 71): "Rabbinic discussions are often at the third remove from central questions of religious importance. Thus the tractate Mikwaoth, 'immersion pools,' does not consider the religious value of immersion or the general reason for purity, much less such a large topic as why the law should be observed. It simply begins with the classification of the grades among pools of water. This does not mean that there were no religious principles behind the discussion; simply that they (a) were so well understood that they did not need to be specified and (b) did not fall into the realm of *halakah*." Now on the basis of this statement we must conclude that Sanders has looked at M. Miqvaot 1:1, perhaps even the entire first chapter of the document. It is true that tractate Miqvaot does begin with classification of the grades among pools of water. But a study of the tractate as a whole reveals that it certainly has its own issues, its own critical concerns, indeed, its own generative problematic.

In fact the shank of the tractate--M. Miq. 2:4-5:6--asks about collections of diverse sorts of water and how they effect purification. A secondary development of the same theme follows: the union of pools to form a valid collection of water, and yet a tertiary development, mixtures of water with other liquids (wine, mud). Therefore the primary interest of the tractate is in water for the immersion pool: What sort of water purifies? Now anyone interested in the document must wonder, Why is it that, of all the possible topics for a tractate on purification, the one point of interest should be the definition of effective water? And the first observation one might make is that Scripture, for its part, would be surprised by the datum of Mishnah-tractate Miqvaot.[8] For, in the opinion of the priestly authorities of Leviticus and Numbers, still water by itself--not spring water, not standing water mixed with blood or ashes, for example--does not effect purification. Water may remove uncleanness, but the process of purification further requires the setting of the sun. Water mixed with blood may purify the leper; water mixed with the ashes of a red cow may purify one made unclean by a corpse. But water by itself

is inadequate to complete purification. At best, Scripture knows
running water as a means of purification. But Mishnah-tractate
Miqvaot stresses the purificatory properties of still water, and
explicitly excludes spring water from the center of its discussion.[9]

My own conception of what it is that Mishnah wishes to say in
this tractate is at best a guess,[10] but it is worth repeating so
that the full character of Sanders's "defense" of this particular
tractate may become clear:

> What is the fundamental achievement of our tractate?
> The Oral Torah [Mishnah] provides a mode of purifi-
> cation different from that specified in the Written
> Torah for the Temple, but analogous to that suitable
> for the Temple. Still water serves for the table,
> living water [approved by Scripture] cleans the Zab,
> and, when mixed with blood or ashes, the leper and
> the person unclean by reason of touching a corpse.
> All those other things cleaned by the setting of the
> sun, the passage of time, in the Oral Torah [Mishnah-
> tractate Miqvaot] are cleaned in the still water [of
> the immersion pool, which, Mishnah makes clear, must
> be] gathered in the ground, in the rains which know
> no time, but only the eternal seasons.[11]

Now it may be that that is the whole story. What follows is my own
obiter dictum on the matter, my conception of the world-constructing
meaning of the laws just now summarized:

> In an age in which men and women immersed themselves
> in spring-fed lakes and rushing rivers, in moving
> water washing away their sins in preparation for the
> end of days, the Pharisees observed the passing of
> the seasons, which go onward through time, immersing
> in the still, collected water which falls from heaven.
> They bathe not in running water, in the anticipation
> of the end of days and for the sake of eschatological
> purity, but in still water, to attain the cleanness
> appropriate to the eternal Temple and the perpetual
> sacrifice [of the very real, physical Temple of
> Jerusalem]. They remove the uncleanness defined by
> the Written Torah for the holy altar, because of the
> conviction of the Oral Torah [Mishnah] that the hearth
> and home, table and bed, going onward through ages
> without end, also must be and can be cleaned, in
> particular, through the rain: the living water from
> heaven, falling in its perpetual seasons, trickling
> down the hills and naturally gathering in ponds,
> ditches, and caverns, for time immemorial. As sun
> sets, bringing purification for the Temple, so rain
> falls, bringing purification for the table.[12]

Now I cite this passage to juxtapose it to Sanders's judgment that
Miqvaot "does not consider the religious value of immersion or the
general reason for purity." I think it does exactly that--in its
own way.

In my view, Sanders finds in Miqvaot no answers to questions
of religious value because he has not asked how Miqvaot asks its

questions to begin with. And that is because he has not allowed
the tractate to speak for itself, out of its own deepest stratum of
conceptions. He has brought to the tractate an alien set of questions and, finding nothing in the tractate to deal with those
questions--that is, no sayings explicitly addressed to them--he has
gone his way. It is true that the tractate does not consider "the
religious value of immersion," and that is because it has quite
separate, and, if I am right, more profound, issues in mind.[13]   To
say, "This does not mean that there were no religious principles
behind the discussion" is not only patronizing, it also is ignorant. To claim that the "principles were so well understood that
they did not need to be specified" is true but beside the point.
Granted that we deal with a system of covenantal nomism, what is it
that that covenant was meant to express? And how did the ancient
rabbis interpret that covenant and its requirements for their own
trying times?

Now I must repeat that I do not propose to criticize Sanders
on the basis of his not having read a book which appeared two or
three years after his own work was completed (which I believe, on
the basis of his discussion and bibliography, to have been in 1973
or 1974). It is to point out, on the basis of an example of his
own selection and what he has to say about that example, that the
promised systemic description simply does not take place. The
claim, in this very context, that religious principles cannot be
discussed in the Mishnah because of the character of Mishnah, would
be more persuasive if there were substantial evidence that Mishnah
to begin with has been studied in its own framework. Sanders says
(p. 71): "We should at least briefly refer to another characteristic of the literature which makes a small-scale analysis of
basic religious principles impossible: they are not discussed as
such. Rabbinic discussions are often at the third remove from
central questions of religious importance." There follows the
treatment of Miqvaot cited above. I contend that it begs the
question to say "basic religious principles" are not "discussed
as such."

Anyhow, why should "the religious value" of immersion be
spelled out by the second-century rabbis in terms immediately
accessible to twentieth-century theologians? Mishnah's audience
is second-century rabbis. How can we expect people to explain to
outsiders ("why the law should be kept" indeed!) answers to questions which do not trouble insiders to begin with. The whole
statement of the question is topsy-turvy. I find deplorable
Sanders's failure to object to the notion of "central questions of

religious importance" and "religious principles." Taken for
granted is the conception that what are central questions to us
are central questions to all "worthwhile" religious literature.
It follows that if we cannot locate what to us are "religious
principles," then we have either to condemn or to apologize for
the documents which lack them. Stated in this way, the implicit
position takes for granted "we all know" the meaning of "religion,"
"religious importance," "religious principles." In the case of
the vast *halakhic* literature, we do not find readily accessible
and immediately obvious "religious principles." When, moreover,
we do find those conceptions, subject to generalization and analysis, which do address issues of common, even contemporary concern,
we sometimes discover a range of topics under analysis more really
philosophical than religious (in the contemporary sense of these
words). An apology for Rabbinic Judaism bypassing the whole of
the *halakhic* corpus which constitutes its earliest stratum is
cosmically irrelevant to the interpretation of Rabbinic Judaism,
therefore to the comparison of that system to others in its own
culture.

The diverse Rabbinic documents require study in their own
terms. The systems of each--so far as there are systems--have to
be uncovered and described. The way the several systems relate
and the values common to all of them have to be spelled out. The
notion that we may promiscuously cite everything in every document
(within the defined canon of "permitted" documents) and then claim
to have presented an account of "the Rabbis" and their opinions is
not demonstrated and not even very well argued. We hardly need
dwell on the still more telling fact that Sanders has not shown
how systemic comparison is possible when, in point of fact, the
issues of one document, or of one system of which a document is
a part, are simply not the same as the issues of some other document or system. That is, he has succeeded in finding Rabbinic
sayings on topics of central importance to Paul (or Pauline theology). He has not even asked whether these sayings form the
center and core of the Rabbinic system or even of a given Rabbinic
document. To state matters simply, How do we know that "the
Rabbis" and Paul are talking about the same thing, so that we may
compare what they have to say? And if it should turn out that
"the Rabbis" and Paul are not talking about the same thing, then
what is it that we have to compare?

Even by 1973 it was clear that the issue of historical de-
pendability of attributions of sayings to particular rabbis had to
be faced, even though, admittedly, it had not been faced in most

of the work on which Sanders was able to draw. I do not wish to
dwell upon the problem of why we should believe that a given abbi
really said what is attributed to him; elsewhere[14] I have discussed the matter at some length. Still, it seems to me that the
issues of historical evidence should enter into the notion of the
comparison of systems. If it should turn out that "the Rabbis'"
ideas about a given theological topic respond to a historical
situation subject to fairly precise description, then the work of
comparison becomes still more subtle and precarious. For if "the
Rabbis" address their thought--for example, about the right motive
for the right deed--to a world in which, in the aftermath of a
terrible catastrophe, the issue of what it is that human beings
still control is central, the comparison of their thought to that
of Paul requires us to imagine what Paul might have said if confronted by the situation facing "the Rabbis."

A powerful motif in sayings assigned to authorities who lived
after the Bar Kokhba war is the issue of attitude: the surpassing
power of human intention in defining a situation and judging it.
In many ways diverse tractates of Mishnah seem to want to say that
there are yet important powers left in the hands of defeated,
despairing Israelites. The message of much of Mishnaic *halakhah*
is that there is an unseen world, a metaphysical world, subject to
the will of Israel. Given the condition of defeat, the despair
and helplessness of those who survived the end of time, we may
hardly be surprised at the message of authorities who wish to
specify important decisions yet to be made by people totally sub-
jugated to the will of their conquerors. Now if we ignore that
historical setting, the dissonances of theology and politics, in
which the message concerning attitude and intention is given, how
are we properly to interpret and compare "the Rabbis'" teachings
on the effects of the human will with those of Paul, or those
assigned to Jesus, for that matter? If they say the same thing,
it may be for quite divergent reasons. If they say different
things, it may be that they say different things because they
speak of different problems to different people.

Now these observations seem to me to be obvious and banal.[15]
But they are necessary to establish the urgency of facing those
simple historical questions Sanders wishes to finesse (by quoting
me, of all people!).[16] If we have a saying assigned to Aqiba how
do we know it really was said by him, belonging to the late first
and early second century? If we cannot show that it does go back
to A.D. 100, then we are not justified in adducing said sayings
as evidence of the state of mind of one late-first- and early-

second-century authority, let alone of *all* the late-first- and
early-second-century authorities—and let alone of "the Rabbis" of
the later first and whole of the second centuries. I cannot concede that Sanders's notion of systemic description, even if it
were wholly effected, has removed from the critical agendum these
simple questions of historical study we have yet to answer.

Nor should we ignore the importance, in the work not only of
comparison, but also of interpreting a given saying, of establishing the historical context in which the saying was said (or at
least in which it was important to be quoted). Sanders many times
cites the famous saying attributed to Yohanan b. Zakkai that the
corpse does not contaminate, nor does purification water purify,
but the whole thing is hocus-pocus. That saying first occurs in
a later, probably fourth-century, Midrashic compilation. Surely
we might wonder whether, at the time of the making of that compilation, issues of magic were not central in Rabbinic discourse.[17]
The denial of efficacy, *ex opere operato*, of a scriptural purification rite, addressed to a world in which magic, including Torah
magic, was deemed to work *ex opere operato*, may be interpreted as
a powerful polemic against a strong current of the fourth-century
Palestinian and Babylonian Jews' life, a time at which Rabbinical
circles, among others, were deeply interested in the magical
powers inherent in Torah. Now I do not mean to suggest that the
proper interpretation of the saying is in accord with this hypothesis,[18] nor do I even propose the stated hypothesis for serious
consideration here. I only offer it as an example of one context
in which the saying is credibly to be interpreted and, more important, as evidence of the centrality of context in the interpretation of each and every saying. If we do not know where and
when a saying was said, how are we to interpret the saying and
explain its meaning?

In my view the meaning of a saying is defined, at the outset,
by the context in which it is meaningful. To be sure, the saying
may remain meaningful later on, so that, cited for other purposes,
the saying takes on new meanings. No one denies that obvious
proposition, which, after all, is illustrated best of all by the
history of the interpretation, but, of greater systemic consequence, the deliberate misinterpretation, of the Old Testament in
Judaism and Christianity. If that is so, then we surely should
not reduce to a fundamentalistic and childish hermeneutical framework the interpretation of sayings attributed to rabbis in Rabbinic
documents of diverse periods, put together, as I said earlier, for

diverse purposes and therefore addressed, it seems to me self-
evident, to historically diverse circumstances.

Since this is one of the most ambitious works in Pauline
scholarship in twenty-five years and since, as I just said, it
does adumbrate initiatives of considerable methodological promise,
we must ask ourselves what has gone wrong with Sanders's immense
project. I think the important faults are on the surface.

First, his book should have been subjected to the reading of
two kinds of editors, a good editor for style and a critical editor for the planning and revision of the book. As a whole, it
simply does not hang together.

Second, I think Sanders pays too much attention to the anti-
Judaism of New Testament scholars. It is true, I suppose, that
there is a built-in bias on the part of some of Christian scholarship on Rabbinic Judaism, leading to negative judgments based upon
fake scholarship. But the motive for a major scholarly project
must be constructive. One must love one's subject, that is one's
sources and scholarly setting.

If, as I believe, Sanders has given us a good proposal on
"the holistic comparison of patterns of religion" (pp. 12-24),
then, third, he should have tried to allow his book to unfold as
an exposition and instantiation of his program of systemic comparison. This he does not do.

Fourth, his approach to the Rabbinic literature covers too
much or too little (I am not sure which). That is, he begins with
a sizable description of methodological problems. But when he
comes to the substantive exposition of the Rabbinic theology important for his larger project, Sanders seems to me to have forgotten pretty much everything he said on method. There are acres
and acres of paragraphs which in sum and substance could have been
lifted straight away from Schechter, Moore, or Urbach,[19] to name
three other efforts at systematic dogmatics in early Rabbinic
religion. I found the systematic theology of the Dead Sea Scrolls
equally tedious but know too little of the problems of working on
those sources to suggest how things might have been done differently and better. But to produce Sanders's substantive results
of the theological discussions, from election and covenant to the
nature of religious life and experience (pp. 84-232), we simply do
not need to be told about critical problems ("the use of Rabbinic
material, the nature of Tannaitic literature") laid out earlier
(pp. 59-83).

Still, in Sanders's behalf it must be repeated: He has defined the work to be done in terms which I think are valid and

fructifying. He has done his scholarly homework with more than routine ambition. He has laid forth an apologetic for Rabbinic Judaism and a powerful critique of ignorant or malicious or out-and-out anti-Semitic reports of, and judgments on, Rabbinic Judaism (or simply "Judaism"). Even though that theological enterprise cannot be deemed consequential for the study of the history of the religious world of ancient Judaism, it surely is not irrelevant to the context in which that history is written. The book is more than a mere compendium of this and that. It is based upon a care-fully thought-through program. Sanders's insistence that when Judaism is studied by Christian scholars, it must be considered without the endemic anti-Judaism characteristic of earlier work, is important for both social and academic reasons. The sort of people who believed that Judaism was depraved also maintained, like Kittel in 1933, that the best solution (if inexpedient) to the Jewish problem was to exterminate the Jews. In its apologetic aspect, Sanders's book addresses itself to a considerable social problem of our age. But, alas, it also is a service to scholar-ship in the history of religions to insist, as Sanders does, that religions, including Judaism, be studied *sine ire et studio*. So as it is a document of the times, Sanders's book is on the side of life and learning.

That is all the more reason to insist that, in regard to Rab-binic Judaism, Sanders's book also is so profoundly flawed as to be hopeless and, I regret to say it, useless in accomplishing its stated goals of systemic description and comparison. No, systems which have not accurately described cannot be compared. And the work of description surely involves critical initiatives in selection and interpretation. But to take up the work of inter-pretation, to design a project of comparison and carry it through, to reckon with the complexities of diverse documents and systems--these are essentially the tasks of our *own* exegesis of these an-cient texts and systems. To effect the comparison of patterns of ancient Jerusalem, what is needed is our self-conscious exegesis of their unself-conscious exegesis. For the history of religions is the exegesis of exegesis.

NOTES

THE USE OF THE LATER RABBINIC EVIDENCE FOR THE STUDY OF PAUL

[1]The polemic against New Testament scholarship on Judaism is a powerful theme which runs through the book and takes many forms. It is difficult to locate a major unit of thought which is not in some way affected by Sanders's apologetic interest. This example should not be thought to exhaust the matter, but shows how, at the very center of the book, issues are defined in contemporary theological terms. As we shall see in a moment, the very work of description itself becomes flawed on this account.

[2]So far as I can see, Sanders is reticent about the meaning of "religion" in this context, and other "*types* of religion" which are not to be found in Palestine before A.D. 70, but which might have been present there, also are not defined or discussed. I find a general lack of precision in terminology. But Sanders's purpose is not to contribute to the theoretical literature of religious studies.

[3]See above, n. 1.

[4]Try to imagine the scholarly agendum if Christianity were the minority religion, Judaism the majority one. Books on "the Christian background of Judaism" and "what Paul teaches us about the world of Mishnah" surely would distort the interpretation of Paul. After all, "Paul and the dietary laws" would not focus upon an issue at the center of Paul's thought, though it might be a principal point of interest to theological faculties. Proof that Jesus made important contributions to Judaism through his disciple, Hillel, or that Jesus was a Pharisee, would seem still more ridiculous, except that, the apologetic mind being what it is, they are written even here and now.

[5]In fact, all descriptions of the Talmuds tell us that the Talmud consists of the Mishnah and the Talmud (or Gemara, the terms are interchangeable), the latter being an exegesis of the Mishnah. I believed that view with perfect faith until I began work on Mishnah-tractates for which we have Talmud and found that, after a certain limited point, the Talmud really is not much interested in Mishnah and does not pretend to be. Still, the Talmud is so put together as to constitute a kind of "commentary" to the Mishnah, and this formal trait, so predominant in the sight of literary theorists, has to be taken seriously.

[6]*A History of the Mishnaic Law of Purities* (Leiden, 1974-77), vols. 1-22.

[7]My present work is on the fifth and third of the six divisions, *A History of the Mishnaic Law of Holy Things* (Leiden, 1979-80), which will be complete in six parts, and *A History of the Mishnaic Law of Women*, complete in five. Diverse volumes of my students' equivalent commentaries and analyses of the first division will appear under the general title, *A History of the Mishnaic Law of Agriculture*. The first of these is Richard S. Sarason, *Mishnah-Tractate Demai* (Leiden, 1979). Why a doctoral program, such as Brown's, calling itself "History of Religions: Judaism" should find its principal intellectual challenges to be those of exegesis, and how participants in that program conceive the purpose of history of religions to be served by their work, are not questions to be dealt with here, although the answers are suggested at the end of this paper.

[8]This is worked out in my *History of the Mishnaic Law of Purities*, vols. 13, *Miqvaot. Commentary*, and 14, *Miqvaot, Literary and Historical Problems* (Leiden, 1976). One of the most complex problems of Mishnah-study is the relationship of the diverse tractates of Mishnah to Scripture. I have dealt with this problem in "From Scripture to Mishnah: The Origins of Mishnah-tractate Niddah," *Journal of Jewish Studies*, in press; "From Scripture to Mishnah: The Exegetical Origins of Maddaf," *Festschrift for the Fiftieth Anniversary of the American Academy for Jewish Research*; "From Scripture to Mishnah: The Case of Mishnah's Fifth Division," *Journal of Biblical Literature* (March 1979); "The Meaning of *Torah shebe al peh*, with Special Reference to Kelim and Ohalot," *AJS Review* 1 (1976): 151-70, and in the various volumes of *Purities*, *Holy Things*, and, in due course, *Women* (cited above, n. 7). I do not understand why Sanders does not begin his work of description with an account of the Old Testament legacy available to all the groups under discussion as well as with an account of how, in his view, each group receives and reshapes that legacy. Everyone claimed, after all, to build upon the foundations of Mosaic revelation ("covenantal nomism"), indeed, merely to restate what Moses or the prophets had originally said. It seems to me natural to give the Old Testament a central place in the description of any system resting upon an antecedent corpus of such authority as the Mosaic revelation and the prophetic writings. Systemic comparison on diverse relationships to, and readings of, Scripture certainly is invited. In this context I must reject Sanders's critique of Vermes (pp. 25-29). His omission of reference to the Targumim because they are "generally late" is not very gallant. He chokes on the gnat of the Targums and swallows the camel of the Midrashim. Sanders says, "Even if generally late, the Targums may, to be sure, contain early traditions. But these must now be sought out one by one." True, indeed. *And the same is so for the whole of Tannaitic literature!* By "Tannaitic literature," Sanders means literature containing sayings attributed to Tannaim, or authorities who are assumed to have flourished before A.D. 200. As I shall suggest in a moment, such "early traditions" as occur in the name of first- and second-century authorities in documents of the third and later centuries also must be sought out, one by one. Sanders's more honest reason follows: "In general, the present state of Targumic studies does not permit the Targums to be used for our purposes." My argument is that the same is self-evidently true of the earlier Rabbinic documents. But Sanders successfully answers his own objection, with his stress on systemic—therefore diachronic—as against merely synchronic, comparison. Omission of the Targums is less damaging than failure to exploit the sizable legacy of the Old Testament, which surely is available, all parties concur, by the first century B.C.

[9]That is the point of the redactor's beginning with the chapter of Miqvaot which Sanders does cite.

[10]It is a tribute to the kindness of the reviewers of my *Purities* that the theory now laid forth has been received with a certain patience. Louis Jacobs, writing in *Bulletin of the School of Oriental and African Studies* vol. 40, no. 2 (1977), very correctly states, "Here, too, there is a fascinating theory about Pharisaic notions of purification, but one which does not necessarily follow from the acute analysis Neusner has given us of the Mishnaic sources." Jacobs then cites the passage before us. Jacobs is surely right that this theory does not necessarily follow from the sources. It is my guess at what the sources *mean*.

[11]*Purities*, 14:204-5.

[12] Ibid., p. 205.

[13] I must concede that it is asking much of scholars to sit
patiently to master the details of the Mishnaic (and other Rabbinic) law and only then to raise the questions of the deeper
range of meanings of that law. But the work of interpretation begins in exegesis and only ends in the formation and history of
ideas. If people find too arduous, or merely dull, the work of
patient exegesis, then of the recombinant history of small ideas,
let them write on some subject other than earlier Rabbinic Judaism.
The legal materials are not easy to understand. They are still
more difficult to interpret as statements of philosophical or
metaphysical conceptions. My message is that only in the work of
exegesis is that task of interpretation to be undertaken, and it
is only through interpretation that the meaning of the law is to
be attained.

[14] "The History of Earlier Rabbinic Judaism: Some New
Approaches," *History of Religions* 16 (1977): 216-36.

[15] Only people wholly ignorant of the way in which context,
both literary and social, affects interpretation of ideas will
even imagine that I here commit reductionism. I need hardly point
out that I do not claim the context exhausts the meaning or even
definitively establishes the parameters of meaning. That is why
I insist these observations are obvious and banal.

[16] See pp. 63-64, 70.

[17] I assemble the evidence on rabbinical wonder working (magic)
in the period under discussion in my *History of the Jews in Babylonia*, vol. 3, *From Shapur I to Shapur II* (Leiden, 1968), pp. 102-
30; vol. 4, *The Age of Shapur II* (Leiden, 1969), pp. 330-63; and
vol. 5, *Later Sasanian Times* (Leiden, 1970), pp. 174-93. There is
some indication that more wonder working or magical stories are
told about third- and fourth-century rabbis than about second-
century ones, and this corresponds to a general rise in magical
activity.

[18] That is, the story is meant as an antimagical polemic or an
effort to claim that the Torah's ritual laws have magical power,
a claim very widely advanced in Rabbinical circles and also in
regard to Jews or Jewish magicians.

[19] Solomon Schechter, *Some Aspects of Rabbinic Theology* (beginning in essays in *Jewish Quarterly Review*, 1894); George Foot
Moore, *Judaism in the First Centuries of the Christian Era: The
Age of the Tannaim* (Cambridge, 1927); and Ephraim E. Urbach, *The
Sages: Their Concepts and Beliefs* (Jerusalem, 1975). I cannot
imagine how Urbach, fifty years after Moore, has advanced the
discussion, except in some matters of detail. Indeed methodologically it is a giant step backward, excluding evidence Moore
included and adding an explicit apologetic layer to the discussion
left by Moore with a (merely subterranean) apologetic implication.

PUZZLING OUT RABBINIC JUDAISM

E. P. Sanders

McMaster University

A few years ago I published a study of what I ventured to call
"patterns of religion" in Paul and in Palestinian Judaism.[1] The
purpose of this present brief essay is to reassess some of my
proposals about Judaism (Paul will be left aside for the present
purpose) in light of scholarly response and, more important, to
identify issues that still need consideration in the attempt to
characterize Judaism in the first two centuries of the common era.
I particularly wish to enter into public dialogue with Professor
Jacob Neusner, whose treatment of my account of Rabbinic Judaism
(above pp. 43-63) is the lengthiest to have appeared.[2]

Neusner's article contains both agreements and disagreements
with my work. I wish not to take up every point, but to single
out the most important for comment. In doing so I must presuppose
that the reader has some knowledge of the contents of at least
part of *Paul and Palestinian Judaism*. A short statement of one of
the main points, however, may not be out of place. I proposed
that, when one asks of Jewish literature from about 200 BCE to
200 CE the question of how one becomes and remains a Jew in good
standing, a common answer emerges. Without unpacking the answer,
I can point toward it by citing some of the key terms: election
(the covenant), law, obedience/disobedience, and atonement.

On the positive side, Neusner characterizes as "wholly sound
and...self-evident" my proposal that Rabbinic literature presupposes the covenant (p. 47). In fact, the entire pattern I call
covenantal nomism is affirmed with the remark that "anyone familiar
with Jewish liturgy will be at home in that statement" (p. 48).

On the other hand, Neusner suggests that I may not have succeeded in uncovering the issues and the system of any of the forms
of Judaism which I studied: "...the issues of election and covenant, obedience and disobedience, do not necessarily define the
generative problematic of any of the Judaisms before us" (p. 49).
With regard to Rabbinic Judaism, I did not do what must be done:
analyze the central documents of the system (in this case primarily
the Mishnah) to discover, or more precisely, "to bring to the fore
what Rabbinic sources themselves wish to take as their principal
theme and generative problem" (p. 50). Thus, for example, the
Mishnah "does not wish to tell us much about election and covenant"

but "does wish to speak about other things" (p. 51).

Similar to this criticism is that of A. J. Saldarini.[3] He grants that "certainly the rabbis read Scripture and accepted the covenant," but argues that "neither their practice nor their self-consciousness centered on it." He continues,

> As difficult as it is for modern scholars--Christian and sometimes Jewish--to understand it, first and second century rabbis shifted their attention and efforts to the development of halaka and in its observance they found their God and guidance for living. Halaka is not derived from covenant in any concrete way in Tannaitic literature; it is itself central and primary.

1.   I have several responses to this line of criticism, but let me begin with a concession. I believe that, in doing my research, I was preoccupied more with what was common to the various forms of Judaism of the period than with what distinguished the various parties, movements, and sects from one another. It is true that I did not give an account of Rabbinic Judaism which would explain why more than one-sixth of the Mishnah is devoted to purity laws. "Covenantal nomism" offers a general explanation of the halaka--the concern to obey the God who chose Israel and gave the law--but not an account of why some elements are elaborated and some introduced while others disappear, nor an account of why concrete halakot differ between, for example, the Rabbis and the authors of IQS. The Mishnah and IQS are both concerned with purity. For my common denominator, that was adequate. I did not explain, nor attempt to explain, why they differ in elaboration and detail.

Along the same lines, there are other *differentia* which I did not account for. I noted, for example, that some authors and perhaps groups were more apocalyptically minded than others.[4] I was more interested in observing that there was agreement among the groups (or authors) on such items as the importance of obedience and the definition of righteousness than in explaining why some emphasized direct revelation and a climactic end to the present order while others emphasized study of the law of Moses and said relatively little about the end.[5] These latter, I am glad to grant, are important questions. In my view, the differences had been overemphasized in previous scholarship, to the point that, for example, apocalypticism had been sometimes treated as almost a separate religion.[6] If I had it all to do over again, I think that I would still emphasize what was common, but I might add more frequently and with greater emphasis that what was different was not getting quite equal attention.

Thus I am glad to have Neusner's consent to the *existence* of the common covenantal nomism and to acknowledge that my treatment of Rabbinic literature does not bring to the fore what is peculiar to it in the way that the program which he outlines would do.

I consider the existence of the common denominator--the agreement on election, law, obedience, atonement and the like--to be very important. For one thing, the framework of grace and atonement has been denied to "the Rabbis" by generations of Christian scholars, so that establishing the presence of that framework in the Rabbinic materials still seems to me something that had to be done. For another, the establishment of the ubiquity of covenantal nomism helps explain something about the continuity of Judaism in the flux of the times. I regard the pattern of election, law, obedience/disobedience, return and the like to be the common inheritance of Judaism from the Bible. My contribution was intended to show that the common inheritance was in fact maintained, both among the Rabbis and among such fringe groups as the Qumran covenanters.[7] That insistence was made in the face of a scholarly tendency to deny the common inheritance and speak about different Judaisms, a phrase which is used by Neusner himself.[8]

2. As a further preliminary to the major issue to be raised here, it should also be emphasized that Neusner and I are asking different questions of the material, although from his essay it might appear that our questions are the same: the world view that emerges from studying the Mishnah. The question that I raised-- and that Neusner does not mention--was how "getting in and staying in" were understood. I think that this difference of question leads to an ambiguity in Neusner's article: on the one hand granting the existence of covenantal nomism and on the other saying that I did not correctly represent the world view of the Rabbis. If the difference in what question is at stake had been more carefully noted, it might have led--and I hope that it still may lead--to a fruitful discussion of the *relative* place of covenantal nomism in the overall world view of the Rabbis. Neusner grants that the covenant was presupposed by the Rabbis, but what is the *relative* importance of that for understanding their entire point of view? This problem remains unaddressed. I granted, and will continue to grant, that the Rabbis did not much discuss how one gets in--or, as far as that goes, out. This may mean no more than that, as I shall propose below, they accepted the givenness of Israel and the election. Alternatively, it may have wider ramifications for understanding the Rabbinic movement. This I must leave as a question for others. I am content that, when the Rabbis did discuss

how one gets in, they saw it in terms of accepting the election and the commandments.

It might be proposed that asking how one gets "in" and stays "in" is to ask the material to answer questions that are foreign to it. This seems to be the significance of Neusner's saying in several places that I impose Pauline categories on the Rabbinic material or that I have "succeeded in finding Rabbinic sayings on topics of central importance to Paul (or Pauline theology)" (p. 56). The fullest statement is this: "Sanders...has not asked what is important and central in the system of Tannaitic-Rabbinic writings. All he wants to know is what, in those writings, addresses questions of interest to Paul" (p. 50). Saldarini has a similar criticism: "Sanders's sketch of rabbinic religion coheres, but it derives from Christian theological interests rather than from second- and third-century Jewish religion."[9]

I reject this charge almost entirely. The "almost" here implies a small concession. I did write in the context of previous scholarship on Paul and Judaism and Christianity and Judaism. It would have been irresponsible to do otherwise. Thus I had to deal with the old contrast of a religion of grace versus one of law, and the like. I tried to make it clear that this sort of comparison is inadequate. Discussing grace and law, I should add, is not entirely foreign to either Jewish material or Pauline, but I regarded that and similar frameworks as insufficient. I sought instead a different framework for comparison, the problem of how getting into the "in" group and staying "in" are understood. I regard that as a relatively neutral question. It could be asked of rather a lot of religions and movements within religions. It is a conscious theme in some literature more than it is in others, but it is not peculiarly Christian or Pauline. In detail, asking that question led me to discuss topics which have often had a place in theological discussions: grace, election, obedience, atonement and the like (Judaism); faith in Christ, righteousness, dying with Christ, remaining blameless and the like (Paul). Those who wish to deal with Judaism and Christianity in non-traditional terms may be put off a little to see such traditional topics come up again; but I would submit that it is perfectly reasonable for them to come up once the question about getting in and staying in is asked.

One of the main topics of the Conclusion of *Paul and Palestinian Judaism* is why some of the principal motifs of the traditional and common Jewish pattern, such as repentance and forgiveness, play so minimal a role in Paul's thought. I do not see how

raising this sort of question can be said to be imposing Pauline
categories on Judaism (Neusner) or to be analyzing Rabbinic religion on the basis of Christian theological interests (Saldarini).
Covenant, law, obedience and atonement are thoroughly traditional
Jewish interests. Discussing them is not discussing topics of
central importance to Paul (Neusner), but discussing what happened
to some of the common concerns of biblical and post-biblical
Judaism.

3.   When one turns to Neusner's program of determining what
Rabbinic Judaism was like, in its particularity, by analyzing the
world view of its central document, the Mishnah, a few questions
arise.   It is under this head that I wish to raise the issue of
how best to proceed with the study of Judaism, in this case
second-century Rabbinic Judaism.   Neusner, it will be recalled,
points out that the Mishnah "does not wish to tell us" very much
about such things as covenant and election.   In response to a
letter from me on the centrality of repentance in all of Judaism,
Neusner pointed out, quite accurately, that, "if you look in all
of Mishnah-Tosefta for the conception of repentance, you may find
it four or five times, never at crucial turnings in the document"
(letter of July 24, 1979).

This observation is entirely in line with what appears to be
Neusner's principal view of the nature of the material, which includes an assessment of the purpose and intention of its authors
(or compilers).   Thus he states elsewhere that the six orders of
the Mishnah constitute "the most important things" which the
Rabbis of the late first and second centuries could specify.[10]
Similarly he writes, "what they put in they think essential, and
what they omit they do not think important."[11]   In particular, the
Rabbinic material is not about "the great issues of theology,"
such as sin and atonement, suffering and penitence, divine power
and divine grace.   There are no tractates on such topics.[12]
Neusner grants, in the lecture from which these quotations are
taken, that some things worth knowing about the Rabbis are not
laid out in their system,[13] but the main thrust of his argument is
that one should take what is there as being of the utmost
importance.

Neusner's point about what is not in the Mishnah--an observation which is also reflected in the passage from Saldarini's
review which was quoted above--is a striking one.   But what does
the observation about what is in the Mishnah and what is not tell
us?   The absence of such terms as "election," "covenant" and the
like has long been cited by Christian scholars as evidence of the

debasement of "late Judaism."[14] I was equally conscious of the
relative absence of direct discussion of such conceptions, but I
drew different inferences, and those different inferences were
based on a different assessment of the nature of the material.

It is also, I believe, a divergence of view about the nature
of the material which is principally at issue between Neusner and
me. Both views are explicitly stated. Neusner's principal view I
have just given. My own was this: the Mishnah includes contentious points or issues requiring clarification, but omits direct
discussion of things which were granted on all hands and which are
thus arguably central to the Rabbinic system.[15] This is, it will
be seen, almost the direct opposite of Neusner's view that what is
there is most important.

It is perhaps foolhardy and presumptuous to maintain this
view in the face of criticism from one whose occupation is precisely a study of the nature of the material under discussion. It
would be simple to say that my work should be judged on the basis
of the "state of the art" as it was in 1974--a point which both
Neusner and Saldarini offer as mitigating some of the deficiencies
of my work[16]--and that, now that Neusner's mature and full view of
the relationship between what is in the Mishnah and what mattered
to the Rabbis is available, I am better instructed than I was when
I wrote. The trouble is that I still think that there is much to
be said for the view of the material that I previously expressed.
In saying this I do not intend to challenge the value of laying
out the world view of the Mishnah on the basis of what is in it.
I still think, however, that it is also important to try to determine what is presupposed in the Mishnah, but perhaps not directly
discussed.

In his essay Neusner does not give a direct evaluation of my
view that what is central is not directly discussed *because* it was
presupposed, but that view has drawn at least one dry criticism:
"I don't see how one could verify or falsify that argument."[17] I
think that I do see how; I do not regard that view of the material
to be based on arbitrary preference or on wishful thinking. Since
the issue of the nature of the material is crucial for its interpretation, I shall offer three observations, which obviously cannot
be definitive, in favor of the view that Rabbinic material, and the
Mishnah in particular, presupposes important agreements that either
are not directly discussed or that play a relatively small role in
the material as a whole.

a. The compilers of the Mishnah, and presumably the
preceding Rabbis whose discussions are often repeated in it,

assumed the entire "repair system" of the Bible. By "repair system" I mean to include both the sacrificial system and the prophetic exhortations to "return," for which the word "repentance" was coined in the post-biblical period. The sacrificial system occupies a prominent place in the Mishnah.[18] Also of importance is the tractate on Yom Kippur, the Day of Atonement, which some-one--I assume the Rabbinic leaders--insisted should still be observed even when the sacrifices were no longer possible. The tractate deals largely with "historical" information about how the Day was observed when the Temple stood (chs. 1-7). One may learn by *inference* from ch. 8, the final chapter, that the Day of Atonement in the post-Temple period involved abstinence from eating and the like (8.1) and repentance (8.8f.). Since sacrifices are mentioned in both contexts (8.3; 8.8), one could conceivably suppose if all we had were the Mishnah tractate, that the statements about abstinence and repentance apply to the observance of the Day only in the period of the Temple. It is in Sifra that the role of repentance in the post-Temple period is highlighted and sharpened.[19] Even the basic rule that the Day was still observed and was still regarded as efficacious, which obviously governed Rabbinic practice, can be derived only by inference from M. Yoma 8; it is not explicitly stated.[20] Again, the explicit statement appears in Sifra.[21] The relevant discussions in Sifra are constructed in such a way as to emphasize Rabbinic practice and to prove exegetically that it is correct, while what comes to the fore in the Mishnah tractate is priestly practice in the Temple (at least as the Rabbis thought it should have been). The importance of the annual observance of Yom Kippur in post-Temple Judaism would be a little hard to reconstruct if we were limited to the Mishnah tractate.

Thus I would offer the observation that behind the tractate on the Day of Atonement lie two major views that are not argued for but are taken for granted: that the Day would be observed without sacrifices and that it was efficacious for those who repented. These were uncontentious points and did not need to be established by halakic debates in the Mishnah. The contrary position, that the Day was not kept or that repentance was not required, would be amazing.

This sort of argument, which could be multiplied, seems to show that the conception of atonement for transgression, including especially repentance in lieu of sacrifice after CE 70, was alive and well among the Rabbis. Atonement for transgression, further, seems to *presuppose* the conception of *sin as disobedience* to *law*.

It further presupposes a prior, given relationship between God and Israel which could be in some way damaged by disobedience. It does not seem unreasonable to call that given relationship "the conception of the covenant"--whether the Rabbis in the Mishnah directly discuss the relationship between God and Israel under precisely that title or not.

b. The Mishnah often contains debates about how and when to do something or other when the "something or other" is not explicitly quoted. I have in mind in particular the saying of the *shema*[c][22] and the praying of the *[c]amidah*.[23] As I indicated above, Neusner grants that covenantal nomism will sound reasonable to anyone at home in the liturgy. Yet the liturgy is not in the Mishnah--only statements about details of how and when elements of it should be said. The Rabbis, in other words, took it for granted that the *shema*[c] should be said and the *[c]amidah* prayed on a regular basis. They do not discuss what one learns from saying them. But can we suppose that, in insisting that the *shema*[c] and the *[c]amidah* must be said, they were blind to their contents and did not consider those contents to be of great, perhaps central importance? The *shema*[c] and the *[c]amidah* taken together contain unmistakably clear references to such conceptions as election, obedience, and repentance for disobedience.[24] Their absence from the Mishnah is due entirely to the fact that its compilers saw no reason to lay out the contents of what they insisted must be said *every* day by *every* practicing Jew. Those contents are simply taken for granted. I do not think that Saldarini can be right that the Rabbis did not connect the halaka with the election. The halakot requiring the repetition of a biblical passage and a prayer that affirm the election seem to stand in direct opposition to that proposal.

When one considers the importance of the *shema*[c] and the *[c]amidah* in daily life, and the importance of Yom Kippur in the annual cycle, it seems strange to deny that the contents indicated by those prayers and practices were consciously related to the making of halaka.

It may be useful here to re-emphasize what is learned from the Mishnah and what is not. One can learn by inference *that* Yom Kippur was observed. One explicitly learns *that* the *shema*[c] and the *[c]amidah* (or its substance)[25] were said--or at least were considered by the makers of the Mishnah to be mandatory. We must go somewhere else, not to the Mishnah itself, to learn what contents the Rabbis were concerned to work into the fabric of Judaism.

c. It is noteworthy that it is in polemical literature

that the topics of election and the requirement of strict obedience to the Mosaic code come to most explicit expression. I have in mind, for example, Jubilees, the principal Dead Sea Scrolls, and the letters of Paul. It is striking that Paul attacks Judaizing precisely on the adequacy of the election of Israel and on the requirement to keep the Mosaic law--two of the principal elements of covenantal nomism.[26] This is simply further proof of how common those elements were in Judaism. When one turns to Rabbinic literature, which is relatively nonpolemical toward outsiders, it is quite understandable to find that these inherited, common features were taken for granted and discussed relatively little. The makers of the Mishnah did not see the existence and status of Israel as being in question in the society which they addressed, and reasonably enough did not defend them. Here, however, one may again see the role of the tannaitic midrashim in supplementing the Mishnah. Since the midrashim discuss the Bible, and since the Exodus, the election, the giving of the law, and the like are in the Bible, we find that they are commented on explicitly *when the subject comes up* in the course of the commentary. It does not seem unreasonable to turn to those comments to discover what was said when such subjects were discussed. I would further venture the opinion that the makers of the Mishnah may have neither disapproved nor excluded from their own view of things the sorts of statements which are made in the midrashim about the relation between law and covenant (for example), even though they had no reason to include them in the Mishnah itself.

These three points should serve to illustrate why I continue to think that the traditional concerns of covenant, atonement, and the like retained their importance in Rabbinic Judaism, even though other things are discussed more often and more explicitly. Further, they show why one must press behind the contents of the Mishnah and attempt to discover what the contents of the Mishnah presuppose.

I believe that there is a very important respect in which Neusner would agree with the last sentence, and I should here turn to another feature of his view of the nature of the material. From the programmatic statements such as those quoted above it might appear that he thinks that what is important is what is *explicitly* there. This is, however, a long way from being the case. It turns out that "what Mishnah wishes to say" includes a metaphysical world view which is not explicitly stated and to which no Orders or even tractates are devoted. Neusner describes as "at best a guess" a statement from his work on Purities about what the Mishnah wishes to say in Miqvaot. The statement is, in part, this: "They [the Pharisees] remove the uncleanness defined by the Written Torah for the holy altar, because of the conviction of the Oral Torah [Mishnah] that the hearth and home, table and bed, going onward through ages without end, also must be and can be cleaned, in particular, through the rain...."[27] The explanation ("because...") of why the Rabbis sought for daily life the purity prescribed for the Temple is a statement of what the Mishnah "wishes to say,"[28] but it is a statement which is not in the Mishnah--nor, as far as I know, in Rabbinic literature. It is a fair inference from what is there, and I consider it insightful; but it is, in my terms, an inference about what the Mishnah implies. Neusner cites this explanation in the context of criticizing me for saying that Miqvaot does not directly tell us what concerns lie behind its detailed prescriptions. I think in fact that we agree, at least to the extent of seeing the need to find out what values the halaka presupposes and implies.

It is beyond the scope of this essay to lay out, much less to analyze, the metaphysical world view which Neusner's study of the Mishnah and Tosefta has thus far led him to posit, but one statement appears to be both seminal in Neusner's own view and important for the present discussion.

> If we stand back from the system of uncleanness and look at the structure of which it is a principal part, we observe a set of balanced circles: Israel at the center, the nations at the periphery; the Land at the center, the lands at the periphery; the Temple at the center, the profane world at the periphery. To these circles the system merely adds, the *haber* at the center, the *'am ha areṣ* at the periphery, a late and unimportant conception generated by societal, not metaphysical considerations. Accordingly, when we enter the system of purity, we come to the pivot of the world: Temple, the holiest place of the holy Land of the holy people, Israel. *We bring the life-sustaining processes of the people into conformity with the world-sustaining processes of the Temple.*[29]
>
> So far as the structure stands upon a pivot, it is the people of Israel, not the Temple, which is pivotal.[30]

The centrality of the people of Israel seems to correspond to the centrality of the covenant and election for which I argued.[31] The method by which the result is reached--the line of argument-- is certainly different, resting as it does on Neusner's systemic analysis of what is in the Mishnah and the Tosefta. Aspects of my own method are sketched in points a., b., and c. above. I argued in part from what is said when the topic of election comes up

(principally in the tannaitic midrashim) and partly from what seems
to be presupposed by what is said on other topics. Thus I inferred
from the discussions of how atonement is obtained that a prior
relation, signified by the word "election," is presupposed.[32] The
method I followed still appears to me viable, particularly given
the question I was asking, and I am glad to see that there is at
least partial agreement with the results produced by systemic
analysis of the Mishnah.

Just as the methods of studying the material and the questions
which were asked of it are different, so also is the terminology
which is employed to describe the values which lie behind it. I
wrote about the traditional concerns of Judaism--election, covenant, obedience and the like. Neusner, drawing partly on anthropology, speaks of a metaphysical world view. I do not want to debate the relative merits of these languages. As I pointed out in
2. above, the relationship of the traditional concerns to the
world view remains an unaddressed question. The brief discussion
of Israel, however, indicates that there is at least some overlap.
The most important point to be made here is the need to press behind the explicit statements of the Mishnah (and the related
literature) to the values and views which are presupposed.[33]

I wish, naturally, that these two reviewers, and one or two
others, had dealt with my work more in terms of my intention and
less in the light of their own programs of how the material should
be studied. This, I am aware, is a standard author's lament.
Nevertheless, these reviews do offer the potential of asking in a
fresh way questions about ancient Judaism. I repeat for the sake
of emphasis the principal questions which arise from this discussion and which seem to me to require further consideration:
1) What is the relationship between the common Jewish pattern that
I designated covenantal nomism and the particular set of concerns
that emerge from systemic analysis of the Mishnah? 2) If one
grants, as I believe Neusner will grant, that the presuppositions
of the makers of the Mishnah often are not discussed directly in
the Mishnah, can their world view be *adequately* reconstructed by
analyzing "what Mishnah wishes to say"? Will one not also have to
give appreciable place to the contents of traditional Judaism,
which they seem to have regarded as not requiring halakic discussion? 3) What is the role of the halakic midrashim in reconstructing the total set of concerns which animated the makers and
redactors of tannaitic literature?

NOTES

PUZZLING OUT RABBINIC JUDAISM

[1] *Paul and Palestinian Judaism: A Comparison of Patterns of Religion* (London/Philadelphia: SCM/Fortress, 1977).

[2] I write "public dialogue," since our discussions have not been limited to what is in print. I was in correspondence with Professor Neusner about what was and was not feasible to do in the study of Rabbinic Judaism in the early 1970's; he kindly sent me a draft of the review article and considered some of my comments on it, and we have continued to discuss the issues. We are, I think, drawing closer in some ways.

[3] Review in *JBL* 98 (1979): 299-303, here 300.

[4] *Paul and Palestinian Judaism*, pp. 423f.

[5] The failure to explain the distinction between direct revelation and study of the law of Moses was well pointed out by John Collins in "The Son of Man Who Has Righteousness," a paper presented to the Society of Biblical Literature Pseudepigraph Seminar, 1979, p. 8 of the typescript (at fn. 65). I am not, however, persuaded that the Similitudes of Enoch, which Collins is discussing, are closer to Paul's pattern of religion than to covenantal nomism, as he proposes.

[6] See the discussions referred to in *Paul and Palestinian Judaism*, p. 423 n. 12.

[7] See *Paul and Palestinian Judaism*, p. 424: "we have been concerned with the question of whether or not there is a basic common ground...."

[8] Above, p.

[9] *JBL* 98 (1979): 300.

[10] Jacob Neusner, "The Talmud as Anthropology," Annual Samuel Friedland Lecture, The Jewish Theological Seminary of America (New York: JTS, 1979), p. 15.

[11] *Ibid.*, p. 31.

[12] *Ibid.*, p. 25.

[13] *Ibid.*, p. 32.

[14] See, for example, *Paul and Palestinian Judaism*, pp. 419-21.

[15] Neusner criticizes me for not asking "what is important and central in the system of Tannaitic-Rabbinic writings" (p.   ), and I am probably meant to be included in the criticism that not a single theologian "begins with consideration of the character of the sources" ("The Talmud as Anthropology": 16 n. 19). I explicitly stated my view of the material in *Paul and Palestinian Judaism*, pp. 76-81, and I moved from that to a statement of what central questions generated the *halaka* (pp. 81-4), a statement which was subsequently elaborated.

[16]Neusner: "We cannot...blame Sanders for not doing what has only just now been undertaken" (Above, p. 51); Saldarini: the "defects will be overcome only by advances in basic research and methodology" (*JBL* 98 [1979]: 303). Neusner accurately noted that the portion of the book dealing with Rabbinic Judaism was completed "in 1973 or 1974" (Above, p. 50). Early 1974 is the correct date. The entire typescript was sent to the press in 1975.

[17]Nils Dahl, Review in *RSR* 4 (1978): 153-57, here 155.

[18]See, for example, the tractates Zabahim, Tamid, Middoth and Kinnim, and such passages as Parah 1.4, Shebuoth 1.5-7. See Neusner's recent summary on the order Qodashim, which deals with the sacrificial system: "From Scripture to Mishnah: The Origins of Mishnah's Fifth Division," *JBL* 98 (1979): 269-83.

[19]See, for example, Sifra Emor *pereq* 14.1 (to 23.27).

[20]J. N. Epstein proposed that most of Yoma 8.9 is a *baraita* added after the principal redaction of the Mishnah (for reference, see *Paul and Palestinian Judaism*, p. 158 n. 57). Even if this is the case, the wording of the opening sentence of 8.9 seems to imply that the Day is still being observed. A similar inference can be drawn from 8.1, 4.

[21]The halaka appears in Sifra Aḥare Mot *pereq* 8.1 (to 16.30).

[22]M. Berakoth 1.1-3.2.

[23]M. Berakoth 3.5-4.7. The ^{c}*amidah* (standing [prayer]) is often called simply the *tefillah* (prayer) or the *shemoneh* ^{c}*esreh* (Eighteen [benedictions]).

[24]It is now recognized that the precise wording, or even the variant wordings, of the ^{c}*amidah* in the second century cannot be recovered. See Richard Sarason, "On the Use of Method in the Modern Study of Jewish Liturgy," *Approaches to Ancient Judaism: Theory and Practice*, ed. W. S. Green (Missoula: Scholars Press, 1978), pp. 97-172, especially n. 34. There would seem, however, to be no doubt that the themes of repentance, forgiveness, the redemption of Israel, and the like always figured.

[25]M. Berakot 4.3.

[26]The adequacy of the election and the Mosaic dispensation: Rom. 3.9; 9.6-8; II Cor. 3.7-18; Gal. 3.19-21; Phil. 3.2-3; the requirement to keep the law: Rom. 4; Gal. 3; and often.

[27]Above p. 54, quoting *A History of the Misnaic Law of Purities* 14 (Leiden: Brill, 1976), p. 205.

[28]Above, p. 54.

[29]*Purities*, 22:297; "History and Structure: The Case of Mishnah," *JAAR* 45 (1977): 184.

[30]*Purities*, 22:299; "History and Structure": 186.

[31]Neusner called my attention to the correspondence in a letter of August 13, 1979.

[32]E.g., *Paul and Palestinian Judaism*, pp. 235f.

[33]Whether or not what is assumed and presupposed in the Mishnah, and implied by it, was *consciously* held is a weightier question and one that is harder to resolve. To deal with it would require a separate study, and so I must pass over it here. It is my view, however, that the constituent elements of covenantal nomism were consciously held. They often go unexpressed because they were assumed. Neusner, if I understand him, would also argue that the drafters of the Mishnah consciously held the world view which he describes: thus, for example, he speaks of what the Mishnah "wants to say."

MISHNAH AND SCRIPTURE:

PRELIMINARY OBSERVATIONS ON THE LAW OF TITHING

IN *SEDER ZERA^{c}IM*[*]

Richard S. Sarason

Hebrew Union College

The central myth of rabbinic Judaism is that of the twofold
Torah. At Sinai Moses Our Rabbi received from God not merely the
Written Torah, Scripture, which at the time of the formation of
rabbinic Judaism was the common heritage of all Jews, he also
received an Oral Torah that was faithfully transmitted by word of
mouth down to the rabbis themselves and finally encapsulated in
Mishnah. The authorities behind both the Mishnah and the Talmuds
view the Oral Torah as in part elaboration and specification of
the Written Torah (that is to say, as filling in the details of
Scripture's general principles), and in part as autonomous of, but
correlative to, the Written Torah.[1] When we as historians of
religion ask about the relationship between "Oral Torah" and
"Written Torah"--between Mishnah and Scripture--we in fact are
asking about the nature of Mishnah as a document and about the
world view of earliest rabbinic Judaism which is embodied therein.
These questions recently have been posed anew by Jacob Neusner in
his studies of the Mishnaic Orders of Purities, Holy Things, and
Women.[2] Here I propose to address them out of my own work in the
Order of Seeds.

Let me begin by putting this topic in perspective and indi-
cating why it must be treated in a fundamentally fresh way. The
question of the relationship between Mishnah and Scripture is as
old as Mishnah itself and generally has been raised in an apologetic or polemical context. The early rabbis had to address this
question in order to substantiate their claims to salvific
authority in the Jewish community as possessors of the true and
complete divine revelation. The link between Written Torah, the
authority of which was generally acknowledged, and Oral Torah was
achieved in two ways: 1) through *post facto* formal exegesis of
Scripture, and 2) through mythic history.

The first is evidenced in the so-called "Tannaitic," halakic
midrashim, particularly in Sifra. Neusner[3] asserts that Sifra as
a document wishes to demonstrate that the rabbinic *halakot* cannot
be discovered solely by human logic, but must be deduced formally
from Scripture. Sifra further claims that the laws of Mishnah

81

were deduced from Scripture--including those laws which, elsewhere
in the rabbinic corpus, are acknowledged to have little to do with
Scripture. "From this [scriptural verse] have they taught"
(*mik'an 'amru*), is a common formulary in Sifra. Through elaborate
and frequently artificial hermeneutics the halakic *midrashim*
ground Mishnah in Scripture.

A second method by which the rabbis establish the authority
of Mishnah is through the myth of the twofold Torah revealed at
Sinai, to which I referred above. This myth, incidentally, pre-
serves the autonomy of the Oral Torah *vis à vis* the Written Torah,
since it claims only that the former is co-equal in antiquity and
authority with the latter, and not that the Oral Torah is derived
from the Written Torah.[4] The history of the faithful transmission
of Oral Torah from Moses to the authorities of Mishnah is related
in the "chain of tradition" in Tractate Abot.

Rabbinism's apologetic need to establish the link between
Mishnah and Scripture, and to demonstrate the reliability of the
rabbinic tradition as a whole, became particularly acute at the
time of the Qaraite revolt against rabbinic authority, beginning
in seventh-century Babylonia. Against the Qaraite claims that the
rabbinic tradition was of human origin and constituted a perver-
sion of the true sense of Scripture, the rabbanites argued that
the Oral Torah indeed was the true interpretation of the Written
Torah. The Qaraite controversy spawned a genre of apologetic histories of rabbinism and the Oral Torah, best represented by the
Letter of Sherira Gaon and Abraham ibn Daud's *Book of Tradition*
(*Sefer haQabbalah*). These became the standard sources, down to
the present day, for rabbinic Judaism's mythic understanding of
its own history.

Of greater moment for our purposes, the question of the relationship between Mishnah and Scripture was raised once again by
nascent Jewish scholarship of the nineteenth century, to be
answered in no less apologetic a fashion than the one just now
noted. Historical and philological scholarship were the tools
for defending Judaism against the polemics of Christian theologians and Biblical scholars, on the one hand. On the other,
historical argumentation for a time proved a congenial mode for
right-wing Reformers such as Zacharias Frankel and "enlightened"
traditionalists such as David Hoffmann and I. H. Weiss to defend
traditional Judaism and its practices against the more radical
Reformers, and to strengthen the perplexed among the faithful in
their adherence to the tradition. The Letter of Sherira Gaon now
was read as a straightforward, factual historical source, its

apologetic and mythic character largely ignored. In general, the
mythic history of rabbinism and the Oral Law was translated, for
no less apologetic reasons, into a "history" no less mythic for all
its *wissenschaftliche* pretenses. In accord with the prevailing
historicism and Hegelianism of the age, rabbinic Judaism was portrayed as the organic and inevitable outcome of the post-exilic
community's acceptance, in the time of Ezra, of the Mosaic Torah
as its constitution. The Oral Law, as the detailed interpretation
of the constitution (it was claimed), grew organically in mono-
linear fashion from the time of Ezra and the scribes to its ultimate codification in Mishnah.[5]

This apologetic view of Mishnah, the scholarly legacy of the
nineteenth century, has been a long time in dying, and persists
overtly or tacitly in some circles today. In light of our present
knowledge of the variety of groups and ideologies in Palestinian
Judaism of the late Second Temple period, it must be fundamentally
rejected. Mishnah is properly to be understood as but one potential system among many. Moreover, as Neusner has insisted,[6]
Mishnah is to be understood as a *system*, as a particular "statement
on the meaning of Scripture" and a particular interpretation of the
world. The importance of this observation is twofold. First,
Mishnah is to be granted its uniqueness. We must be wary of comparisons with non-rabbinic sources from the late Second Temple
period that yield overly hasty generalizations about "the *halakah*"
of Palestinian Judaism. What the various groups and authors possess in common is Scripture. Scripture can yield the same or
similar meanings for different groups through different exegetical
techniques, as Lawrence Schiffman has shown,[7] or even through
similar techniques without one group necessarily "influencing" the
other. As Samuel Sandmel, Morton Smith, and Jacob Neusner have
insisted,[8] we should be comparing entire systems of thought--coher-
ent world views--and not simply this detail and that rule.
Obviously the same detail or ruling can take on entirely different
meanings in the context of different systems.

A second point logically follows from the first. If we wish
to analyze Mishnah as a system of ideas and rules--as a document
with a particular point of view--then we must ask not only where
Mishnah depends on Scripture and where it does not, but also which
parts of Scripture interest Mishnah and which do not; and, finally,
what it is that Mishnah wants to say *about* Scripture and Scripture's laws. We must distinguish, then, between Scripture's
topics, on the one hand, and Mishnah's *interests*, on the other.

Bearing in mind these observations, we now turn to the Mishnaic
law of tithing.

I begin by noting that, with the exception of Tractates Berakot and Demai, the topics of Mishnah's tractates in $Zera^{c}im$ originate in Scripture. But the choice of topics also indicates Mishnah's interests. The tractates deal with the various agricultural
gifts--to the priests, to the Levites, to the poor--that must be
given from produce grown in the soil of the Holy Land of Israel,
as well as with the various taboos that apply to such produce.
Excepting Peah (gifts to the poor), each of these topics represents
an aspect or a kind of holiness that can pertain to types of produce, grown in the Land, on which God has a claim. We shall see
below that Mishnah's primary interest is in the process of sanctification, and the interaction in this process between human and
divine will and action.

My focus is on the tithing laws, which comprise roughly half
of the Order. Mishnah's system of tithes begins in a unitary,
harmonistic reading of the Torah literature's diverse pericopae on
tithing.[9] The tithe of grain, wine, and oil that Numbers 18
assigns to the Levites is juxtaposed by Mishnah with the Deuteronomic tithe (Deut. 14:22f.), which must be taken to Jerusalem and
eaten there by the farmer and his family "before Yahweh your God."
In Mishnah, the Levitical and Deuteronomic tithes become first and
second tithe, respectively, each a tenth part of the produce.
Additionally, the Deuteronomic "welfare" tithe, which is stored up
in the towns every three years for "the Levite, the resident alien,
the fatherless, and the widow" (Deut. 14:28-29; 26:12f.), becomes
Mishnah's poor man's tithe, separated instead of a second tithe in
the third and sixth years of each sabbatical cycle and given to
the poor. Finally, the "tithe from the tithe" ($ma^{c}a\acute{s}er\ myn$
$ha-ma^{c}a\acute{s}er$) that Numbers 18 requires the Levites to give to
"Aaron the priest" from the tithe they receive becomes Mishnah's
"terumah from the tithe" ($terumat\ ma^{c}a\acute{s}er$; cf. Num. 18:28: Kn
$trymw\ gm\ 'tm\ trwmh\ LYHWH\ mkl\ m^{c}\acute{s}rwtykm$).

So far there is nothing unique about Mishnah's understanding
of Scripture's "facts." A unitary reading of Scripture will yield
the same information to any group or author. In fact, the same
systematization of the scriptural tithes is found in the Books of
Tobit and Jubilees, and in Josephus' *Antiquities*, the only difference being that Josephus and some versions of Tobit hold that the
tithe for the poor is to be separated triennially as an additional
third tithe. (Jubilees does not refer to this tithe.)[10]

In addition to these tithes, Mishnah knows three agricultural offerings that are given to the priest: the dough-offering (*hallah*) of Numbers 15:17-21; the first fruits (*bikkurim*) of Numbers 18:13, Deut. 26, ex. 23:19, 34:26, and Neh. 10:36; and the *terumah*, usually and incorrectly translated as "heave-offering."[11] The derivation from Scripture of this last offering depends in part on the distinctive use of terminology at Num. 18:12-13, which assigns to the priest "all the best (*ḥlb*) of the oil, and all the best of the wine and of the grain, the first (or "best") part (*r ̆sytm*) they give to the Lord.... The *first ripe fruits* of all (*bkwry-kl*) that is in their land, which they bring to the Lord...." Mishnah distinguishes between the *re'ŝyt* of v. 12 and the *bikkurim* of v. 13, and holds that these are two distinct offerings. In fact, the passage from Numbers probably did bear this meaning originally.[12] It is certain in any case that this is how Mishnah reads Scripture, since the heave-offering is referred to at M. Ter. 3:7 and T. Ter. 3:18 as *terumat re'ŝyt*. It is also the case that Mishnah's usage of the term *terumah* to designate this particular offering to the priest is distinctive; to my knowledge, the term does not occur with this meaning in any of the extant non-rabbinic sources from the Second Temple period.[13]

These, then, are the scriptural data--the facts--with which Mishnah chooses to deal. But the important question, as I have indicated before, is, What does Mishnah propose to do with these facts? What does it want to know about tithes and *terumah*? What, in short, is its agendum? To begin with, it is not quite the same as Scripture's, although the basic tithing system remains the same. The various scriptural pericopae on tithing, of course, are not of a piece, and there are shifts of emphasis among them, particularly between those in Deut. and those in the Priestly Code. Nonetheless, the following generalizations can be made: Yahweh is conceived as the owner of the Land of Israel and as ruler of the people Israel. The people, as tenant farmers on Yahweh's Land (who also are concerned to insure the Land's ongoing fertility), owe to Yahweh, through his priestly agents, the first ripe fruits of each year's harvest (*bikkurim*) and the first, or best, portion of their grain, wine, and oil (*re ̆syt*) and of their dough (*re ̆syt ᶜarysah*; *hallah*). The fruit of a newly-planted vineyard in its first year of harvesting (the fourth year of its growth) also is dedicated to Yahweh. The Deuteronomic tithe, while not given to the priests,[14] is eaten by the farmer, his family, and the local Levites as a cultic meal "before Yahweh" in Jerusalem, and is designated as holy (Deut. 26). On the other hand, the triennial

welfare tithe of Deuteronomy and the Priestly Code's Levitical
tithe (Num. 18) are not offerings to Yahweh, but taxes paid to
support the needy and the Levites. Scripture thus describes only
some offerings as holy to Yahweh, and Mishnah closely adheres to
the distinctions of Scripture. Mishnah's system of agricultural
offerings remains that of Scripture (read harmonistically, as a
unitary text). But the documents differ in their emphases and
interests. Scripture's emphasis, particularly at the stage of
final redaction, is with the care and feeding of the priesthood
and the Levites, that is, with the cultic system and the ultimate
disposition of the agricultural offerings. This concern is particularly evident in Num. 18, the *locus classicus* on priestly and
Levitical perquisites from the soil, and in Neh. 10, where the
returning exiles vow to bring "our contributions, the fruit of
every tree, the wine and the oil to the priests, to the chambers
of the house of our God; and to bring the Levites the tithe from
our ground" (10:37).

When we turn to Mishnah, we discover that a shift of interest
has taken place. While Mishnah by no means is indifferent to the
proper disposition of the *terumah* and tithes, *its* primary concern
is with the process of sanctification of the various agricultural
offerings, and, particularly, in the part man plays in the process
of sanctification. In this respect, I think it hardly coincidental
that the lengthiest tractate in the Order of Seeds is Terumot,
which deals with that offering regarded by Mishnah as holy *par
excellence*. Nor is it coincidental that Mishnah devotes a tractate
to second tithe, which is deemed holy, but not to the Levitical
first tithe, which is not sanctified. The tractates on tithing
give us a kind of geometry or logic of the sacred and sanctification in the realm of agricultural practice. A careful analysis of
these tractates will show that Mishnah's theory of the holiness of
produce that grows from the soil of the Land of Israel is transactional. That is to say, holiness does not naturally inhere in
produce. Rather, God and man are the agents of sanctification.
God, as owner of the land, has prior claim on its produce. But
man must acknowledge God's ownership and validate God's claim by
actively designating and separating God's portions. Additionally,
holiness is to be understood primarily in functional rather than
substantive terms, i.e., that which is deemed holy belongs to God
(and frequently is allotted by God to his priests), and must not
be used by ordinary Israelites. Sacrilege thus is conceived as a
violation of God's property rights.[15]

The authorities behind Mishnah primarily are interested in spelling out the role of human action and, particularly, intention in the process of sanctification. That role, as I shall indicate, is determinative throughout the process. To begin with, the locus of susceptibility to sanctification is determined with reference to man's actions and intentions (cf. Tractate Maaserot). Not everything that grows in the soil of the Land of Israel is liable to the separation of heave-offering and tithes. Liability falls only on produce which is cultivated for human food (M. Ma. 1:1). This notion, of course, begins in Scripture, which requires Israelite farmers to offer to God, as owner of the Land, the best part of their grain, wine, and oil, and to feed the priests and Levites, who do not farm the land. Mishnah expands the liability to include all edible produce.[16] The tithing laws, then, are food laws. Only produce which can be human food enters the system of tithing and sanctification.

Similarly, the point at which produce becomes liable to the separation of *terumah* and tithes (i.e., becomes *ṭebel*; see below) is the point at which it becomes edible (M. Ma. 1:2). But man's actions and intentions further determine liability at this juncture. For before edible produce has been fully harvested or processed, it may be eaten randomly without incurring liability to tithing. Only if a man eats the produce as a regular meal before it is harvested must he tithe it. Furthermore, the point at which produce is considered to be fully harvested and liable to tithing also is determined by human intention regarding its ultimate disposition. If the farmer intends to bring his produce to market, it becomes liable to tithing when it is in that condition in which it will be brought to market--sifted, stacked, tied in bundles, etc. If, on the other hand, he intends to bring the produce home to be eaten by his household, it does not become liable to tithing until it enters his private domain--the house or the courtyard (M. Ma. 1:5, 3:5; cf. T. Ma. 2:4).

Finally, produce becomes holy (i.e., God's property) only through man's act of consecration. This is made clear by considering the status of *ṭebel*, i.e., produce which has become liable to the separation of *terumah* and tithes, but from which these offerings have not yet been separated. Such produce must not be eaten by man, nor may benefit be derived from its use. But this is not because the produce now is deemed "holy," rather because it is now susceptible to sanctification, where previously it had not been.[17] The whole is deemed "bonded" to God[18] until his portion has been designated by the farmer's verbal declaration, and then

separated. Even the priest, the ultimate recipient of the most
holy portions (*terumah*, *terumat ma^{c}aśer*) has no share in them until
they actually have been separated (T. M.S. 3:11). Before that
time, these offerings exist only *in potentia*.[19] For the same reason, *ṭebel* is treated as unconsecrated produce, rather than as
terumah, regarding removes of uncleanness--the *terumah* does not
come into being until it has been designated (T. Toh. 1:7).

The consecration of produce is effected through two actions,
one verbal; the other, physical. The farmer, in a verbal declaration must explicitly designate the exact location in the produce
of each offering (cf. M. Ter. 3:5, T. Ter. 4:9-11, M. Dem. 4:4,
5:1-2, 7:1-6). His words, once uttered, immediately take effect
(cf. M. Dem. 7:6). The declaration localizes the various offerings and consecrates the holy portions (*terumah*, *terumat ma^{c}aśer*,
second tithe). It is accompanied, or followed, by the physical
separation of the offerings. The physical act of separation is
particularly crucial in the case of *terumah*, the precise measure
of which is not fixed (unlike that of the tithes). The farmer, by
his act of separation, determines how much of the produce actually
has been consecrated as *terumah*.[20] That the holiness of produce
is not immanent, but the result of man's act of consecration,
further is illustrated by the ruling that *terumah* and tithes for a
particular batch of produce need not be separated from that batch
itself. They may be taken from any tithable batch of produce, so
long as natural taxonomic categories are not violated (cf. M. Ter.
2:4, 6). This notion, not found in Scripture, is spelled out at
length in Tractate Terumot.[21] For Mishnah, then, it is man who
consecrates produce by his word and deed.

The act of tithing, however, is not merely formal. Mishnaic
law also assigns to human intention an important role in the process of sanctification. Thus Tractate Terumot asks about categories of people who may or may not validly separate *terumah* (M.
Ter. 1:1-3-3:5). Only people with understanding (and therefore
with presumed proper intention) may do so--this excludes children
and imbeciles. Additionally, a man's intentions and his words
must correspond for the designation of *terumah* and tithes to be
valid (M. Ter. 3:8, cf. T. Ter. 4:11). So, too, regarding the
sanctification of *terumah*, the precise quantity of which is not
prescribed, we take into account the farmer's prior intention to
separate a particular amount of produce. If he thereafter turns
out to have separated a smaller amount than intended, the separation is deemed valid (and he may separate an additional amount if
he so wishes). But if he turns out to have separated more than he

originally intended, the separation is deemed invalid, since the
intention has been violated (T. Ter. 5:5-6; cf. M. Ter. 4:4, T.
Ter. 5:4).[22]

To summarize: Mishnah's theory of holiness in *Seder Zera^{c}im*
is transactional rather than immanentist.[23] Nothing (except perhaps for God) is inherently sacred. The Land of Israel is sanctified through its relationship to God. The produce of the Land is
sanctified by man, acting under God's commandment, through verbal
designation and separation of the various offerings. Man, through
his action and intention, additionally determines what is susceptible to sanctification (i.e., liable to tithing as human food),
and the point at which it is susceptible (i.e., edible, at the
point of completion of processing or harvesting, or the point of
intention to make a fixed meal). Mishnah's primary concern in the
tractates under investigation is that man should separate properly
that which is due to God, so that non-priests will not inadvertently eat produce bonded to God or consecrated to him. Mishnah's
authorities further wish to examine in detail man's role in the
process of sanctification, and to specify the power of his will,
word, and deed. The Mishnaic law of tithing begins in Scripture's
facts and conceptions, but has its own distinctive interests and
thrust.

NOTES

MISHNAH AND SCRIPTURE

* An earlier version of this paper was read at the Fourth Max
Richter Conversation on Ancient Judaism, held at Brown University
on June 27, 1978. I am grateful to my teacher and colleague,
Professor Jacob Neusner, for inviting me to deliver a paper at
that conference. I have benefitted from seminar papers on Tractates Terumot, Maaserot, Maaser Sheni, and Bikkurim read by Mr.
Alan Peck, Mr. Martin Jaffee, Rabbi Peter Haas, and Ms. Margaret
Wenig Rubenstein, respectively, although the synthesis put forth
here is my own. I have also benefitted from discussions on tithes
in the ancient Near East and in the biblical literature with my
former colleague at Brown, Professor S. Dean McBride, Jr., now of
Northwestern University. In revising the paper for publication, I
have profited immensely from discussions with my colleagues,
Professors Horst R. Moehring and Sumner B. Twiss, and from critical
insights and comments offered by the following participants in the
Richter Conversation: Professors Morton Smith, Columbia University; Baruch Levine, New York University; Jonathan Z. Smith,
University of Chicago; and Mr. Daniel Schwartz, Hebrew University
of Jerusalem. I bear sole responsibility for any errors which
remain. Part of the research for this paper was supported by a
1978 Summer Research stipend from the National Endowment for the
Humanities.

[1]M. Hag. 1:8: "[The rules about] release from vows hover in
the air and have no [scriptural] basis. The rules of Sabbath,
festivals, and sacrilege are like mountains hanging by a hair, for
they consist of scant Scripture and numerous *halakot*. The proper-
ty-laws and [the rules of] the Temple service, and [the rules of]
cleanness and uncleanness, and [the rules of] forbidden intercourse
have [scriptural] basis. They are the essentials of Torah."

Cf. b. Hag. 11a: "[The laws concerning] leprosy-signs have
considerable scriptural basis and few *halakot*. [The laws concerning defilement through] overshadowings have scant scriptural basis
and numerous *halakot*."

Tanh. Noah (=*Pirqoi ben Baboi*: a Geonic text): "The Written
Torah [consists of] general principles. The Oral Torah [consists
of] concrete details."

[2]Jacob Neusner, *A History of the Mishnaic Law of Purities*,
Parts I-XXII (Leiden, 1974-77); *A History of the Mishnaic Law of
Holy Things*, Parts I-VI (Leiden, 1978-   ); *A History of the
Mishnaic Law of Women*, Parts I-V (Leiden, forthcoming). See also
the following articles by Neusner: "The Meaning of *Torah Shebeᶜal
Peh* with Special Reference to *Kelim* and *Ohalot*," in J. Neusner,
Early Rabbinic Judaism (Leiden, 1975), pp. 3-33, and in *AJS Review*,
I (1976), pp. 151-70; "Scripture and Mishnah: The Exegetical
Origins of *Maddaf*," in *Festschrift of the American Academy for
Jewish Research* (forthcoming); "From Scripture to Mishnah: The
Origins of Tractate Niddah," in *Journal of Jewish Studies* (forth-
coming); "From Scripture to Mishnah: The Origins of Mishnah's
Fifth Division," in *Journal of Biblical Literature* (forthcoming).

[3]Neusner, *Purities*, VII.

[4]Cf., for example, M. Peah 2:6, "Nahum the Scribe said: I have received a tradition from R. Meashah, who received it from his father, who received it from the *zugot*, who received it from the prophets as a *halakah* given to Moses at Sinai, that if a man sowed his field in two kinds of wheat...." Cf. also M. Ed. 8:7, M. Yad. 4:3. No claim is made that the *halakah* in question is derived from Scripture, only that it goes back to Moses at Sinai.

[5]See J. Neusner, ed., *The Modern Study of the Mishnah* (Leiden, 1973).

[6]Neusner, *Purities*, XXII; *Holy Things*, VI; *Women* V.

[7]Lawrence H. Schiffman, *The Halakhah at Qumran* (Leiden, 1975), p. 134. It is, of course, anachronistic to speak of "the halakah" at Qumran!

[8]Samuel Sandmel, "Parallelomania," in *JBL*, 81 (1962), pp. 1-13; Morton Smith, *Tannaitic Parallels to the Gospels* (Philadelphia, 1951); Neusner, *Aphrahat and Judaism* (Leiden, 1971), pp. 188-95, and see n. 6.

[9]Numbers 18; Deut. 12:17-19, 14:22-29, 18:4-5, 26:1-19; Lev. 27:30-33; Ex. 23:19, 34:26; cf. also Ez. 44:30, 45:13-17, Neh. 10:35-39, 12:44-47, 13:10-12. For a detailed analysis of these pericopae, see Otto Eissfeldt, *Erstlinge und Zehnten im Alten Testament* (Leipzig, 1917).

[10]Tobit 1:5-8 (Codices Vaticanus, Alexandrinus); Jubilees 13: 25-27, 32:9-15; Josephus, *Antiquities*, IV, 68, 205, 240. The Septuagint version of Deut. 26:12 also holds that the tithe for the poor is given every three years *in addition to* the Jerusalem tithe, and not instead of the latter. Diverging from Code, Jubilees 13:25-27 assigns "a tenth of the first fruits (*asrata kadame*) to the Lord...to the priests." Since no Levites are mentioned, this passage seems to confuse the tithe with the priestly gift, the "first fruits." Josephus (*Ant.* IV, 68, 208) assigns the tithe to the Levites *and priests*. If these various texts in any way reflect at this point the reality of tithing in the late Second Temple period, as I think they do, we see the further eclipse of the Levites by the priests, and the assimilation of the Levitical tithe to the priestly offering of the "first" or "best" part (*re šyt*). See Eissfeldt, pp. 130-131, 133, 138, 141, 145; and Martin Hengel, *Judaism and Hellenism* (Philadelphia, 1974), I, p. 49; II, pp. 38-39, n. 385. Mishnah and Tosefta depict a situation in which the Israelite common fold (*ʿamme ha ares*) scrupulously separate the priestly *terumah* (= the biblical *re šyt*), but cannot be relied upon to separate the Levitical tithe or the second tithe (cf. M.-T. Demai, T. Sot. 13:10)--thus the only offering separated is given to the priests. Against this practice, the rabbis behind Mishnah require the proper separation and distribution of *all* scriptural tithes (according to their particular reading of Scripture, of course). While this requirement has the effect of supporting the otherwise neglected Levites, Tractate Demai and T. Sotah (13:10) make it clear that the major concern of the authorities behind Mishnah lies elsewhere. The problem with the tithing practice of common folk is that, by not separating the Levitical tithe, they also fail to separate the *terumat maʿaśer*, which is God's property and no less holy than the *terumah*. (*Terumat maʿaśer*, like *terumah*, is given by God to the priests.) Produce from which *terumat maʿaśer* has not been separated is still "bonded" to God and must not be eaten by man. Meticulous tithers therefore must designate all tithes in produce acquired from, or sold to, an *ʿam ha'areṣ* (cf. M. Dem. 2:2). This procedure insures

the separation of *terumat maᶜaśer* and prevents the inadvertent consumption of God's property by man.

[11]The term *terumah* refers to a "specific type of obligatory cultic contribution to be conveyed to the priests"; see Baruch A. Levine, *In the Presence of the Lord* (Leiden, 1974), p. 17, and p. 6, n. 6; cf. Ludwig Kohler and Walter Baumgartner, *Lexicon in Veteris Tesamenti Libios* (Leiden, 1963), p. 1040, s.v. *terumah*.

[12]Cf. Eissfeldt, pp. 81-83. Eissfeldt holds that the character of these two gifts can be distinguished from one another. On philological and contextual grounds, he views the *re šyt* as a kind of tax, the "best" or "first" portion of the grain, wine, and oil, to be paid to the priest. The *bikkurim*, on the other hand, as the first ripe fruits of the harvest, are a ceremonial, cultic offering. Cf. also Roland de Vaux, *Ancient Israel* (New York, 1961), pp. 404-5, and the discussions of George Buchanan Gray, *Numbers* [International Critical Commentary], 1903, p. 235; and N. H. Snaith, *Leviticus and Numbers* [Century Bible], 1967, p. 270. Smith is not sure that Numbers 18:12-13 describes two distinct kinds of offerings. See further my discussion in *A History of the Mishnaic Law of Agriculture: III. A Study of Tractate Demai. Part One: Commentary* (Leiden, 1978), pp. 6-8, and note 8 there; and p. 274.

[13]The Mishnaic usage of the term *terumah* (which in Scripture refers in general to a cultic offering or contribution) in this restricted, technical sense is to be understood in the light of such biblical passages as Num. 18:8, 11, 19, 26-29 (particularly the latter, where the priestly gift the Levites separate from their tithe is referred to as a *terumah* parallel to that which the Israelites give to the priests from their grain, wine, and oil), as well as Deut. 12:6, 11, 17, and Neh. 10:38-40. A harmonistic reading of Scripture can easily assimilate *terumah* in these passages. Eissfeldt, pp. 89, 92f., 110, 113, notes that the terms *terumah* and *re šyt* in fact are not sharply distinguished from one another in the later biblical sources themselves (particularly in Ezra-Nehemiah and the Chronicler). Additionally, the Mishnaic use of the term *terumah* may be shorthand for *terumat re šyt* (cf. T. Ter. 3:18). Extant non-rabbinic literary sources from the late Second Temple period and the first Christian century do not use the term *terumah* in this sense, as I noted, but preserve the Hebrew *re'šyt* in the Greek ἀπαρχή (LXX; Tobit 1:6; Judith 11:13; Testament of Levi 9[?]; Philo, *De Specialis Legibus*, II, 141, 152; Josephus, *Antiquities*, IV, 69-71[?]). Cf. Eissfeldt, pp. 112-13, 119, 122, 126, 134-35, 142-43. (Elsewhere in some of these sources ἀπαρχή renders the Hebrew *bikkurim*.)

[14]Eissfeldt, pp. 49-50, and de Vaux, p. 381, hold that, in spite of D's silence on this matter, the priestly officiants at the Jerusalem sanctuary must have received portions of the tithe.

[15]I am particularly grateful to Professor Morton Smith and Daniel Schwartz for drawing me out on this point and forcing me to rethink an earlier formulation.

[16]Scripture also may refer to a wider range of produce than simply "grain, wine, and oil." The latter phrase is formulaic, and occurs as well in the Ugaritic texts which deal with (royal) tithes. See the following texts in Jean Nougayrol, *Textes accadiens et hourrites des archives est, ouest, et centrales* [*Le palais royal d'Ugarit, III*] (Paris, 1955): 16.244, 16.238, 16.132, 16.153.

[17]If we understand liability to tithing in terms of susceptibility to sanctification, we may easily account for Mishnah's
ruling that *terumah* and tithes may be separated for any batch of
produce from another batch so long as both batches are liable to
tithing (M. Ter. 1:5, M. Dem. 5:3-11; see below, notes 21, 24).
Produce which is exempt from tithing is not susceptible to sanctification, i.e., it is not "bonded" to God and therefore lacks the
potential to be made *terumah* or tithe. A useful analogy may be
drawn here to the purity laws, which distinguish between that
which has been rendered clean or unclean, that which has been
rendered susceptible to uncleanness, and that which is insuscep-
tible to uncleanness.

[18]I am grateful to my colleague Professor Horst R. Moehring,
who suggested this metaphor, and to Daniel Schwartz, who pressed
me on this point.

[19]Cf. the dispute in the same pericope between Rabbi (Judah
the Patriarch) and Yosé b. Judah, two late second-century authori-
ites, over the case of a man who eats [b. Qid. 58b, b. Ned. 84b:
"steals (Ned.: and eats)"] his fellow's *tebel*. Rabbi requires the
offender to pay back the full value of the produce, including that
of the *terumah* and tithes which have not yet been separated. Yosé
b. Judah, on the other hand, requires repayment of the value of
only the unconsecrated portion of the produce (*hulin sebo*). He
apparently holds that we take seriously God's prior claim to a
portion of the produce. Professor Morton Smith writes, "The thief
stole not only from the human owner, but also from God. The theft
from man can be repaid, that from God cannot."

[20]T. Ter. 4:9 maintains in this case as well that the verbal
declaration, and not the physical act of separation, actually
effects the consecration of the produce.

[21]M. Ter. 1:4-5; 8-10; 2:1-6; T. Ter. 2:4-9, 14; 3:7-10,
14-19; 4:3-5; M. Dem. 5:3-11; T. Dem. 5:6b-11; 8:15-17. The
notion that tithe can be separated from one batch of produce for
another while unknown to Scripture, nonetheless bears some logical
affinity to Deuteronomy's claim that the holiness of tithe can be
transferred from produce to coins. Cf. Moshe Weinfeld, *Deuteronomy
and the Deuteronomic School* (Oxford, 1972), pp. 214-15:

> The book of Deuteronomy also contains a less
> sacral conception of the tithes than the other
> Pentateuchal sources. The tithe, which the
> Priestly document designates as 'holy to the
> Lord' (Lev. 27:30-33), and which according to
> a second tradition accrues to the Levites
> (Num. 18:21-32), remains by deuteronomic legis-
> lation the property of the original owner
> (14:22-7) [on this point, see note 14, above].
> Furthermore, it may be secularized and employed
> for profane purposes on payment of its equivalent
> monetary value (without the addition of the
> fifth-part required by P (cf. Lev. 27:31). This
> provision seems to be yet another expression of
> the liberation of the cultus from its intimate
> ties to nature. The sanctity of the tithe is not
> conceived as an inherent quality of the grain
> or animal, as in the Priestly document (Lev. 27:
> 30-3); for it is man who consecrates it and may,
> if he wishes, secularize it through redemption.

> In the deuteronomic view, sanctity is not a
> taboo that inheres in things which by nature
> belong to the divine realm but is rather a
> consequence of the religious intentions of
> the person who consecrates it.

[22]On the other hand, human intention to separate a particular
amount of produce is irrelevant in the case of first tithe, second
tithe (or poor man's tithe), and *terumat ma^{c}aśer*, since the precise quantities of these offerings are fixed by Scripture, as
interpreted by Mishnah (10% of the produce as first tithe, 10% of
the remainder as second tithe or poor man's tithe, 10% of the
first tithe [= 1% of the whole] as *terumat ma^{c}aśer*). Here God's
claim is to a specific amount of produce, and this claim must be
validated by man's acts of separation and consecration. If the
farmer fails to separate just those prescribed amounts which
Scripture dictates, the produce or tithe will be spoiled for non-
priestly consumption, since part remains "bonded" to God as poten-
tially consecrated produce (*terumat ma^{c}aśer*, second tithe). Thus
if an insufficient amount of produce is separated as tithe, the
remainder is spoiled for eating by non-priests, since it contains
potential *terumat ma^{c}aśer* (and second tithe). If, on the other
hand, too much is separated as tithe, the tithe is spoiled for
consumption by Levites, since some of the first tithe should be
consecrated second tithe (T. Dem. 8:13; cf. T. Ter. 4:10). Similarly, in separating tithe from one batch of produce for another,
we must be careful that the batch from which the tithe is to be
taken is large enough to contain (at least) the precise quantity
of potential tithes needed to render unconsecrated the other produce. (The arithmetical calculations involved can be quite elaborate; see T. Dem. 8:15-17a, and my *Demai*, pp. 256-60.) Otherwise
a portion of the produce in this case as well remains "bonded" to
God as potential *terumat ma^{c}aśer* and second tithe.

[23]Once produce has been consecrated by divine command and
human action (i.e., set aside as God's property), it is deemed to
be tangibly different from unconsecrated produce. Thus *terumah*
which falls into a batch of unconsecrated, fully tithed produce is
deemed to retain its integrity in the mixture, and, if we do not
know where it is located, to render the entire mixture prohibited
for consumption by non-priests (*meduma^c*; unconsecrated produce put
into the status of *terumah*). But if the ratio of consecrated to
unconsecrated produce in the mixture is one to one hundred parts,
the *terumah* is neutralized, and the mixture may be eaten by non-
priests. Professor Morton Smith astutely points out that the concept of *meduma^c* is best to be understood not in terms of the con-
taminating effects of material holiness, but in the context of a
theory of mixtures which bears striking affinities to those of
Aristotle and the Stoics (on Aristotelian *synthesis*, and on both
Aristotelian and Stoic *mixis* and *krasis*, cf. S. Samburski,
Physics of the Stoics, London, 1959, pp. 11-15 and 121-22, and
Harry A. Wolfson, *The Philosophy of the Church Fathers: I. Faith,
Trinity, Incarnation*, Cambridge, Mass., 1956, pp. 372-86; and cf.
Neusner, *Purities*, XII, pp. 207-9). Depending on the physical
characteristics of the mixture, the *terumah* will be deemed either
as thoroughly intermingled with the unconsecrated produce, and
therefore as present throughout the mixture (as in a mixture of
liquids or granules), or as physically circumscribed in a definite,
but unknown, location (as in a collection of figs; cf. M. Ter.
4:8-9). In the latter case, none of the discrete items may be
eaten, lest *terumah* inadvertently be consumed. But if there is
no doubt as to where the *terumah* is located, we of course must
remove it. The ruling that *terumah* is neutralized in a mixture of
one part *terumah* to one hundred parts of unconsecrated produce

recalls Aristotle's notion of "predominance," viz., that "if one
component is predominant in bulk,...then the mixture results in
fact in a change of the weak component into the predominant one"
(Sambursky, p. 12, referring to Aristotle, *De Generatione et
Corruptione*, I, 10, 328a, 11; cf. Wolfson, pp. 377-79, 382-83).
Yet, as we have noted, the Mishnaic ruling also applies to mixtures of discrete items when the location of the *terumah* is
unknown or in doubt (cf. M. Ter. 4:11).

CONTEXT AND MEANING IN RABBINIC "BIOGRAPHY"

William Scott Green
University of Rochester

The first step in the construction of any history of rabbinic Judaism must be critical reflection on the nature and character of the sources that contain the primary data about the ancient rabbis. Without a clear picture of the various rabbinic documents, of their modes of formulation, redaction, and organization, of their biases and preoccupations, of the world views they reflect and promulgate, it is difficult, if not impossible, to decide how to evaluate the quality of the evidence they provide. The search for rabbinism's past, then, begins not with a gaggle of historical queries but with literary criticism. It is the delineation of the textual facts of rabbinic documents, the straightforward characterization of the evidence, which generates a theory of the sources, the prerequisite to all critical research. Our theory of the sources, our informed notion of how their contents were transmitted, of how they were put together, and of what they want to say, in turn shapes the questions we bring to them and the sorts of historical problems they can be expected to solve. This means that the propriety of any method for the study of rabbinic history ultimately must be justified at the level of theory.

The central role of a theory of the sources in the study of rabbinic history is particularly evident in the enterprise of rabbinic "biography," an inquiry into rabbinism's past that focuses on the lives and teachings of individual sages. Modern scholarship on this matter is methodologically diffuse, exhibiting a number of techniques and procedures. What should command attention, however, is not the fact of variety, but the question of the legitimacy of these different approaches and of the adequacy of the theories and presuppositions that underlie and claim to justify them. The purpose of this brief paper is to examine one current set of assertions about rabbinic "biography" and to assess its utility.

That rabbinic documents block our perception of development, of change or growth over time, in the life or thought of any rabbinic master now appears a generally accepted view among historians of rabbinism. Acknowledging this, Reuven Kimelman suggests that a proper tactic of historical research on individual teachers is the "Bacher-like organizing of a sage's dicta under what appears to be

the most salient topics."[1] That is, one way to understand the
thought of a given rabbinic teacher is to cull his sayings from the
various rabbinic documents and to categorize them under appropriate
conceptual headings. Kimelman argues that this method does not
misrepresent rabbinic materials, and he legitimates it by reference
to its use in the study of patristic literature.

> Why such concern [with the categorization of rabbinic
> teachings under abstract, conceptual headings] should
> do more violence to rabbinic sources than it would do
> to patristic, or, say, Neo-Platonic ones is puzzling.
> ...Are the rabbis, as a whole, any less consistent
> than the Church Fathers, as a whole? Is, for example,
> Urbach's *The Sages* any less coherent in its own way
> than, say, Wolfson's *The Philosophy of the Church
> Fathers*? Does systematizing that which was recorded
> unsystematically necessarily do violence to the material?[2]

This proposal presumes the viability of three unstated theoretical
presuppositions on which its force and credibility depend. In
what follows, these are considered in turn.

First, the appeal to patristic materials necessarily supposes
that rabbinic and patristic writings constitute two monolithic
literary *corpora* so similar to one another that the same methods
of investigation and analysis, without differentiation or modifi-
cation, can be applied equivalently to each. But the writings of
the Church Fathers are not all of a piece, and few of the literary
forms present in patristic documents--dialogue, apology, commentaries, letters, etc.--are replicated in rabbinic literature.
Likewise, despite their superficial similarity to one another,
rabbinic documents also do not represent a single type of literature. The form and style of exegetical and homiletical collections
surely are distinct not only from one another but also from the
argumentation of the *gemara* and the terse, truncated formulary
patterns of Mishnah. Moreover, much of early Christian literature
is defensive and apologetic, aiming to prove the truth of the new
religion to Jews and pagans or to demonstrate the superiority of
one version of it to another. This certainly is not the case with
rabbinic documents, most of which address the Jewish, particularly
the rabbinic, world of antiquity. Finally, a significant number
of early Christian documents are authored by single individuals.
Indeed, the proportion of singly authored works in patristic literature is sufficiently large that Goodspeed preferred to classify
the bulk of early Christian literature by author rather than literary form.[3] This feature of patristic literature makes some of
those materials suitable for the study of individual Church
Fathers, but there is nothing comparable to it in rabbinic documents, which almost without exception are anonymous and

collective. Rabbinic and patristic literatures are internally
differentiated and are dissimilar to one another in important ways,
and to speak categorically of rabbinic and patristic sources is
highly misleading.

Second, Kimelman implies that the contents of rabbinic documents were "recorded unsystematically" and that "systematizing"
them will make their meaning clear. This assertion suggests that
the organization of rabbinic documents is at best idiosyncratic,
at worst random, and that, in any case, the patterns of arrangement in these texts exhibit no larger structure or structuring of
ideas. This view casts rabbinic redactors as mere collectors ar-
bitrarily aligning discrete materials. The fundamental error of
this assertion has been demonstrated by Jacob Neusner's research
into Mishnaic law. Among other things, Neusner shows that a number
of clear-cut systems of ideas, often involving elaborate corres-
pondences between heaven and earth, undergird Mishnah's discrete
legal teachings and determine the organization of the document as
a whole. To be sure, rabbinic modes of classification may differ
from our own, but they are not "unsystematic" on that account. At
issue here is the autonomy, integrity, and coherence of rabbinic
documents, each of which has its own theological, ideological, and
literary agendum.[4] The portrayal of rabbinic literature as an
undifferentiated whole does not distinguish between and among
documents, and this yields a highly ethnocentric characterization
of rabbinic materials.

Insufficient attention to the documentary divisions of rabbinic literature generates a third theoretical supposition, which
in some ways is the most problematic of all. To propose the construction of "Bacher-like" thematic lists necessarily assumes that
the discrete dicta and teachings of rabbinic masters carry a uni-
vocal meaning and accurately reflect what the master actually
thought. That is, it supposes that the teachings of individual
rabbis are immune from their documentary contexts and that by
extracting them from their present settings and re-cataloguing
them, it is possible to chart the range and foci of a rabbi's
interests and thereby to limn his intellect. To this notion,
two objections can be raised.

First, there are no grounds to claim that the extant materials
about any rabbinic master constitute the whole of his teaching.
Consequently, there is no control data against which to measure
and evaluate the configuration of interests represented by the
preserved sample in any given case. This problem is complicated
by the curious mixture in rabbinic documents of anonymous and

attributed materials. No theory fully accounts for this discrepancy, but if, as the Talmud itself suggests, redactors excised masters' names from rulings whose general acceptance they wished to guarantee,[5] important opinions of a given master may now appear anonymously. This means that even if it were possible to demonstrate that the preserved materials do reflect what a master actually said or thought, the individual intellectual context of that thought is impossible to recover. The result is a list of opinions that points nowhere beyond itself.

Second, and more important, because of the thoroughgoing legal character of most of rabbinic literature, the bulk of opinions attributed to any given master will consist of rulings on specific, concrete cases. These rulings usually are unaccompanied by justification or explanation, and their rationales are not self-evident. The larger meanings these rulings now may appear to reflect, the abstract, conceptual ideas they appear to represent, do not emerge from the language of the teachings themselves but from their documentary context, from their location in the text, from their relationship to the other rulings and opinions that surround them. Since that context is not the creation of the master himself but is the work of redactors and editors, even if it could be shown that all the opinions of a given rabbinic teacher actually derive from him, it would be impossible to demonstrate that the abstract ideas they now appear to exhibit were in his mind. Moreover, even if a precise correspondence between specific rulings and general principles would be firmly established, that correspondence would not prove that the latter generated the former; coincidence is not causality.

Since this last objection is the least obvious, it requires documentation. The following examples illustrate something of the difficulty of determining the meaning of a master's discrete legal ruling outside of its documentary context.

(i)

A.   Until when are they called saplings?

B.   R. Eleazar b. Azariah says, "Until they cease to be sacred (^{c}d $\check{s}yhwlw$)."

C.   R. Joshua says, "Seven years old (bt $\check{s}b^{c}$ $\check{s}nym$) [L: *Until* seven years old; U: *Until* seven years; K: *Until* ninety years; M: *Until* nine years (See TKZ, p. 487, note 36)]."

D.   R. ^{c}Aqiba says, "A sapling is according to its name ($k\check{s}mh$)."

E.   "A tree which was razed and puts forth shoots--from
     a handbreadth and downwards, like a sapling; from a
     handbreadth and upwards, like a tree," words of R.
     Simeon.

M. Shev. 1:8

During the sabbatical year all work on the land is prohibited.
M. Shev. 1:6-7 state that a field containing ten saplings or ten
gourds to a *se'ah*'s space may, in the sixth year, be plowed until
the New Year and not, as usual, only until Pentecost. The pericope
before us then raises the problem of the definition of a sapling.

The question of A assumes that the definition of a sapling
will be determined by time, not size or some other category.
Eleazar's lemma at B links the definition of sapling to the scriptural law of ^{c}*orlah*, which states that the fruit of newly planted
trees is forbidden in the first three years of its life, is
sacred in the fourth, and may be consumed as common produce only
in the fifth. In Eleazar's view, then, a new growth is considered
a sapling until the fifth year of its life. When it enters the
fifth year, it ceases to be sacred and consequently no longer is
regarded as a sapling; it is a tree.

Joshua's lemma at C is incomprehensible if read independently,
so its meaning depends on the context established by A and B. The
version of C in the printed editions ("Seven years old") reads
like a gloss of B. The MSS versions that begin with "until" respond directly to A. In either case, the time supplied in C must
read as the time until which plants are regarded as sapling. In
Hebrew, the years of age are computed from the time of birth so
that, for instance, a calf becomes three years old in the beginning of the third year of its life and not, as in English, at
the end of the third year (See M. Par. 1:3). Therefore, whether
we take the substance of Joshua's rule to be "seven years" or
"seven years old," the meaning is the same: a growth is considered
a sapling until the seventh year of its life. The word "until"
(^{c}*d*), however, presents an ambiguity because it apparently can
connote either "up to and including" or "up to but excluding" (see
Jastrow, p. 1042). Its meaning here, therefore, will have to be
deduced from its use in context. In B the latter meaning ("up to
but excluding") clearly operates; a plant is a sapling until the
fifth year but not in the fifth year. Joshua's lemma, accordingly
means that a plant is considered a sapling up to but excluding the
seventh year of its life. When it becomes seven years old, that

is, when it enters the seventh year of its life, it no longer is
regarded as a sapling.

The meaning of ^cAqiba's lemma in D is unclear. It apparently
offers a common sense definition: a plant is a sapling if people
are accustomed to call it one. Bert. and TYY take this to mean
one year, but their interpretation obscures the fact that ^cAqiba's
lemma does not share the presupposition of the question in A.
Although Simeon's lemma (E) deals not with saplings but with new
growths from felled trees that are "like saplings," it seems to
presuppose a definition of sapling that is based on size, not time.
In his view, a new growth less than a handbreadth in height is
regarded as a sapling, but if it is taller, it is regarded as a
tree.

The pericope has not been redacted smoothly. Formally it
resembles M. Ber. 1:1-2 (See *Eliezer* I, pp. 18-20): a brief question followed by various terse responses, each exhibiting the form
Rabbi X says: In Berakot the questions assumed previously decided
matters of law, and the Yavneans glossed what appeared to be antecedent legal traditions. In our pericope, however, the question
of A serves as a redactional device to provide a context for the
various opinions. It does not succeed. Eleazar's lemma repeats
A's "until," and therefore requires and directly responds to the
superscription. Joshua's lemma, as we saw, is totally dependent
on the context of A and B. But the statements of ^cAqiba and
Simeon are grammatically complete without A, and, moreover, do not
share its supposition of a temporal definition of sapling. D and
E clearly are appendages and it is doubtful that the pericope ini-
tially was constructed with them in mind.

Let us now return to Joshua's ruling of C. To better assess
it and its place in the Mishnaic pericope, we need to consider the
following passage from Tos. Shev. 1:3 (ed. Lieberman, p. 166,
lines 14-16):

1. What is a sapling (*'y zw hy' nṭy^ch*)?

2. R. Joshua says, "Five years [old] (*bt ḥmš*), six years
   [old] (*bt šš*), seven years [old] (*bt šb^c*)."

3. [Said Rabbi, "For what reason did they say, 'Five years,
   six years, seven years']

4. "Rather, I say, vines--five years, fig trees--six years,
   and olives--seven years."

In the Toseftan passage Joshua lists three ages that, in the context provided by 1, are definitive of a sapling. In context,
Joshua's lemma says that a five, six, or seven-year-old plant is a
sapling. It seems reasonable to suppose that growths younger than

five also would be considered saplings, but, because of the language of 1, that cannot be specified here. It is clear, however,
that growths older than seven are not saplings. Lieberman (TKZ,
p. 487) following y. Shev. 33c, regards Rabbi's comment (3-4) as
an explanation of, rather than a disagreement with, Joshua's rule
in 2. To list five and six appears redundant because they are
presupposed by seven, but Joshua lists all three to specify that
he refers to different plants which mature at different times.
According to this interpretation, five and six, as well as seven,
are definitive because they indicate the maximum age of a sapling;
a vine older than five is not a sapling, it is a tree, and so on.
Rabbi's comment therefore is not only an explanation of the Tosefta
version of Joshua's rule, it is also an endorsement of it. In
Rabbi's view, Joshua's listing of the three ages is essential because it makes an important point: there is no single age which
in all cases defines a sapling. Different species are to be
treated separately.

   The Mishnaic and Toseftan pericopae do not offer identical
representations of Joshua's view. In Mishnah, Joshua holds that
all plants cease to be saplings at the beginning of the seventh
year. According to that rule, a seven-year-old sapling is impossible. But in Tosefta, seven-year-old olive trees are saplings.
Let us compare the two versions of Joshua's ruling in their respective contexts and try to determine their relationship.

	Mishnah		*Tosefta*
A.	Until when are they called saplings?	1.	What is a sapling?
B.	R. Eleazar b. Azariah says, (-). "Until they cease to be sacred."		_____
C.	R. Joshua says, "Seven years old."	2.	R. Joshua says, "Five years old , six years [old], seven years [old]."

The exact relationship between the two versions is not easy to
obtain. Since the Toseftan passage treats Joshua alone and does
not reproduce the question of Mishnah's A, it is difficult to con-
strue it as a development of the Mishnaic pericope. But does
Tosefta stand behind Mishnah here? If so, how is the alteration
to be explained? In Tosefta the context is established by 1,
which asks, "What (or, perhaps, Which--'*y zw hy*') is a sapling?".
Joshua's list in 2 is a formally and substantively appropriate
answer to that question. Indeed, the Toseftan superscription is
singularly apposite to Joshua's rule and probably was generated

by it. But in Mishnah Eleazar's lemma dominates, and the superscription of A clearly was designed to accommodate it. The question of A consequently anticipates a temporal limit, the last possible time until which all plants can be considered saplings.
Since it supplies a particular time, Joshua's answer in Mishnah (C)
is formally correct in the pericope.

But if 2 of Tosefta has been abbreviated to form C of Mishnah,
then the Mishnaic redactors have altered the plain sense of the
Toseftan version to make it conform to the context constructed
around Eleazar's lemma. Moreover, they have done so either in
opposition to or in ignorance of Rabbi's interpretation of 2.
In Rabbi's view, the point of Joshua's rule is that no single time
will serve to define all saplings; each plant must be considered
individually. As we observed, this conflicts with the presupposition of the question of A. The contexts of the two passages are
mutually contradictory, and it is doubtful that Tosefta has been
revised to serve the needs of Mishnah.

It therefore appears that two independent versions of Joshua's
rule about saplings have survived, one in Mishnah in conjunction
with Eleazar, the other in Tosefta, supported by Rabbi.

The substance of Joshua's "original" lemma, whatever it was,
consisted of ages which determine the definition of a sapling, but
its meaning now depends entirely on the redactional structure in
which the ruling is set. Because the two extant structures differ,
the substance of Joshua's rule and the principle upon which it is
based cannot be precisely determined.

(ii)

A. Three things they said before R. ^{c}Aqiba,

B. two in the name of R. Eliezer and one in the name of
R. Joshua.

C. Two in the name of R. Eliezer:

D. A woman may go out [on the Sabbath] with (b) a "city
of gold" [a tiara shaped like Jerusalem -- Danby].

E. And pigeon-flyers [those who race pigeons for money]
are unfit to give testimony.

F. And one in the name of R. Joshua:

G. The [dead] creeping thing is in the mouth of a weasel,

H. and it [the weasel] walks on loaves of Heave-offering --

I. [There is] doubt whether it [the creeping thing] touched
[the loaves] or did not touch them --

J. Its [matter of] doubt is [deemed] clean.

M. Ed. 2:7 (M. Toh. 4:2;

b. Hul. 9b)

The pericope contains three discrete rulings bonded together
by the redactional devices of A-B, C, and F. The rulings themselves (D, E, and G-J) are substantively unrelated and formally
dissimilar, and this suggests that the pericope was neither designed to illustrate a legal theme or principle nor generated
by a particular literary form. The redactor's aim, indicated by
the redactional components, evidently is to identify ^{C}Aqiba as the
master to whom opinions of Joshua and Eliezer were transmitted and
perhaps to establish a line of tradition or authority. That the
redactional interest is in ^{C}Aqiba rather than in the substance of
Joshua's and Eliezer's rulings is confirmed by ^{C}Eduyyot's second
chapter. ^{C}Aqiba is central in seven of its ten pericopae, and M.
Ed. 2:7 inaugurates a cluster of four passages whose combination
is justified only by their common attribution to him. This sort
of arrangement, typical of ^{C}Eduyyot but alien to most of Mishnah,
means that Joshua's ruling will be explained neither by its context in the pericope nor by the pericope's in the tractate.

G-J *verbatim* appears anonymously at M. Toh. 4:2, however, and
the context provided there may help to elucidate it. The ruling
is preceded by M. Toh. 4:1:

1. He who throws [an] unclean [thing] from place to place --
2. a [clean] loaf among the [unclean] keys, an [unclean]
    key among the [clean] loaves --
3. it is clean.
4. R. Judah says, "A [clean] loaf [thrown] among the
    [unclean] keys is unclean.
5. "An [unclean] key [thrown] among the [clean] loaves --
    [the loaf] is clean."

And it is followed by M. Toh. 4:3, which reads in part:

6. The [dead] creeping thing is in the mouth of the weasel,
7. and carrion is in the mouth of the dog --
8. and they passed among the clean [things],
9. or the clean [thing] passed between them --
10. their matter of doubt is [deemed] clean
11. because the uncleanness has no [resting] place.

This combination of pericopae makes clear the redactor's conception of the problem. At issue is the effect of movement on the
relation between the clean and the unclean. The particulars of
each case, key, loaf, weasel, etc. are important not in themselves
but as illustrations of the more general problem, the resolution
of doubt when either the clean or unclean thing is not stationary.
Judah (4) and the rules of 2-3 and 9-10 disagree about resolving
doubt if the clean thing is in motion. But all parties can agree

on the principle stated at 11: "if something unclean is in transit, matters of doubt are deemed clean (*Purities* XII, p. 174)."
Apparently, the firm determination of contamination requires a
definable locus for the unclean thing. Within the context of
Tohorot, then, it is possible not only to explain the meaning of
G-J but also to identify the rationale which apparently stands
behind it.

On this basis it is tempting to suppose that Joshua held or
concurred with the principle of 11, but several considerations
restrain such a conclusion. First, however relevant, 11 itself is
not formally integral to M. Toh. 4:1-3. The rulings of 4:1-3 do
not require it, and its position following the concluding judgment
of 10 makes it look like a *post facto*, explanatory gloss. Second,
it is the redactional context of M. Toh. 4 which has determined
the problem 4:2 (=G-J) treats, not the language of the pericope
itself. The following example suggests how the ruling of J might
be explained without reference either to the problem of the movement of the unclean thing or to the principle of 11. Tos. Toh.
4:6 resembles G-J and reads as follows:

> T1. R. Simeon b. Leazar says, "A creeping thing in the
>   mouth of the snake --
>
> T2. "it is crawling on top of loaves of heave-offering --
>
> T3. "there is doubt whether it touched or whether it did
>   not touch --
>
> T4. "its matter of doubt is [deemed] clean.
>
> T5. "For thus it is the way of the snake, to raise its
>   head and crawl along."

T1-T4 parallel G-J almost exactly except that T1 has "snake" in
place of "weasel" in C. In T5, however, the rationale for T4 is
not the movement of uncleanness or the lack of a resting place for
the dead creeping thing but the characteristics of the snake.
Since the snake raises its head when it crawls, it is unlikely
that the creeping thing has touched the loaves, and they therefore
are regarded as clean. T1-T4 easily could have replaced G-J in
the series of M. Toh. 4:1-3, and without T5 the principle of 11
could be applied to the ruling at T4. Likewise, perhaps some
characteristic of the weasel could be used to explain the ruling
of J. The near identity of T1-T4 and G-J and the attribution of
the former to Simeon b. Leazar, an Ushan, demonstrate that the
language of the case itself is paradigmatic and not unique to
Joshua.

Third, the absence of Joshua's name from M. Toh. is an incon-
venient fact that admits of no obvious explanation. The redactor

of M. Toh. either did not know 4:2 to be Joshua's or deliberately
suppressed his name. If the latter, he did so out of hostility to
Joshua or to give the ruling the authority of consensus which
comes with anonymity. Finally, the likelihood that G-J actually
derives from Joshua is further diminished by the observation that
all the named masters in M. Toh. 4 are Ushan and that M. Toh. 4:
1-3 appear to belong to the Ushan stratum of Mishnaic law
(*Purities* XII, pp. 174-175). However Joshua's absence from M.
Toh. is explained, the fact remains that the redactor who knows
both G-J and the principle of 11 attributes neither to Joshua,
and the redactor who knows Joshua is ignorant of the principle
behind this rule. This analysis indicates how the meaning of an
individual's ruling can depend on its redactional context. Even
were it possible to prove that G-J derives from Joshua himself,
the larger meaning of that utterance, at best, would be ambiguous.

Tosefta's version of the passage, which follows, does not
clarify matters.

Ta. Three things they said before R. ^CAqiba.

Tb. two in the name of R. Eliezer and one in the name
of R. Joshua,

Tc. and he [^CAqiba] did not say to them either forbidden
or permitted, fit or unfit, unclean or clean.

Td. Two in the name of R. Eliezer:

Te. A woman -- may she go out [on the Sabbath] with a "city
of gold?"

Tf. And he [^CAqiba] did not say concerning her either forbidden or permitted.

Tg. R. Eliezer permits,

Th. and sages forbid.

Ti. Pigeon-flyers -- may they give testimony?

Tj. And he [^CAqiba] did not say concerning them either
fit or unfit.

Tk. And R. Eliezer declares fit,

Tl. and sages declare unfit.

Tm. One in the name of R. Joshua:

Tn. The [dead] creeping thing is in the mouth of the weasel,

To. and the weasel walks on loaves of heave offering --

Tp. [There is] doubt whether it [the creeping thing]
touched [the loaves] or did not touch [them] --

Tq. R. Eliezer declares clean,

Tr. and R. Joshua declares unclean

Ts. and sages say, "What is certain is unclean, what is in
doubt is clean (*wd'y ṭm' spq ṭhr*).

Tos. Ed. 1:10-12, ed. Zuckermandel,
p. 456, ls. 1-8

The Toseftan passage is a formal jumble. Te and Tg-Th, Ti
and Tl-Tm, and Tn-Tr are independent disputes that have been incor-
porated into a list of "three things said before R. ^cAqiba." It
seems unlikely that followers of either Eliezer or Joshua would
have preserved and reported views contrary to those of their
masters, and this makes Tb, Td and Tm look improbable. Tc, Tf and
Tj indicate that the interest of the pericope's final redactor was
to report ^cAqiba's view. The passage contains nearly all the elements present in the Mishnaic pericope (Ta, Tb, Td, Te, Tg, Ti,
Tk, Tm-Tp, Tr), and it is difficult to imagine that the two versions are unrelated. If so, then the formally corrupt version of
Tosefta is apt to have preceded the smoothly redacted Mishnaic one.

The Toseftan pericope presents a special problem because the
view it assigns to Joshua in Tr contradicts the view given him in
Mishnah's J. G-I and Tn-Tp are virtually identical, but in Mishnah Joshua holds the matter of doubt clean, in Tosefta unclean.
This sort of contradiction, susceptible of a number of plausible
explanations, obstructs any useful historical speculation about
Joshua's view. If the Mishnaic pericope in fact is a reworking of
the Toseftan version, then the Mishnaic redactors have made Joshua
represent the view of Eliezer and sages. It is difficult to say
why this should be so. Taken together, the materials of M. Ed.
2:7 and its versions hardly constitute evidence of scrupulous and
reliable transmission. M. Ed. 3:7, which follows immediately, is
relevant to this problem.

(iii)

A.   Four matters of doubt R. Joshua declares unclean
      and sages declare clean

B.   Under what circumstances (kysd) [Missing from Tosefta]?

C.   The unclean [person or thing] stands and the clean
       person or thing passes by --

D.   The clean [person or thing] stands and the unclean
      [person or thing] passes by --

E.   The uncleanness is in the private domain and the
      cleanness is in the public domain --

F.   The cleanness is in the private domain and the
      uncleanness is in the public domain --

G.   [There is] doubt whether it touched or did not touch --

H.   [There is] doubt whether it overshadowed or did not
      overshadow --

I.   [There is] doubt whether he shifted [it] or did not
      shift [it] --

J. R. Joshua declares unclean,

K. and sages declare clean.

> M. Ed. 3:7 (M. Toh. 6:2;
> Tos. Ed. 1:18, ed. Zuckermandel,
> pp. 456-457, ls 32, 1-3)

The superscription (A-B) suggests that the redactor intends C, D, E, and F to be read as four discrete cases to which the possibilities of contagion in G, H, and I are to apply. But A-B is a somewhat misleading introduction. D is the inverse of C, and F the inverse of E, so the four segments actually constitute two units, each of which treats a different mode of disparity between the clean and the unclean. In C-D the problem is motion: one item (either clean or unclean) is stationary, the other in transit. In E-F the problem is location; one item is in the private, the other in the public, domain. The general language of each segment, and the placement of G-I after all four of them indicate that the pericope's interest is not in concrete, particular cases, but in abstract patterns of relationship between the clean and the unclean. The problem is how to resolve questions of doubt when the clean and the unclean are in unequal relation to one another. Joshua judges such matters of doubt to be unclean; sages deem them clean.

Predictably, the pericope's context in Eduyyot does nothing to elucidate the reasons behind Joshua's ruling. M. Ed. 3 contains twelve pericopae on unrelated subjects; six rulings (3:1-6) are attributed to Dosa b. Harqinas, three (3:9-11) to Gamaliel II, and one apiece to Ṣadoq (3:8), Eleazar b. Azariah (3:12) and Joshua. It is difficult to discern the redactional stratagem, if any, that has formed the chapter. But in M. Toh. 6 the pericope is part of an extended subtractate on doubts in the public and private domains, and the operative principle there is that matters of doubt in the public domain are deemed clean, those in the private domain unclean (*Purities* XI, pp. 8-11; XII, pp. 161-165). This principle certainly could help to explain E-F, but it plainly is irrelevant to C-D, which has nothing whatever to do with location. So the issue that dominates the context in Tohorot did not motivate the pericope's redactor, and the passage will have to explain itself. It is clear that Joshua's rulings on C-D and E-F, if treated separately, are susceptible to interpretations not justified if the two pairs are examined together. This means that the redactor's combination of the two sets is itself an act of interpretation. The end result is not Joshua's philosophy or attitude, but an editor's view of how his discrete rulings ought

to interact and of the larger issues they raise or reflect. In
this rendition Joshua rules that when (and perhaps because) the
clean and unclean are in unequal relation, matters of doubt are
deemed unclean. The best that can be said of that picture of
things is that it is a redactor's perception. Showing that this
principle motivated Joshua's rulings or that he even thought in
those terms is another matter entirely.

As these examples suggest, the redacted character of rabbinic
materials make unwarranted the supposition that the dicta and
rulings of individual rabbinic masters can be lifted whole out of
their present documentary contexts and transported to thematic
catalogues or the pages of a history book. Each datum about an
individual rabbinic master has a complex history of its own. In
many cases, that history is beyond recovery. Rabbinic redactors
were skilled literary artisans, and in many instances their mani-
pulation of inherited materials for their own purposes makes our
recovery of the process of contextualization impossible to perform.
Examples of that process, however, are sufficiently numerous to
justify caution in the way discrete teachings of individuals
are used.

Kimelman's proposal concludes with an appeal for methodological tolerance.

> Why any student of rabbinic literature has to argue
> for a methodological exclusivism is perplexing.
> Preferably, there should be a receptivity to a
> methodological pluralism which presumes that various
> questions may require different methods for their
> respective responses.[6]

To be sure, different historical questions do require different
methods and procedures, but the important issue is whether or not
the questions are appropriate to the data in the first place. The
assumption that rabbinic materials can answer any and all historical
questions and that all methods are equivalently applicable to them
obscures distinctive traits of the literature, bypasses problems of
textual classification, definition, and analysis, and oversimplifies
the enterprise of rabbinic history.

NOTES

CONTEXT AND MEANING IN RABBINIC "BIOGRAPHY"

[1] Rueven Kimelman, Review of Gary G. Porton, *The Traditions of Rabbi Ishmael*, *Association for Jewish Studies Review*, July 1977, p. 26.

[2] Ibid.

[3] E. J. Goodspeed, *A History of Early Christian Literature*, Revised and Enlarged by Robert M. Grant (Chicago, 1966), p. 5.

[4] W. S. Green, "What's In a Name? -- The Problematic of Rabbinic 'Biography,'" in W. S. Green, ed., *Approaches to Ancient Judaism: Theory and Practice* (Missoula, 1978), pp. 77-96.

[5] Robert Goldenberg, *The Sabbath Law of Rabbi Meir* (Missoula, 1978), p. 203.

[6] Kimelman, op. cit., p. 27.

RABBI AQIVA AND BAR KOKHBA

Peter Schäfer

University of Cologne

Until now historians have always assumed that Rabbi Aqiva, the
hero of ancient Judaism, played an important part in the Bar Kokhba
rebellion.[1] In the opinion of most authors, Aqiva was one of the
keenest supporters of the rebellion, journeyed throughout the
Jewish Diaspora looking for resources and sympathizers for his
revolt against Rome, proclaimed Bar Kosiva, as Bar Kokhba, to be
the Messiah, was imprisoned as a result of his active support of
the rebellion, and finally died a cruel martyr's death because of
his convictions.[2]

There is little point in discussing in detail the literature
on the subject of Rabbi Aqiva and Bar Kokhba; for the most part it
is fanciful and not critically sound. The first critical evaluation was attempted by G. S. Aleksandrov in his essay, "The Role of
[c]Aqiba in the Bar Kokhba Rebellion,"[3] and his critical evaluation
was then taken a step further by Jacob Neusner in his article
about Aqiva in the *TRE*.[4] Unfortunately, Aleksandrov's essay concerns itself hardly at all with the sources themselves and therefore, despite a good deal of justified criticism of the secondary
literature, does not contribute very much to the subject itself.
Soundly based conclusions about Aqiva's role in the Bar Kokhba
rebellion can only be drawn if the relevant sources together with
their parallels in the corresponding contexts are carefully analysed. I have attempted to do this in a lengthy appraisal of the
subject,[5] and this essay offers some examples and conclusions from
that larger work. At the same time, I hope that certain fundamental methodological views about the possiblity and impossibility of
interpreting rabbinic sources historically will emerge as a result.

I shall deal in detail with the following subject areas:

I.   Aqiva's journeys.

II. The proclamation of the Messiah.

III. Aqiva's messianic expectations

IV. Aqiva and Tineius Rufus.

V.   Aqiva's imprisonment.

VI. Aqiva's martyrdom, death and burial.

I. Aqiva's Journeys

Many texts describe Aqiva's journeys to the various parts of
the Jewish Diaspora. A number of scholars--from Frankel, Graetz,
and I. H. Weiss to Mantel and Avi-Yonah[5]--have put forward the
theory that Aqiva undertook these journeys for political reasons
(especially in Rome) or else to make preparations among the Jews
for the rebellion against Rome. It is true that an impressive
itinerary on the part of Aqiva can be deduced from various allusions found throughout rabbinic literature. However, the question
is whether a clearly defined political purpose to these journeys
can be inferred from largely fragmentary details.

Aqiva's journeys can be summarized in the following groups:

1. Aqiva journeys with other rabbis by ship

This is a clearly defined collection of texts that can
be recognized by the reference to a group of four rabbis (mostly
Rabban Gamaliel, R. Joshua b. Hanania, R. Eleazar b. Azaria and
R. Aqiva) as well as by certain formulas as *Rabban Gamliel weha-
zeqenim* and, above all, *šehayu ba'in ba-sefinah*.[7] The texts also
have something else in common. All of them provide precedents for
halakhic questions, in which prescriptions concerning the Feast of
Tabernacles predominate. Whether there were one or more journeys
cannot be inferred from the texts. Similarly, there are no details about the destination, purpose, or date of the journey or
journeys. It would therefore be unwise to impute a definitely
political purpose to these journeys.

2. Aqiva with other rabbis in Rome

The travellers on this journey or journeys are once
again the well-known group of four (with some variations), and the
destination this time is certainly Rome.[8] In contrast to the
above-mentioned group of texts, many scholars believe that both the
date and purpose of this journey can be narrowed down more accurately. They base this claim on an episode which appears at b.
A. Z. 10b and Deuteronomy Rabbah 2:24 about a certain Qeti[c]ah b.
Shalom (in Deuteronomy Rabbah he is a "senator") who opposes an
anti-Jewish decree by the Emperor, is executed, and who circum-
cises himself immediately before his execution. This Qeti[c]ah b.
Shalom is supposed to be none other than the Consul of 95 C.E.,
Clemens Flavius, who, together with his wife Domitilla, was
accused by Domitian of having Jewish tendencies and was executed
in 95 or 96 C.E. (Domitilla was exiled). The journey of the
Rabbis would therefore have to have taken place in 95 or 96 C.E.[9]
It furthermore is claimed that the announcement of the imminent
misfortune of the senate's decision led the rabbis to journey to

Rome "in order to avert the danger threatening their own nation."[10]
This theory is hardly convincing. It stands or falls on the identification of Qeti^{c}ah b. Shalom as Clemens Flavius, which is based
on pure speculation and is substantiated neither linguistically
nor factually. Linguistically, the senator's name is not a proper
name, but a paranomasy. Factually, it is by no means proven that
Clemens Flavius and Domitilla had Jewish tendencies; they may well
have had leanings toward Christianity. A political purpose to the
journey or journeys therefore seems unlikely, and the suggestion
by M. D. Herr that the rabbis' journeys were "normally for political purposes"[11] is not supported by close reference to the sources.

3. Aqiva alone in Rome

Among this group of texts is the famous episode in ARN
(Version A, Chap. 16) which I should like to quote in detail because its interpretation is typical of a certain kind of historiography:

> And do not be astonished at Rabbi Zadok, for lo, there
> was [the case of] Rabbi Aqiva, greater than he. When
> he went to Rome, he was slandered before a certain
> hegemon. He sent two beautiful women to him. They
> were bathed and anointed and outfitted like brides.
> And all night they kept thrusting themselves at him,
> this one saying: 'Turn to me,' and that one saying:
> 'Turn to me!' But he sat there in disgust and would
> not turn to them. In the morning they went off and
> complained to the hegemon and said to him, 'We would
> rather die than be given to this man!' The hegemon
> sent for him and asked, 'Now why did you not do with
> these women as men generally do with women? Are they
> not beautiful? Are they not human beings like yourself?
> Did not He who created you create them?' 'What could I
> do?,' R. Aqiva answered, 'I was overcome by their breath
> because of the forbidden meats they ate!'[12]

This text shows Aqiva in a situation brought about by a
Roman hegemon. M. D. Herr concludes that Aqiva visited Rome "on
an official mission," in other words, to conduct political negoti-
ations.[13] He takes the text to be historically reliable, and this
judgment is not shaken even by the fact that immediately preceding
this account, an almost identical story is told about R. Ṣadoq
(who, as is well known according to rabbinic tradition, came to
Rome as a prisoner). This text, too, is taken literally by Herr:
"Such was the spirit of the time that his reply struck a respon-
sible chord in the heart of the matron, who thereupon liberated
him 'with great honours.'"[14] This is an uncritical and positivistic
reading of the texts and hardly stands up to literary critical
analysis. It is far more likely that the same story (a rabbi
resists "human" temptation and this "unnatural" steadfastness
arouses the suspicion and incomprehension of the gentiles) was

attributed to various individuals. The setting (individuals, date, and place) then is variable and can be altered to suit the particular circumstances.[15]

Apart from the assumption that Aqiva was at some point in Rome--and even this cannot be conclusively proven from the text as the story could have been attributed to Aqiva because of his well-known journeys--the historical value of the information in this text is zero.

4. Aqiva visits various places in the Diaspora

Besides Rome, various other places are mentioned, which Aqiva, in most cases alone, is supposed to have visited. I will summarize them as follows:

(1) According to Leviticus Rabbah 5:4[16] and parallel sources Aqiva was with Eliezer and Joshua in Antiochia. The purpose of this journey is indicated in the phrase *magbit ḥakamim*; this refers to the gathering of collections, probably for needy rabbis in Palestine. Political or religious motives cannot be deduced from the text; similarly the date of the journey cannot be established.

(2) According to several sources[17] Aqiva went to a town which cannot be identified with certainty (Zifirin, Zifronah etc.). Neither an exact place, nor date, nor pupose of the journey can be ascertained.

(3) The Talmud[18] mentions a visit by Aqiva to Caesarea Mazaca, the capital of Cappadocia. Nothing further can be established.

(4) Arabia, Gallia, and Africa are mentioned in the Bavli[19] as being on Aqiva's itinerary, but the parallel version in the Yerushalmi,[20] which a similar tradition links with R. Levi, throws doubt on the authenticity of the report. This does not prevent Avi-Yonah and Safrai from speculating in their atlas as to why Egypt is not mentioned on this journey. In their opinion Aqiva left out Egypt "because the Jews there had still not recovered from their rebellion at the time of Trajan."[21]

(5) According to Mishnah[22] Aqiva went to Nehardea in order to intercalate the year. I do not propose here to go into the complicated problem of whether and under what circumstances intercalation was possible outside Palestine. But it certainly seems to me that the text gives us no reason to believe that Aqiva's journey had anything to do with the Bar Kokhba rebellion.

(6) Finally, mention is also made of Ginzak or Gazaka in Media as a place that Aqiva is supposed to have visited.[23] Even if Aqiva really did go there--which is quite doubtful--again

no conclusions as to the date or, more importantly, the purpose of the journey can be drawn from the sources.

This is a general survey of the journeys which Aqiva, according to rabbinic sources, is supposed to have undertaken. To sum up: in some cases the destination of the journey cannot be established with certainty; in others it is not clear *who* undertook the journey (i.e. whether it was really Aqiva who was the traveller). The dates of the journeys cannot be reckoned with any degree of accuracy and, so far as the purpose of the journeys is concerned, in none of the texts can even a political purpose be identified, let alone the preparation of the Bar Kokhba rebellion. Such a theory is based on pure speculation. It is far more likely that Aqiva's journeys, if they took place, were to various Jewish communities and served such internal purposes as the settling of halakic problems, collections, questions of self-government and the like.

11. *The Proclamation of the Messiah*

Aqiva's famous proclamation of Bar Kokhba as the Messiah is one of the most important texts bearing on the present subject. It appears in three versions, all of which are cited below.

1. *y. Ta. 4:8*

R. Simeon b. Yohai taught, "My teacher Aqiva used to expound, '*There shall step forth a star out of Jacob* (Num. 24:17)-- thus Koziva steps forth out of Jacob!'

"When R. Aqiva beheld Bar Koziva, he exclaimed, 'This is the king Messiah.'" R. Yohanan b. Torta retorted, "Aqiva, grass will grow between your cheeks and he still will not have come."

2. *Lamentations Rabbah 2:4*

R. Yohanan said, "My teacher used to expound, '*There shall step forth a star out of Jacob* (Num. 24:17)--thus, read not *kokab* (star), but *kozeb* (liar).' "When R. Aqiva beheld Bar Koziva, he exclaimed, 'This is the king Messiah.'"

R. Yohanan b. Torta retorted....

3. *Lamentations Rabbah, ed. Buber, p. 101*

R. Yohanan said, "When R. Aqiva beheld Ben Koziva, he said, '*There shall step forth a star out of Jacob* (Num 24:17)-- Kokhba steps forth out of Jacob. This is the king Messiah!'"

R. Yohanan b. Torta retorted....

These three versions of the so-called proclamation of the Messiah by Aqiva are the only sources in rabbinic literature in which Aqiva and Bar Kokhba are brought into direct contact with one another. Since parallel versions of this episode are missing, an adequate historical evaluation of the text is almost impossible. Progress can be made, if at all, only by a careful comparison of the three versions.

1.   In y. Ta. the "authors" are R. Simeon b. Yohai, who hands down Aqiva's interpretation of Numbers 24:17, and R. Yohanan b. Torta, who contradicts Aqiva. In Lam. R. and Lam. R. Buber, on the other hand, Yohanan b. Torta not only contradicts Aqiva but also hands down the interpretation of Numbers 24:17. Since there is no other evidence that Yohanan b. Torta was a pupil of Aqiva (in fact they were probably contemporaries), it seems that Lam. R. and Lam R. Buber offer a secondary, revised text with regard to the "authors."

2.   The literary composition of the texts supports this view. One cannot help noticing that in y. Ta. and Lam. R. Aqiva's inter-pretation of Numbers 24:17 and Yohanan's contradiction both appear in Hebrew, while the middle part--the explicit application of the interpretation to Bar Koziva--is written in Aramaic. Lam. R. Buber reduces what apparently was originally a three-part construction to the argument between Aqiva and Yohanan by combining the middle part with the interpretation of Numbers 24:17 (whereby linguistically a mixture of Hebrew and Aramaic is the result). It is therefore more likely, from the literary point of view, that the Aramaic middle part in y. Ta. and Lam. R. was added at a later date between Aqiva's interpretation and Yohanan's retort and therefore can be rejected as a marginal comment. Accordingly, the argument between Aqiva and Yohanan b. Torta is probably the literary essence of the texts that have been handed down. Whether this controversy is based on an historical argument between Aqiva and Yohanan is not clarified by this assertion. Nevertheless, Yohanan's saying is so closely con-nected with the situation, as well as referring to Aqiva's inter-pretation, that an editorial juxtaposition of the two sayings seems hardly likely.

3.   The intention of Aqiva's interpretation of Numbers 24:17 is, as Yohanan's answer shows, undoubtedly messianic. A messianic interpretation of this verse is basically not new or even unusual, in fact it has a long tradition.[24] Without going into detail, I would only refer to the Septuagint on Numbers 24:17,[25] the Targu-mim[26] and the Damascus Document (7:18f.).[27]

4.   What is unusual and singular, however, is the concretiza-tion of the traditional messianic interpretation of Numbers 24:17 in one, very specific person. The name of this person in all the texts (despite varying spellings) is Bar Koziva (with a *zayin*. Since Bar Kokhba, as the letters from Nahal Hever show, was

originally called Shimon bar or ben kosiva (with a *Samek*, in the
Greek letter Chōsiba),[28] all the versions of the text reflect the
rabbinic change of meaning of Bar Kosiva's name to Bar Koziva (in
other words to "son of a liar," see especially Lam. R.)[29] and
therefore the situation after the Bar Kokhba rebellion. Aqiva's
original interpretation, if indeed there was one, therefore appears
in none of the three versions, but must have appeared as"

> *There shall step forth a star (kokab) out of Jacob* (Num 24:17)
> --Kosiva steps forth out of Jacob.

The change of name from Bar Kosiva to Bar Kokhba ("son of the
star") as it appears in Lam. R. Buber, is more likely to have been
a conclusion rather than the original content of Aqiva's interpretation.

5.   What is then the historical essence of the texts? The
analysis of the various literary versions showed the actuali ation
of a verse of the Bible traditionally given a messianic sense in
the person of Bar Kokhba, through Aqiva, and the opposition of his
contemporary, Yohanan b. Torta. That this interpretation stems in
reality from Aqiva can be neither proved nor disproved with certainty. The fact that it is not mentioned in older sources does
not necessarily exclude the possibility,[30] since the sources are
rather meager, and--as our text shows too--editorial changes made
at a later date to the detriment of Bar Kokhba must be allowed for.
On the other hand, there is always the possibility that later
editors put these words into Aqiva's mouth because his connection
with the Bar Kokhba rebellion had become a permanent part of the
tradition. If, however, the interpretation does go back to Aqiva,
one cannot help ascribing to it a politically explosive quality,
for it is certainly not a mere academic play on words. Nonetheless, it is by no means a solemn proclamation of Bar Kokhba as the
Messiah nor does it support any of the other dramatic actions with
which biographers of Aqiva or Bar Kokhba may care to connect it;
it provides no information about the real relationship between Bar
Kokhba and Aqiva or about any active support the latter may have
given to the rebellion.

III. Aqiva's Messianic Expectations

There are very few messianic utterances that can be ascribed
to Aqiva. I will refer only to the well-known section in M. Sanh.
10:3, in which Aqiva excludes the generation of the deserts, the
company of Korah, and the ten tribes from the redemption of the
world to come.[31] J. Heinemann has understood this text, I think
rightly, as proof of the concrete national and earthly nature of
Aqiva's messianic expectations, in which no utopian features can
be identified.

> There is no doubt, therefore, that Aqiva's determination
> that the ten tribes are not destined to return had
> practical implications for the messianic aspirations
> and activities of his time....He who saw in Bar Kokhba
> the king Messiah...and held that the process of
> redemption had certainly begun, was forced to utterly
> disavow all utopian and unrealistic elements of the
> messianic redemption and to remove them from the
> first stages.[32]

It is perhaps also worth remarking that Aqiva pleads for an
extraordinarily short messianic period (only 40 years)[33] and that,
as the following text suggests, he is clearly one of those who
calculated the end.

> It has been taught: R. Nathan said, "This verse
> pierces and descends to the very abyss: *For there
> is yet a vision for the appointed time; and at the
> end it will come in breathless haste, it will not
> fail. If it delays, wait for it; for when it comes
> will be no time to linger* (Hab. 2:3). Not as our
> Masters...nor as R. Simlai...nor as R. Aqiva, who
> expounded [the verse] *One thing more: I will shake
> heaven and earth* (Hag. 2:6)."

We may not know Aqiva's actual interpretation, but we can say from
the context (see also Hag. 2:7: *I will shake all nations*) that he
is definitely one of those who calculated the end (*meḥaŝŝbe ha-qeṣ*),
and whose calculations, in the opinion of the author or editor,
proved incorrect and even detrimental (this is also Aleksandrov's
opinion). There hardly can be any doubt that the actual background to these words is the Bar Kokhba rebellion, and that
Aqiva's messianic expectations that related to this rebellion are
condemned.

IV. *Aqiva and Tineius Rufus*

Numerous texts in rabbinic literature report dialogues between Aqiva and Tineius Rufus (mostly known in the sources as
twrnws rwpws, the Governor of Judaea in the time of the Bar Kokhba
war. The subjects of these dialogues are some of the classical
topoi of dialogue literature: the election of Israel,[35] the precepts of the Sabbath[36] and circumcision,[37] God's providence and
justice.[38] There are parallels to all these subjects with varying
participants. A particularly significant question is why circumcision is not laid down in the Ten Commandments. It is not only
asked by Tineius Rufus of Aqiva, but also by the famous matron of
R. Yose b. Ḥalafta[39] and by Aqilas the proselyte[40] or King Agrippa
of R. Eliezer.[41] These are without doubt literary *topoi* with
different speakers, whose historical background is to be found in
the Gentile-Jewish controversy. All attempts to identify the
various questioners are of little use and sometimes lead to absurd

conclusions. When, for example, M. D. Herr discovers in Agrippa King Agrippa II,[42] does this mean that Aqilas put the same question to the same R. Eliezer, and similarly the (or a) matron to Yose b. Ḥalafta, or Tineius Rufus to Aqiva? Herr is convinced that the discussions between Aqiva and Tineius Rufus actually took place. The problem posed by the fact that the same Tineius Rufus con- demned Aqiva to death and had him martyred most cruelly is "solved" by a displacement of time: "These discussions with R. Akiva, which demonstrate the interest of Roman statesmen and en- lightened citizens in the religion and people of Israel, must obviously have been conducted while he still enjoyed his freedom, before the Bar Kokhba rebellion (there being no evidence whatever that they took place during R. Akiva's imprisonment)."[43] This way of arguing is on a par with the fanciful biography of Aqiva by Finkelstein, who even makes the two of them friends, whose friend- ship, however, comes to a tragic end: "...I thought of Tineius Rufus and the part he played in that tragedy, in the execution court of Caesarea....He had liked Akiba, and would have preferred to spare the old man; but naturally the interests of the Empire came first."[44] On the basis of this kind of "critical" discussion and "historical" evaluation of rabbinic texts, what prevents us from accepting the tradition that Aqiva married Tineius Rufus' wife[45] as historical fact as well? Apparently nothing else but the difficulty of reconciling this "fact" with the rest of infor- mation known about Aqiva's life!

V. Aqiva's Imprisonment

Many texts in rabbinic literature have been handed down in which Aqiva's imprisonment is mentioned. I shall deal with them under three aspects.

1. When was Aqiva taken prisoner and how long did he re- main in prison? M. D. Herr (in his essay "Persecutions and Mar- tyrdom in Hadrian's Days")[46] seeks to draw conclusions from T. Sanh. 2:8,[47] where we read that R. Aqiva, *šehayah ḥavuš bevet ha- 'isurin*, made three consecutive years leap years. Herr concludes from this that Aqiva was imprisoned in about 131-132 C.E. and re- mained in prison for about three years (this also means that, according to Herr, he was executed before the end of the rebel- lion).[48] This conclusion cannot be regarded as convincing because the text nowhere states when Aqiva carried out the intercalations, i.e., whether he intercalated three years at one time (= fixed the calendar) or three consecutive years at different times. But be- yond this, there is the fundamental question of how far the texts

can be used as proof of the historical fact that Aqiva was imprisoned. In some of the texts, at least, the real subject is not
Aqiva's imprisonment but a particular halakic question (intercalation, ḥaliṣah, divorce) which is being presented to Aqiva.[49] It
is therefore more than likely that in some texts the imprisonment
is presupposed as a *topos* and was not linked with the various
halakic questions until a later date. If this supposition is correct, we must be careful about any inferences we draw about the
duration of Aqiva's imprisonment.

2. Why was Aqiva imprisoned? The only source that gives a
reason for Aqiva's imprisonment is the well-known narrative in the
Bavli[50] according to which Aqiva was arrested because he disobeyed
the prohibition of teaching the Torah in public. In Herr's opinion
this reason is a "Babylonian legend...of later origin...that arose
at the beginning of the third century C.E."[51] Herr arrives at this
judgment because the text does not conform to his chronological
framework, according to which Aqiva was arrested at the beginning
of the rebellion, when the decrees were not yet in force. The
final point, however, is the real problem. The questions of whether
there ever was an official prohibition of teaching Torah in public
in connection with the Bar Kokhba rebellion, and, if so, when it
was put into effect have not yet been settled, and the entire matter has to do with the much-discussed problem of the reasons for
the Bar Kokhba rebellion.[52] So long as the texts are not critically
analysed in terms of a wider formulation of the question about the
reasons for and consequences of the Bar Kokhba rebellion, they can
not be adduced as evidence for the date of the prohibition of
Torah or for the reasons for Aqiva's arrest. Without actually
attempting such an analysis, it may be assumed that the rabbinic
representation of events appears in certain established patterns of
the "religious persecution" *topos*, and that a comparison with the
Jewish interpretation of the persecution under Antiochus IV
Epiphanes might prove instructive.

3. Under what conditions was Aqiva kept in prison? This
question is particularly interesting. We have several texts in
which we read that certain people visited Aqiva in prison. For
example, b. Eruv. 21b mentions a servant named Joshua ha-Garsi, who
is supposed to have been by his side continually. b. Pes. 112a
describes a visit from Simeon b. Yohai, who wanted to learn Torah
from Aqiva (in prison!). y. Yev. 12:6 mentions that Yohanan ha-
Sandlar, disguised as a pedlar, puts forward a halakic question,
and according to b. Yev. 108b the Rabbis finally hire men to take
on the great risk of presenting another halakic question to Aqiva

for his judgment. If one attempts to put these texts into chronological order, it seems fair to infer an increase in unrestricted
contact with visitors at the beginning of the imprisonment, until
the ban on visitors (a ban that could be circumvented relatively
easily at first). This was followed by a drastic tightening up of
prison conditions at the end of the period of imprisonment and before the execution. This is exactly what M. D. Herr argues:
"During R. Akiva's early imprisonment, his students were generally
permitted to visit him; and before the decrees of persecution were
enacted, he had even been permitted to teach him Torah.... Only
after the decrees of persecution had come into force was this
privilege abolsihed."[53]

This interpretation is certainly a logical attempt at producing a unified picture from all the given "facts" in the sources.
However, the proof that these "facts" are to be evaluated as historical facts ought to be the starting point rather than the conclusion of this quasi-logical interpretation. Altogether, it seems
to me that Herr's argumentation is not untypical of a kind of historical evaluation of rabbinic sources which, in an uncritical,
even naive way, treats odd details as historical facts, without
taking into account the literary character of the sources, i.e.
above all the dynamics inherent in every motive and the particular
bias of each individual text.

VI. *Aqiva's Martyrdom, Death and Burial*

Here too I only summarize the most important points.

1. Many texts mention the fact that Aqiva was martyred before his death. The most important are y. Ber. 9:7 and b. Ber.
61b.[54] A comparison of these two texts reveals substantial differences. Both of them agree that Aqiva died reciting the *Shema*,
but only the Bavli mentions details of the martyrdom (his flesh
was combed with iron combs). Since the Bavli also extends the
whole episode to include a heavenly voice, ministering angels, and
God himself, the oldest available version of the death of Aqiva
appears to be found in the Yerushalmi, and the substance of the
story appears to be a martyrdom of which no further details are
known except that Aqiva died reciting the *Shema*.

2. A very strange tradition surrounding Aqiva's death is
found in *Midrash* ᶜ*asarah haruge malkut*[55] and *Midrash Mishle*.[56]
Here the prophet Elijah announces to Joshua ha-Garsi, known from
other sources to be Aqiva's servant: "I have come to tell you
that (your teacher) Aqiva has died (in prison)." This story is
without doubt both legendary and late; however, a tradition may

be assumed here which knew nothing of martyrdom in connection with Aquiva's execution.

3.   The only text to actually mention the place of Aqiva's death by name is the tractate Semahot (8:9):[57] "When R. Aqiva was killed in Caesarea (*qysryn*) the news came to R. Juuda b. Baba and R. Hanania b. Teradyon." The authenticity of the source of this text is doubtful; among other things, it is presupposed here that Aqiva's death was a "sign" for the expected war, which means that he was executed before the outbreak of the Bar Kokhba rebellion. The mention of Caesarea as the place of Aqiva's execution is therefore more likely to be a conclusion on the part of the later redactor (If Aqiva was executed it was most probably in Caesarea, the seat of the Roman Governor and the headquarters of the Commander Julius Severus during the war.) and is hardly an historically reliable fact.

4.   Aqiva's burial is only mentioned by the late Midrashim *Elleh ezke-rah*,[58] *c Asarah haruge malkhut* and *Midrash Mishle*.[59] They tell how Elijah, together with Joshua ha-Garsi, buried Aqiva in a cave in Caesarea that was afterwards sealed in a miraculous way. These texts belong to the group of Elijah legends, and the influence of the story of Moses' burial can be traced in several details.[60] They do not contribute to the historical questions surrounding Aqiva's death and burial.

Finally I should like to summarize the results of my survey in the following short points:

1.   Aqiva's journeys provide no suggestion that they served any political purpose.

2.   If the interpretation of Numbers 24:17 can be traced back to Aqiva, the messianic implications of the verse only allow one conclusion: that Aqiva understood and approved of the rebellion as a messianic movement.

3.   The few messianic utterances ascribed to Aqiva reveal a national and earthly messianic expectation on Aqiva's part which is directed toward a point in the near future.

4.   The discussions between Aqiva and Tineius Rufus are part of the dialogue literature found in the Gentile-Jewish controversy, and in view of the individuals involved, are without any historical value.

5.   From the texts about Aqiva's imprisonment practically the only fact that can be extracted is *that* Aqiva was probably in prison in connection with the Bar Kokhba rebellion. Most of the sources are not primarily concerned with Aqiva's imprisonment, but presuppose this, and are therefore of no historical value beyond the mere fact of the imprisonment.

6. The same is true of Aqiva's martyrdom and burial. The fact that Aqiva was executed in connection with the Bar Kokhba rebellion is presupposed in all the texts. Concrete details about the date, time, and other circumstances are doubtful and seem to result from the need to link the (existent) tradition of Aqiva's execution with generally known historical information. The core of the tradition consists of various cycles of legends, behind which the historical reality can only be guessed at, not reconstructed.

7. And finally, to sum up, one last remark about methodology: a condition of any historical evaluation of rabbinic texts is the consistent and rigorous application of literary criticism. Historical reality is not revealed by adding together isolated pieces of information from which all contradictions have been painstakingly removed. It is only after careful analysis of the context and all versions of a tradition that the historical value of each individual item of information can be ascertained.

NOTES

RABBI AQIVA AND BAR KOKHBA

[1] For a survey of the rebellion see E. Schürer-G. Vermes-
F. Millar, *The History of the Jewish People in the Age of Jesus Christ*, Vol. I (Edinburgh, 1973), pp. 534-557, and E. Smallwood, *The Jews under Roman Rule* (Leiden, 1976), pp. 428-466.

[2] Cf. M. Avi-Yonah, S. Safrai, *Carta's Atlas of the Period of the Second Temple, the Mishnah and the Talmud* (Jerusalem, 1966), p. 81 with map 122; D. J. Bornstein, "Akiba," *EJ* II (Berlin, 1928), col. 7-22; J. Derenbourg, *Essai sur l'Histoire et la Géographie de la Palestine*, Vol. I (Paris, 1867), pp. 418ff.; J. Devir, *Bar Kokhba ha-'is we ha-mašiah* (Jerusalem, 1964), pp. 114ff.; L. Finkelstein, *Akiba: Scholar, Saint and Martyr* (repr. Cleveland/ New York-Philadelphia, 1962); Z. Frankel, *Darkhe ha-Mišnah* (Leipzig, 1858/59), pp. 120f.; L. Ginzberg, "Akiba ben Joseph," *JE* I (New York, 1901), pp. 304-310; H. Graetz, *Geschichte der Juden*, Vol. IV (Leipzig, ²1866), pp. 148f.; M. D. Herr, "Persecutions and Martyrdom in Hadrian's Days," *Scripta Hierosolymitana* 23 (1972), pp. 85-125 (hereafter "Persecutions"); I. Konovitz, *Rabbi ᶜAqiva* (Jerusalem, ²1965); M. Lehmann, *Akiba: The Story of Rabbi Akiba and His Times* (New York, ²1961); H. Mantel, "The Causes of the Bar Kokhba Revolt," *JQR* 59 (1967/60), pp. 290f., D. Spiegel, *Die Kaiser Titus und im Talmud und Midrasch sowie bei den zeitgenössischen Geschichtsschreibern* (Wien, 1906), p. 36f.; I. H. Weiss, *Dor dor wedoršaw*, Vol. II (Wilna, 1904), p. 3; J. S. Zuri, *Rabbi ᶜAqiva* (Jerusalem, 1924/25).

[3] Published in English in J. Neusner, *Eliezer ben Hyrcanus*, Vol. II (Leiden, 1973), pp. 428-442 and in *REJ* 132 (1973), pp. 65-77.

[4] *Theologische Realenzyklopädie*. Vol. II (Berlin-New York, 1978), pp. 146-147.

[5] See my article, "Rabbi Aqiva und Bar Kokhba," in my *Studien zur Geschichte und Theologie des Rabbinischen Judentums* (Leiden, 1978) (AGAJU, Vol. XV), pp. 65-121.

[6] See note 2.

[7] Cf. M.M.S. 5:9; b. Suk. 41b (Tos. Suk. 2,11; Sifra *emor pereq* 16, fol. 102c); M. Shab. 16:8; Midrash Tannaim, p. 172; Tos. Shab. 13 (14):14; y. Suk. 2:4 (52d) (b. Suk. 23a).

[8] Cf. M. Eruv. 4:1; Tos. Bes. 2,12; Sif. Dev. § 318, p. 361; b. Mak. 24af.; EkhaR 5:18; RutR 1:8, ed. Buber, p. 42; Yalq. Jes. § 410, p. 779a); ShemR 30:9; b. A.Z. 10b (b. Ned. 50af.); DevR 2:24.

[9] Cf. Graetz, *op. cit.*, pp. 119ff.; Derenbourg, *op. cit.*, pp. 334ff.; H. Vogelstein-P. Rieger, *Geschichte der Juden in Rom*, Vol. I (Berlin, 1896), pp. 28f.; H. J. Leon, *The Jews of Ancient Rome* (Philadelphia, 1960), pp. 35f.; Ginzberg, *op. cit.*, p. 305.

[10] Graetz, *op. cit.*, pp. 121f. and pp. 435ff.

[11] "The Historical Significance of the Dialogues between Jewish Sages and Roman Dignitaries," *Scripta Hierosolymitana* 22 (1971), p. 139 (hereafter "Significance").

[12]Translation, J. Goldin, *The Fathers According to Rabbi Nathan* (New Haven, 1955), p. 84.

[13]"Significance," pp. 136f.

[14]"Significance," p. 137.

[15]Another example is QohR 10:7 (translation A. Cohen, *Midrash Rabbah, Ecclesiastes* [London, [3]1961], pp. 267f.): "R. Akiba went up to Rome where a eunuch of the court met him and said to him, 'You are the Rabbi of the Jews?' He replied, 'Yes.' He said to him, 'Infer three things from me, *viz.* he who has ridden upon a king's horse, or upon the ass of a son of a free man, or has sandals on his feet, is a human being; but he who has none of these things, a man buried in his grave is better than he.' He answered, 'You have mentioned three things; hear from me three things in their stead. The beauty of the face is the beard, the joy of the heart is a wife, *Children are a heritage of the Lord* (Ps. 128:3) - woe to the man who lacks these three things.' ...When the eunuch heard this, he dashed his head against the wall and killed himself." Here we have a parallel in b. Shab. 152a on R. Joshua b. Qorḥa and a eunuch (translation I. Epstein, *The Babylonian Talmud, Seder Mo^ced*, Vol. 1 [London, 1938], pp. 775f.): "A certain eunuch [*gawzaah*] said to R. Joshua b. Karhah [Baldhead]: 'How far is it from here to Karhina [Baldtown]? 'As far as from here to Gawzania [Eunuchtown],' he replied. Said the Sadducee to him, 'A bald buck is worth four *denarii.*' 'A goat, if castrated, is worth eight,' he retorted. Now, he [the Sadducee] saw that he [R. Joshua] was not wearing shoes, [whereupon] he remarked, 'He [who rides] on a horse is a king, upon an ass, is a free man, and he who has shoes on his feet is a human being; but he who has none of these, one who is dead and buried is better off.' 'O eunuch, O eunuch,' he retorted, 'you have enumerated three things to me, [and now] you will hear three things: the glory of a face is its beard, the rejoicing of one's heart is a wife; *the heritage of the Lord is children* [Ps. 128:3]; Blessed be the Omnipresent, Who has denied you all these!' 'O quarrelsome baldhead,' he jeered at him. 'A castrated buck and [you will] reprove!' he retorted." What is the "historical reality" of these episodes? Did Aqiva speak with the eunuch or R. Joshua, or both? Or, and this seems to me more likely, was the same story attributed to R. Aqiva and R. Joshua and perhaps transferred from Joshua b. Qorḥa (!) to Aqiva?

[16]Cf. also y. Hor. 3:7 (48a); DevR 4:8; Yalq. Prov. § 956, p. 990b.

[17]Cf. y. A.Z. 2:4 (41b); b. B.Q. 113a; SifBam § 4, p. 7 (y. B.Q. 9:15 fol. 7a; Yalq. *naso* § 701, p. 444b).

[18]Cf. y. Yev. 16:4 (15d) (b. Yev. 121a; QohR 11:1).

[19]b. R.H. 26a; cf. also b. Yev. 98a; b. Ḥul. 47b.

[20]y. Ber. 9:1 fol. 13c.

[21]*Op. cit.*, p. 81, map 122.

[22]M. Yev. 16:7; cf. also b. Yev. 115a; b. Ber. 63af.; y. Ned. 6:13 (40a); y. Sanh.1:2 (19a); b. Sanh. 11b.

[23]b. A.Z. 34a; b. Ta. 11b (mentions Mar ^cUqba instead of Aqiva); b. A.Z. 39a; BerR 33:5; b. Ber. 8b.

[24] Cf. G. Vermes, *Scripture and Tradition in Judaism* (Leiden, 1961), p. 59; E. E. Urbach, *HZ"L* (Jerusalem, 1969), p. 606, note 80; = *The Sages* (Jerusalem, 1975), p. 999, note 81; M. Hengel, *Die Zeloten* (Leiden/Köln, [2]1976), pp. 243ff.

[25] "A star shall step forth out of Jacob, and a *man* shall arise out of Israel."

[26] Targum Onkelos: "When a *king* shall arise out of Jacob, and the *Messiah* be anointed from Israel"; Targum Pseudo-Jonathan: "When a *mighty king* of Jacob's house shall reign, and the *Messiah* and a *powerful sceptre* be anointed from Israel"; Fragmentary Targum: "A *king* is to arise from the house of Jacob, and a redeemer and ruler from the house of Israel"; Codex Neofiti (like Fragment Targum).

[27] CD 7,18ff.: "The *star* is the Interpreter of the Law who shall come to Damascus; as it is written, *A star shall come forth out of Jacob and a sceptre shall rise out of Israel*" (Num. 24:17) (DSSE, p. 104).

[28] Cf. Y. Yadin, *Bar Kochba* (Hamburg, 1971), pp. 124ff., especially p. 132; S. Abramsky, *Bar-Kokhba', nesi' Yisra'el* (Tel Aviv, 1961), pp. 53f.; *idem.*, "Bar Kokhba," *EJ* (Jerusalem, 1971), Vol. IV, col. 228ff.

[29] Cf. also b. Sanh. 93b.

[30] Cf. Neusner, *op. cit.*, p. 147.

[31] Cf. also Tos. Sanh. 13:9ff.; y. Sanh. 10:4ff. (29c); b. Sanh. 110b; ARNA, ch. 36, pp. 107f.

[32] *'Aggadot wetoledotehen* (Jerusalem, 1974), p. 108.

[33] PesR, p. 4a (b San 99a; Midrash Tehillim 90·17; Tan. *ᶜaqov* § /).

[34] b. Sanh. 97b. Translation I. Epstein, *The Babylonian Talmud, Seder Nezikin*, Vol. III (London, 1935), pp. 658f.

[35] Tan. *terumah* § 3.

[36] BerR 11:5 (PesR, p. 119bf.; b. Sanh. 65b; Tan. *ki tissa'* § 33; Yalq. Gen. § 16, p. 10b).

[37] Tan. Buber *tazriaᶜ* § 7 (Tan. *tazriaᶜ* § 5; Yalq. *tazriaᶜ* § 547, p. 326b); Bereshit Rabbati, Gen 17:1, p. 72f.

[38] b. B.B. 10a.

[39] PesR, p. 117a.

[40] PesR, p. 116bf.

[41] Tan. *lek leka* § 20.

[42] "Significance," p. 146, note 127.

[43] "Significance," p. 135; cf. also S. Lieberman, "The Martyrs of Caesarea," *Annuaire de l'institut de philologie et d'histoire orientales et salves* 7 (1939/44), p. 421, with note 29.

[44] *Op. cit.*, p. XV; cf. also p. 276.

[45]b. A.Z. 20a.

[46]See above, note 3.

[47]Cf. also b. Sanh. 12a.

[48]"Persecutions," pp. 111f., note 88.

[49]Cf. Tos. Sanh. 2:8; b. Sanh. 12a (intercalation); y. Yev. 12:6 (12d); b. Yev. 105b (*ḥaliṣah*); b. Yev. 108b (divorce).

[50]b. Ber. 61b (Tan. *tavo'* § 2).

[51]"Persecutions," p. 111 and 112, note 88.

[52]Cf. Schürer-Vermes-Millar, *op. cit.*, pp. 535ff.; Smallwood, *op. cit.*, pp. 428ff., 465f.; L. W. Barnard, "Hadrian and Judaism," *JRH* 5 (1969), pp. 285-298; J. Brand, *"Ha-'im hitkawwen Hadrianus livnot bet ha-miqdaš?,"* *Sinai* 53 (1962/63), pp. 21-30; H. Mantel, "The Causes of the Bar Kokba Revolt" *JQR* 58 (1967/68), pp. 224-242, 274-296; *JQR* 59 (1968/69), pp. 341-342; D. Rokeah, *"He[c]arot kozbiyot,"* *Tarbiz* 35 (1965/66), pp. 122-131.

[53]"Persecutions," p. 112, note 88.

[54]Cf. also y. Sot. 5:7 (20c); Tan. *tavo'* § 2; b. Men. 29h.

[55]*Bet ha-Midrasch*, ed. A. Jellinek (Jerusalem, [2]1938), Vol. VI, pp. 27f.; cf. also ibid., pp. 33f.

[56]Ed. Buber, pp. 61f.; printed ed. to Prov 9:1; cf. also Yalq. Prov. § 944, p. 980b.

[57]Ed. Higger, pp. 154f.

[58]*Bet ha-Midrasch*, Vol. II, pp. 67f.

[59]See note 55 and 56.

[60]Cf. K. Haacker-P. Schäfer, "Nachbiblische Traditionen vom Tod des Mose," *Josephus-Studien, Festschrift Otto Michel* (Göttingen, 1974), pp. 147-174.

A ROMAN PERSPECTIVE ON THE BAR KOCHBA WAR[*]

G. W. Bowersock
Institute for Advanced Study

Without demeaning the great archaeological discoveries of recent decades, a Roman historian can only feel perplexity at the enthusiasm shown in some quarters for the achievement of Bar Kochba. Although the rebel proclaimed himself "Prince (*nasi*) of Israel," few would care to follow Professor Yadin in rendering this arrogated title as "President of Israel" - the first president.[1] One has naturally too much respect for subsequent holders of that title and for the much larger constituency they have represented. Over the past decades new evidence, as well as reconsideration of the old, has suggested that substantial revision was called for in modern accounts of the Jewish revolt under Hadrian. If we examine what we actually know about the war and its causes, it will look very different from the tale all of us once learned.

The extraordinary discoveries in the region of the Nahal Hever, as well as the documents from the Wadi Murabba'at and the new finds in the Wadi ed-Daliya, have aroused great interest in Bar Kochba and his time. We now possess letters of Bar Kochba, if not in his own hand yet almost certainly in his own words.[2] He sounds rather like a pious thug, keeping his sacred observances and threatening his men. A startling impromptu excavation in Israel by a New York tourist turned up, not long ago, a fine statue of Hadrian that revives the important question of Hadrian's role in Palestine (and his visit there) on the eve of the revolt.[3] All this new material takes its place with the well known and relatively rich coinage through which the rebels announced the freedom of Israel together with the name of its would-be prince.

Let us review briefly the traditional account that dominates even the most recent and authoritative book. Avi-Yonah, in the English translation, which he oversaw, of his *Geschichte der Juden im Zeitalter des Talmuds*, wrote "Arms were accumulated, fortifications prepared in the field, funds were collected ... The rebels forced the Roman garrison of Jerusalem to leave. A whole legion, the XXII Deiotariana disappeared in the course of the war ... We lack a Josephus to give us a just appreciation of the Bar Kochba War."[4] All of this, except the last remark, is probably wrong; and the longing for a Josephus of the Hadrianic age never stops. Mordechai Gihon, in his survey of the war for that bibliographical *monstrum, Aufstieg und Niedergang der römischen Welt*, says

wistfully, "Wohl kaum einem der sich mit dem Bar-Kochba Krieg
befasst hat ist nicht einmal der Seufzer entschlüpft: Warum hat
nicht auch der Bar-Kochba Krieg seinen Josephus gehabt?"[5] Josephus
was neither a simple soul nor a straightforward reporter. Any
Josephus of Bar Kochba's day would probably not have provided much
help. After all, even with the real Josephus, the scholarly world
is unable to agree on the year in which Masada fell.[6]

It will be convenient to look at the evidence for the Bar
Kochba war under five headings, which are obviously interconnected.
The perspective is deliberately Roman, but that is not for lack of
interest in the rabbinic sources. It is rather, as Dr. Schäfer
demonstrates so admirably in his paper,[7] that there is, for the
most part, no authentic history to be drawn from them. (It is
worth remembering that the name of Akiba appears nowhere in the Bar
Kochba documents.) Before proceeding to the various individual
topics, it will be helpful to recall the one and only literary
allusion to the war by a contemporary of Hadrian. Here we have no
problems of literary tradition, transmission, redaction, or the
like. The epistolographer Fronto, boring as he is, was intelligent,
observant, and well placed. He lived through the period of the war
and wrote after Hadrian's death to his young pupil, Marcus Aurelius:
*Avo vestro Hadriano imperium obtinente, quantum militum a Iudaeis,
quantum ab Britannis caesum?*[8] These were the disasters of the reign,
balanced equally in Fronto's mind. Judaea and Britain were two
troublesome provinces at the periphery of the empire. The Jewish
revolt has had ample publicity, whereas even with Hadrian's wall
the British has not. No writer since Fronto has been known to
state that the British revolt disturbed Hadrian's reign just as the
Jewish one did. Fronto gives us the Roman perspective.

I. *Armies in Palestine*

The deployment of military forces in Palestine was once traditionally invoked in accounts of the Jewish revolt. Until about
twenty years ago it was generally assumed that Judaea was not a
consular province when war broke out, but was transformed into one
at the end by an angry Hadrian. The new status represented the imposition of a second garrison legion in addition to the X Fretensis
that had been there before. The elevation of the province and the
presence of two legions had been seen as part of the emperor's punishment of the Jews. But it was an Israeli scholar who first
recognized the implication of a new fragment of the Ostian fasti
giving the consular year of Q. Tineius Rufus as A.D. 127.[9] Rufus
was governor of Judaea when Bar Kochba launched his rebellion

and was therefore, incontrovertibly, a consular at the time. The
province's status had clearly been changed before the war. Evidence
for the presence of a second legion before the fighting was also at
hand. Inscriptions from the Caesarea aqueduct and the Caparcotna
road revealed the VI Ferrata in Judaea in A.D. 130.[10] A question
arose as to whether these alterations were now to be seen as a provocation. Several writers were, however, quick to observe that as
early as the end of Trajan's reign a consular, the Moor Lusius
Quietus, is found in charge of Judaea.[11] The issue now seems
to have been settled by the recent discovery of a milestone 13 km
southeast of Acre with proof of the II Traiana in Judaea in A.D.
120.[12] This establishes the presence of two legions in Judaea by
that time.

The accumulated information about Tineius Rufus, the VI Ferrata, and the II Traiana makes it not only reasonable but necessary
to assume that the transformation of Judaea belonged, not to the
context of the Bar Kochba war, but to the context of the so-called
Polemos of Quietus, the great uprising of Diaspora Jews that lasted
from A.D. 115-117.[13] One of the mysteries of that Trajanic revolt,
which is well documented for places like Cyrene, Cyprus, and Mesopotamia,[14] is the apparent absence of major tumult in Palestine itself. It now appears certain that by raising the status and doub-
ling the garrison of the Jewish province the Romans were able to
block the kind of violence that swept across the diaspora. In any
case, on the present showing the military reorganization of Judaea
must be explained in terms of the revolt under Trajan. It can no
longer provide any help in judging the irritants that may have
affected Bar Kochba and his followers.

Scholars who wish to claim that the twenties of the Second
Century were a time of increasing pressures and persecutions in
Palestine will have to rely on intuition instead of evidence.[15]
The disappearance of the XXII Deiotariana legion proves nothing.
It is last attested in Egypt in A.D. 119.[16] We do not know how
much longer it remained there, nor do we know where (if anywhere)
it was sent. There is not the slightest reason to think that the
Roman coins overstruck by the Jewish rebels came from the paychest
of the XXII Deiotariana, which they are imagined to have annihi-
lated.[17] There is no indication that the legion was in Palestine
under Hadrian at any time, still less that it or any other legion
was wiped out entire. The II Traiana, which appears to have taken
the XXII Deiotariana's place in Egypt, was already installed there
by A.D. 127.[18] If it was, as we have noted, in Judea at the beginning of the decade, it must accordingly have passed from Judaea

to Egypt sometime between A.D. 120 and 127. The dissolution of
legions remains an obscure matter, but destruction of a whole
legion at the hands of an enemy was unlikely to have occurred without huge publicity. The losses of Varus under Augustus and of
Fuscus under Domitian are cases in point. If the XXII Deiotarians
had been eliminated in Palestine, the event would have been among
the most noteworthy in the whole war.

II. *Hadrian in Palestine*

The activities of the II Traiana on the Caparcotna road in
A.D. 120 as well as of the VI Ferrata on the Caesarea aqueduct and
the Caparcotna road in A.D. 130, were undoubtedly part of the
grand preparations for the Palestinian tour of the emperor Hadrian
on his way from the other side of the Jordan over into Egypt. By
late in the year he had left Palestine and did not go back before
the outbreak of the war in 132.[19] We have no reason to think that
Hadrian was received in Palestine with any less enthusiasm than
elsewhere on his tour. The concomitants of such an imperial
adventus are regularly the appearance of special buildings, new
(or renamed) games, and cults, together with salutations of the
emperor as *restitutor*, *sōtēr*, *euergetēs*, or something similar.
The attitude of the Jews toward Hadrian at this time shows up in a
much neglected source, the fifth Sibylline Oracle, which is a
vaticinium ex eventu composed by a Jew before the end of Hadrian's
reign (and presumably before the Bar Kochba war).[20] Hadrian is
praised in the most extravagant terms:

> ἔσται καὶ πανάριστος ἀνὴρ καὶ παντα νοήσει.
> καὶ επὶ σοί, πανάριστε, πανέξοχε, κυανοχῖτα,
> καὶ επὶ σοισι κλάδοισι τάδ᾽ ἔσσεται ἤματα πάντα.
>
> (11.48-50)

Schürer long ago recognized the importance of Hadrian's visit
to Palestine, precisely because it shows the conventional expressions of honor: Hadrianea at Caesarea and Tiberias, a *panēgyris
Hadrianē* at Gaza, coins celebrating *adventus Aug. Iudaeae*.[21] The
newly discovered statue of Hadrian from the vicinity of Beth-Shean
may well be another reflection of his visit.[22] Finally the renam-
ing of Jerusalem and the transformation of the city into a *colonia*
are most plausibly explained as souvenirs of the emperor's passage;
but here, of course, there are traditional interpetations to be
overcome.

III. *Aelia Capitolina*

The foundation of *colonia Aelia Capitolina* is said by Cassius Dio to have been one of the causes of the Jewish revolt. He therefore dates it before the outbreak, whereas Eusebius sees it as a punishment inflicted after the war.[23] The *Chronicon Paschale* also presents the foundation as subsequent to the war; but since it dates the war to A.D. 119 little faith can be placed in its testimony (which can obviously be manipulated to support either an early or a late date).[24] The path of least resistance, often disguised as "reconciliation of the sources," leads to the assumption that the colonial foundation was announced before the war and carried out after it. But Dio, insofar as we can ascertain from the epitome of Xiphilinus what he wrote, clearly dated Aelia before the war and, it would appear, in the context of Hadrian's tour. The earlier date is now confirmed beyond doubt by the presence of a coin of Aelia Capitolina in a hoard of Bar Kochba denarii from the Judaean desert.[25] The honor to Jerusalem, as it was from the Roman point of view, would naturally belong to the year A.D. 130. It was in the causal connection with the revolt that Dio or, more probably, his epitomator may have erred, for two years elapsed between the two events. There must have been a more immediate provocation.

The razing of the temple site as part of the foundation of the city has sometimes seemed to students of the rabbinic texts a great provocation.[26] If the Romans had really done this, it would have been; but all that can be said is that on *colonia* coins a priest ploughing with a team of oxen is depicted to commemorate the traditional Roman rite of *circumductio* which marks out the pomerium of the city.[27] The ploughing motif has nothing to do with razing a site, and such an interpretation could only have arisen, mistakenly, much later and become absorbed in the Jewish tradition. It may tell us something about the time in which it was concocted and circulated, but it certainly tells us nothing about the time to which it refers.

If the foundation of Aelia Capitolina is to be detached from the Bar Kochba war, only to be linked with it for the first time later, a provocation between A.D. 130 and 132 remains to be found. It has been seen, most plausibly, in Hadrian's ban on circumcision, known from the *Historia Augusta* and the *Digest* (which provides the needed support for the testimony of the *Historia Augusta*).[28] The ban was by no means confined to Jews and doubtless reflected a personal distaste of the emperor, not unlike Domitian's aversion to castration. Since, as Schürer pointed out, the regulation

affected far more than Jews,[29] it would be wrong to assume that
Hadrian was singling them out for oppression. Yet it was not surprising that they perceived things that way. Professor Smallwood
has shown that Hadrian's measure seems not to have been in force
as late as A.D. 128,[30] and it is therefore not unlikely that
Hadrian issued it as a result of discoveries he made during his
visit to the Near East. The period between 130 and 132 would be
just right for the measure.

IV. *The Taking of Jerusalem*

Of Jerusalem, Schürer declared, "It was held by the rebels
during the first and second year."[31] Likewise Avi-Yonah: "Bar
Kochba established his government in Jerusalem."[32] In his article
on "Jérusalem sous la domination romaine" for the *Aufstieg und
Niedergang* series the late Baruch Lifshitz maintained the same
position.[33] Mary Smallwood had, however, displayed exemplary caution when she noted, "There is no explicit literary reference to
the Jewish recovery of Jerusalem."[34] Professor Smallwood knew
that the often cited text of Appian (*Syr.* 50) says nothing of a
rebel capture of the city. It simply says that the city which had
been settled (*oikistheisa*) by the Jews had been three times under-
mined--by Ptolemy, Vespasian, and Hadrian. No one could dispute
that.

The entire modern tradition of the rebel capture of the city
turns on the numismatic evidence. Schürer put the case concisely:
"The liberation of Jerusalem was extolled by Simon [Bar Kochba]
coins. But there are others from the same time which, besides the
date Year I of the Liberation of Israel or Year II, bear only the
name of the city of Jerusalem. These, therefore, were minted by
the city in its own name, from which it is clear that it was held
by the rebels during the first and second year."[35] In a lecture
delivered at Zürich in late 1976 and published in the following
year, a distinguished numismatist, Leo Mildenberg, established conclusively that the coins of the city of Jerusalem without the names
of Simon Bar Kochba or (as in some cases) the priest Eleazar were
die-linked to those that have the names.[36] We are therefore dealing exclusively with rebel coinage emanating from one mint, which
begins its advertising of Jerusalem with coins of Year I of the
Liberation of Israel, in other words as soon as the war broke out.
Furthermore the legend "For the freedom of Jerusalem" (*lhrwt yrwšlm*)
appears on undated coins from Year III. It is a legend that makes
more sense as an aspiration than as a statement of fact. More
than this, no Bar Kochba coin has ever been found in Jerusalem--

not for want of looking. Mildenberg draws the only acceptable conclusion from his results. The rebels proclaimed on their coinage, from the start, their ambition to take Jerusalem, but we have no reason to think that they succeeded. "Dass die Eroberung Jerusalems und der Wiederaufbau des Tempels ein Hauptziel Bar Kochbas war, das künden die Münzen in ganz unmissverständlicher Weise. Unsere Quelleanalyse hat aber keinen Beweis dafür ergeben, dass es ihm auch gelungen ist, Jerusalem wirklich zu erobern und zu halten."[37] Although there was a siege at Bethar,[38] there was none at Jerusalem.

V. *The temple of Zeus (Jupiter)*

Deeply entrenched in the Bar Kochba tradition of modern times is Hadrian's shameless construction of a temple to Zeus (Jupiter) on the very site of the Jewish temple.[39] Yet in recent years it has been repeatedly observed that there seemed to have been no such temple there. Francesco Grelle, John Wilkinson, and I have pointed out that eyewitnesses consistently reported that there were only two statues on the site.[40] All, including Origen (an early observer), agreed that one of the statues represented Hadrian. Jerome said that the other was of Zeus, whereas Origen and the Bordeaux pilgrim identified the second statue variously. The differences of interpretation are immaterial. There was no temple. The temple of Zeus was in fact built farther west, as Wilkinson now shows.[41]

The sole evidence for the construction of a pagan temple on the site of the Jewish temple is Xiphilinus' epitome of Dio, in which the project is linked with the foundation of Aelia as a cause of the Bar Kochba war.[42] The words of the Byzantine epitomator need to be scrutinized closely before we ask whether Dio was simply in error: ἐς τὸν τοῦ ναοῦ τοῦ θεοῦ τόπον ναὸν τῷ Διὶ ἕτερον ἀντεγείραντος. The expression ἐς τὸν τοῦ ναοῦ τοῦ θεοῦ τόπον has been universally understood to mean "on the place of the temple of the (Jewish) god." But accustomed as we are to reading classical Greek, we forget that in Roman and Byzantine style εἰς τὸν...τόπον means no more and no less than "in place of," "instead of."[43] The language of Xiphilinus, which could be that of Dio, means only that Hadrian built a temple of Zeus to replace the temple of the Jewish god. That was, of course, inflammatory enough; and that is what he did. A rabbinic tradition in Genesis Rabba that Hadrian once thought of actually rebuilding the Jewish temple may conceivably be connected with a misunderstanding of what Dio wrote but is much more probably a confusion with the

story of Julian's plan to rebuild the temple.[44] There remains no
evidence whatever for Hadrian's construction of a temple on the
place of the Jewish temple, and there is positive evidence
against it.

Summary

The Bar Kochba war was as fierce, protracted, and difficult
as guerilla wars can be. The cost in lives was high on both sides,
and the banishment from Jerusalem that Hadrian imposed on the Jews
was a fearful deprivation. The advertised aim of Bar Kochba may
well have moved him to take this step. But with all its horrors,
the war was historically rather different from what was once
thought. The imposition of a second legion in Judaea and the
province's elevation to consular rank belong to the circumstances
of the Trajanic, rather than the Hadrianic revolt. There is no
evidence for any tensions in the 120's or underground preparation
for war. The foundation of Aelia Capitolina was a natural part of
Hadrian's tour of Palestine and not the cause of revolt. (Perhaps
the ban on circumcision was.) There is no evidence for the loss
of a Roman legion, none for a rebel capture of Jerusalem, and none
for a Roman temple on the site of the Jewish temple. But it was a
serious war nonetheless. We may recall that for Fronto it was
comparable to that which ended with the building of Hadrian's wall.

A ROMAN PERSPECTIVE ON THE BAR KOKHBA WAR

[*]I am grateful to Professor Jacob Neusner for the pleasure and honor of presenting this paper at the Fourth Max Richter Conversation at Brown University in June 1978. I should also like to thank Professor George W. E. Nickelsburg, Jr. for courteously calling my attention to the evidence for Second Revolt occupation he uncovered in northern Judaea at the Wadi ed-Daliya: cf. P. W. and N. L. Lapp, *Discoveries in the Wadi ed-Daliyeh*, Annual of the American Schools of Oriental Research 41 (1974), especially 49ff.

[1]Y. Yadin, *Bar Kokhba* (1971), pp. 14-15, 122. His exact wording is "President over Israel."

[2]See Y. Yadin, *IEJ* 11 (1961), 40ff., and 12 (1962), 248ff. Cf. P. Benoit, J. T. Milik, R. de Vaux, *Discoveries in the Judaean Desert II: Les Grottes de Murabba'at* (1961), 124ff.

[3]The statue was found in fragments in the remains of a Roman building south of Beth Shean in 1975. See G. Foerster, *Qadmoniot* 7 (1975), 38-40.

[4]M. Avi-Yonah, *The Jews of Palestine* (1976), pp. 12-13. The story of the collection of funds has been well treated in Dr. Schäfer's paper, above pp. 113-130. The other points are considered in this paper.

[5]Forthcoming.

[6]The traditional date is spring 73, but W. Eck has proposed spring 74 in his *Senatoren von Vespasian bis Hadrian* (1970), pp. 93-111. Cf. G. W. Bowersock, in support of 73, in *JRS* 65 (1975), 183-184, elaborating arguments advanced by C. P. Jones in *Gnomon* 45 (1973), 689 and in *AJP* 95 (1974), 89-90.

[7]Above, pp. 113-130.

[8]Fronto, *de bello Parth*. 2, p. 206 van den Hout.

[9]B. Lifshitz, *Latomus* 19 (1960), 109ff.

[10]*Ibid.* Cf. H.-G. Pflaum, *IEJ* 19 (1969), 225 suggesting a transfer of the VI Ferrata in 123. For a suggestion that the VI Ferrata was in Arabia in 125 (at Jerash), see G. W. Bowersock, *ZPE* 5 (1970), 43. M. Speidel, *ANRW* II.8 (1977), 698 argues that only a detachment may have been involved and that the evidence must be judged inconclusive. I agree with him.

[11]M. Avi-Yonah, *IEJ* 23 (1973), 209ff.: L. F. J. Keppie, *Latomus* 32 (1973), 359ff. Cf. G. W. Bowersock, *JRS* 65 (1975), 184.

[12]B. Isaac and I. Roll, *ZPE* 33 (1979), 149-55. See also the same authors on "Judaea in the Early Years of Hadrian's Reign," *Latomus* 38 (1979), 54-66. But cf. J. R. Rea, *ZPE* 38 (1980), 220-1, calling for reconsideration of the letters on the stone said to mention II Traiana.

[13]On this war see especially A. Fuks, *JRS* 51 (1961), 98ff.

[14] For Cyrene, note S. Applebaum, *Greeks and Jews in Ancient Cyrene*, published in Hebrew in 1969 and due to appear in English translation. For Cyprus and Mesopotamia, see the references in E. M. Smallwood, *The Jews under Roman Rule* (1976), 412ff. Cf. also J. Neusner, *ANRW* II.9.1 (1976), 46ff.

[15] E.G. H. Mantel, *JQR* 58 (1967/8), 224ff., 274ff.; 59 (1968/9), 341f.

[16] *BGU* 1. 140.

[17] A. Kindler, *Numismatic Studies and Researches* 2 (1968), 68.

[18] *CIL* 3. 42.

[19] Cf. P. Strack, *Untersuchungen zur römischen Reichspragung des zweiten Jahrhunderts II: Die Reichsprägung zur Zeit des Hadrian* (1933), 128ff.; E. Schürer, *The History of the Jewish People in the Age of Jesus Christ*, rev. by G. Vermes and F. Millar (1973), pp. 541-2. Hadrian did return to Syria in 131, but not to Palestine; he spent the winter of 131-2 in Athens.

[20] On the composer and the date of composition of the fifth oracle, see the excellent treatment by Rzach in *P-W* II. 2. 4, cols. 2134-2140. The poet's lines about the destruction of the Temple leave no doubt that he is a Jew. The sequence of emperors stops with Hadrian, apart from line 51, which refers to Pius, Marcus, and Lucius in words that duplicate exactly *Orac. Sib.* 12. 176. As Rzach shows, this line must be an interpolation, not least because the author's view of Hadrian would undoubtedly have been different under the succeeding emperors. I am very grateful to David Potter for emphasizing to me the importance of the fifth oracle for the antecedents of the Bar Kochba war.

[21] For references and discussion, see Schürer (n. 19 above), p. 542.

[22] See note 3 above.

[23] Dio 69. 12. 1; Eus., *HE* 4. 6. 4.

[24] *Chron. Pasch.* I. 474.

[25] Y. Meshorer, *Jewish Coins of the Second Temple Period* (1967), pp. 92-3.

[26] Cf. Schürer (n. 19 above), p. 551, n. 163; Smallwood (n. 14 above), p. 459, n. 122.

[27] L. Kadman, *The Coins of Aelia Capitolina* (1956), p. 53, cf. p. 80, no. 1. On the Aelia coin Hadrian himself appears to be the priest. For other examples of the *colonia* type, depicting ploughing, see, for example, B. M. Levick, *Roman Colonies in Southern Asia Minor* (1967), pp. 36-37.

[28] *HA* Hadr. 14. 2: *moverunt ea tempestate et Iudaei bellum quod vetabantur mutilare genitalia.* Cf. *Dig.* 48. 8. 2. 4 (Hadrianic ban on *spadones*), together with *Dig.* 48. 1. 11 pr.: *Circumcidere Iudaeis filios suos tantum rescripto divi Pii permittitur: in non eiusdem religionis qui hic fecerit, castrantis poena irrogatur.* J. Geiger, *Zion* 41 (1976), 139-147, argues that this is not a relaxation, in respect to the Jews, of an earlier general prohibition but rather a ban against proselytizing. Geiger seems to have forgotten that Jews and Judaizers were not the only people

to practice circumcision. Moshe David Herr, *Zion* 43 1978, 1-11, accepts, however, that Hadrian's ban on circumcision was the primary cause of the Bar Kochba war. Dr. Mildenberg very kindly called my attention to the Herr article.

[29]Schürer (n. 19 above), p. 539.

[30]Smallwood (n. 14 above), p. 429, invoking Juv. 14. 99: *mox et praeputia ponunt.*

[31]Schürer (n. 19 above), p. 545.

[32]Avi-Yonah (n. 4 above), p. 13.

[33]B. Lifshitz, *ANRW* II. 8 (1977), 482ff.

[34]Smallwood (n. 14 above), p. 444.

[35]Schürer (n. 19 above), p. 545.

[36]L. Mildenberg, *Schweizer Münzblätter* 27 (1977), Heft 105, 1ff. See his forthcoming article in *Harv. Stud. Class. Phil.* 84 (1980).

[37]*Ibid.*, p. 6.

[38]Cf. Eus., *HE* 4. 6. 3: also Smallwood (n. 14 above), p. 455.

[39]E.g. Schürer (n. 19 above), p. 554; Smallwood (n. 14 above), pp. 434 and 459.

[40]F. Grelle, *L'autonomia cittadina fra Traiano e Adriano* (1972) 226ff.; G. W. Bowersock, *JRS* 65 (1975), 185; J. Wilkinson, *PEQ* 108 (1976), 77-8, and *Archaeology* 31 (1978), p. 7. Note Origen, *GCS* Orig. 12, pp. 193-4 (two statues, one of Hadrian, the other identified in one version as of Gaius, in another as of Titus; Jerome, *CCL* 73, p. 33: *ubi quondam erat templum et religio Dei, ibi Hadriani statua et Iovis idolum collocatum est*; also *CCL* 77, p. 226 (an equestrian statue of Hadrian). For the pilgrim, *CCL* 175, p. 16.

[41]J. Wilkinson, *Jerusalem as Jesus Knew It* (1978), pp. 178-9: "[Hadrian] left the Temple in ruins ... and erected on the site a statue of himself. This negative treatment of the Temple site was balanced by the erection of a Capitol with the offical Roman temple to Jupiter Capitolinus, Juno, and Minerva in another part of the city." Note the two other deities conjoined with Zeus-Jupiter.

[42]Dio 69. 12. 1.

[43]See Sophocles' lexicon s. v. *topos* for examples with *eis* and the definite article from Diodorus, Dionysius of Halicarnassus, and Nicolaus of Damascus. More in Stephanus s.v., col. 2308.

[44]Genesis Rabba 64. 10. For discussion of the *Letter of Barnabas* 16. 3-4 in this connection, see Smallwood (n. 14 above), p. 435, with notes 28 and 29. Cf. Lifshitz, *ANRW* II. 8 (1977), 473ff.

THE *TEMPLE SCROLL*

IN LITERARY AND PHILOLOGICAL PERSPECTIVE

Lawrence H. Schiffman

New York University

The philological and literary study of the texts of Judaism has a long and distinguished history. Biblical, Talmudic, and medieval texts have been subjected to such inquiry throughout the centuries of Jewish history. In almost all cases this research has had only one purpose, the discovery of the precise meaning of the text. Classically, philological and literary studies were limited to the disciplines of grammar, lexicography and exegesis. To be sure, great strides were made in these fields, and the heritage that modern scholars have received is both prodigious and overwhelming.

The rise of the *Wissenschaft des Judentums*, with its emphasis on the historical method, opened new vistas for philological and literary research. While it is certainly true that our twentieth century conception of historical study and method has advanced far beyond the paths tread by the great scholars of the *Wissenschaft*, our debt to them for opening up this avenue of investigation must be acknowledged. At the same time, developments in the fields of historical philology and literary criticism, especially in regard to the study of the Semitic languages and literatures, have widened our perspective on the study of Jewish texts. Needless to say, the many archaeological discoveries, especially of epigraphic material and manuscripts, have greatly enriched the data that form the basis for our research.

The purpose of this paper is not to deal with the classical areas of grammar, lexicography, and exegesis. What concerns us is the wider implications of philological and literary research, specifically as they can serve as handmaidens to historical study.

Close study of texts from a philological or literary point of view has provided the historical critic with valuable information regarding the date of the material before him. This dating has not only been approximate (This is biblical; this is Second Temple.) but also has led to much more precise results.

In the study of Judaism in late antiquity, literary and philological characteristics may also serve as a clue to the affinity of ideologies among the authors of various texts. It might be objected that one should not expect differing ideological interests

143

to be reflected in philological features. After all, Democrats and Republicans speak the same English. But the facts for our material are otherwise. Let us take a closer look.

While implications of the documentary hypothesis for biblical studies are still a matter of great debate, we can accept with certainty the fact that throughout First Temple times there were schools of thought that can be distinguished by their literary style and even by grammatical and lexicographic patterns. To be more specific, linguistic and literary investigation can fix the ideological provenance of a text or of a given part of a text. Hence, we can trace the work of the priestly and Deuteronomic schools throughout the First Temple period.

Let us look briefly at Second Commonwealth dialectology. I do not mean here to attempt to unravel the complex history of Hebrew in this period, but only to make some general observations.

Our sources, incomplete as they are, indicate four basic dialects. Mishnaic Hebrew was in its incipient stages, developing from tendencies found in the latest of the biblical books. It is possible that many of the features observable in this dialect were colloquialisms in earlier periods.[1] In many of the Qumran texts we find a dialect that seems to be a hyperdevelopment of proto-massoretic, biblical Hebrew. This is the dialect usually referred to as the language of the Dead Sea Scrolls.[2] We also find in the Dead Sea Scrolls another dialect, which seems to be much closer to that of the massocretic Bible. Finally, the Samaritans had their own dialect. Certainly, this survey does not in any way cover the dialectology of this period, yet we can already see that here again the dialectology is linked to ideological affinities.

As we move to the tannaitic period itself we also encounter similar phenomena. The long-standing theory about the different exegetical approaches of Rabbi Akiba and Rabbi Ishmael is certainly oversimplified and in need of re-examination. However, there is no question that exegetical terminology in the texts themselves betrays intellectual and religious trends.[3] Beyond this, our manuscripts of tannaitic Hebrew and the inscriptions, letters, and documents from Bar Kokhba and his followers lead us to believe that there may also have been a complex of dialects within tannaitic circles. Unfortunately, the state of our materials makes investigation from this point of view premature. One can certainly imagine, however, that if there were to be discovered Hebrew materials written by non-tannaitic Jews in the tannaitic period, these would also reflect a dialect different from that of the *tannaim*.

In regard to literary features in Second Temple and tannaitic times, the various literary genres that have come down to us certainly can serve as clues to provenance. The literary character of the Qumran sectarian compositions and of the apocalyptic texts is well known. The thorough study of the literary forms of the tannaitic material, something the earlier texts still await, has been carried out in recent years. An experienced student of this literature can recognize and identify literary affinities that go hand in hand with ideological factors.

One might be tempted to assign all these differences in philological and literary character to the date of composition rather than to ideological considerations, but this argument is patently false. A comparison of securely dated materials reveals that such distinctions operate even in contemporaneous literature. In this regard, texts from the Judean Desert are most helpful.

The recently published *Temple Scroll*, edited by Yigael Yadin,[4] affords us an excellent text from which to illustrate the value of this method. Before discussing the linguistic and literary features of the *Scroll*, we shall outline its archaeological background and Yadin's argument for the composition of the *Scroll* by the sectarian inhabitants of the caves of Qumran.

Yadin assumes that this text was authored by the Dead Sea sect, which, in his view, is identical to the Essenes of Philo and Josephus. Indeed, other fragments of this text were found at Qumran under controlled archaeological conditions. While the main manuscript was written in two Herodian hands, fragments preserved in the Rockefeller Museum indicate that the text was already extant in Hasmonean times. This dating generally accords with that of the other material found at Qumran. In addition, the scribal techniques and practices described in such detail by Yadin also are of the kind familiar from the Qumran collection. Therefore, Yadin concludes that this manuscript of sixty-seven columns emerged from the Qumran caves and that it was, at some time, part of what Cross has so aptly called "the ancient library of Qumran."[5]

It cannot be emphasized enough, however, that presence in a library does not indicate authorship by the librarian. On the contrary, throughout history libraries have attempted to preserve the writings of their own cultures as well as related groups.[6] The fact that Apocryphal and pseudepigraphal works and numerous other compositions are preserved at Qumran does not indicate that they were authored by the sect. Texts are also preserved by a group as part of its literary heritage, but such manuscripts need not have been composed by the group. Who would imagine, for example, that the biblical texts found at Qumran were authored by the sect?

For the Qumran corpus there is one additional factor. The vast bulk of the material gives evidence of having been copied by the sect. This can be shown by both the technical aspects of linguistic forms known to be characteristic of the Qumran sect's own compositions. Despite the arguments about the alleged scriptorum and inkwells of Qumran,[8] the fact is that the texts were copied somewhere, and it seems most logical that they were copied at the sect's headquarters at Qumran. If so, the sectarians would have made efforts to collect as much as possible of Jewish literature, which they would have copied and placed alongside their own sectarian texts, in the caves. This they would have done either for storage, as some have proposed, or, in the view of others, for protection from the onslaught of the Roman legion that eventually destroyed Qumran.[9]

In Yadin's argument for composition of the *Temple Scroll* by the sect, he views the text as representing the ideology and *halakah* of the Qumran group. As we noted, the presence of this text in the Qumran corpus, even in copies made at Qumran, will not be enough to substantiate his view. Yadin is obligated to demonstrate a much more extensive set of affinities. Linguistic phenomena are one factor that can help in determining the author(s) of the material.

Once Yadin assumes that the text was authored by the Qumran sect, he defines its purpose. The scroll, he says, "describes the teachings regarding the Temple which God gave to Moses--like the teachings of the Tabernacle--as a commandment to the children of Israel throughout their generations, which is the same teaching revealed to David, as is alluded to in I Chron. 28:11ff."[10] In other words, he sees the text as describing a Temple that the children of Israel "are about to build," as opposed to the Messianic Temple. The *Temple Scroll* and other Qumran material, as well as Jubilees and Enoch, indicate that the Messianic Temple will be built by God Himself.[11] What Yadin seems to be saying--and he is not clear here--is that this scroll was the ideal picture of how the sect would run the Temple if they were in control of it. After all, the sect had abstained from Temple offerings because they viewed the procedure of the Jerusalem Temple as faulty and the priests as impure.[12]

Yadin further proposes, after a brief discussion of the problems of canon at Qumran, that the author of the scroll and the members of the sect regarded the scroll as "the genuine Torah of

God." He even goes so far as to propose possible identifications
with the *Sefer He-Hagu/i*, the *Sefer Ha-Torah He-Ḥatum*, or the
Sefer Ha-Torah Ha-Shenit mentioned in the sectarian texts from
Qumran. His final conclusion is that the *Temple Scroll* was written
by the Qumran sect, which, he says, with new evidence from this
text, are to be identified with the Essenes. He does consider the
possibility that "sect" is too narrow a designation and that we
might be dealing here with a wider group or stream of thought. [13]

Central to Yadin's entire approach and to his interpretation
of particular texts is the assumption that this text was authored
by the Qumran sect. His method, however, is faulty. Instead of
beginning with an assumption about the authorship of the text and
using this assumption to interpret the *Temple Scroll*, Yadin first
should have subjected the scroll to thorough study and then determined its provenance based on such study. One central area of
concern must always be the language, style, and literary character
of the text. Our study will show that in these areas Yadin's conclusion is highly questionable, and in the course of our work we
hope to illustrate the use of philological and literary study for
historical research.

Language and Style

The linguistic and syntactic characteristics of the Qumran
sectarian literature are well known. It can, I think, be stated
that the dialectical characteristics of these texts, as shown by
their peculiarities in phonology and morphology, are a *sine qua non*
for the assumption of sectarian authorship. Hence, the book of
Jubilees found at Qumran must be excluded. On the other hand,
Qumran-like forms would be expected to creep into other texts
copied and handed down by the sect, as evidenced in the biblical
scrolls.

Our text does have some of these characteristics, but to a
limited degree. This observation is made by Yadin. Basing ourselves on his detailed lists, [14] we will survey the linguistic
features of the *Temple Scroll*.

Like the scribes of the Qumran compositions, our text tends
to plene *waw* and *yod*. Unlike the sectarian texts, medial *'alef* in
rosh and its forms remains. On the other hand, while sectarian
texts write *ky'*, this text, with one exception, writes *ky*. *Hu'*
and *hi'* are written as in MT, unlike the sectarian *hu'ah* and *hi'ah*.
While spellings of the plural of *goy* are similar to those found at
Qumran (with *'alef*), Rabbinic texts attest to the same spelling.
'Alef has clearly lost its glottal character, as it has in the

other dialects of the period. Yet in regard to spelling, Rabbinic
texts are more conservative than our text or the sectarian documents. Elision of *he'*, present in the sectarian texts, especially
in the *hif^cil*, is very common in this text. Substitution of final
yod for final *he'* vocalized with *segol* (massoretic pointing) occurs
frequently here, as it does in the sectarian texts. The inter-
change of *sin* and *samekh*, so common in tannaitic texts, is rare
here, as in the sectarian texts. As at Qumran, the pronominal suf-
fixes *-kem* and *-hem* are written *-kema* and *-hema*. Finally, our
text uses pausal forms in medial position (*yišmoru* for *yišmeru*),
a phenomenon also attested in the sectarian texts.

Yadin has correctly stated "that before us is a text the
author of which tried hard to imitate biblical language, except
that there were included in it unintentionally syntactic and linguistic usages which were widespread at the time of composition of
the scroll, and especially obvious is the difference between the
language of the Bible and that of the scroll."[15] Yadin further
notes the closeness of the text to late biblical Hebrew and to the
language of the tannaim.[16]

A major feature of this text is the use of forms of *hyh* followed by participles to indicate past or future meaning, often
durative. Indeed, the presence of such forms in Second Temple
biblical Hebrew shows that these forms were coming into vogue then
as well. Although extremely common in mishnaic Hebrew and in the
Temple Scroll, these forms are rare at Qumran.

In regard to lexicography, a number of features may be
observed. First, there is a large number of words in the *Temple
Scroll* that appear rarely in biblical Hebrew but are found in tannaitic sources with greater frequency. A few examples drawn from
Yadin's list are: *'esel*, the root *bdl*, and the forms *^casuy* and
re'uyah (spelled here without the medial *'alef*). There is also a
long list of technical terms connected with the Temple and its
structures that are found only in Rabbinic sources. Some examples
are: *ḥel*, *taba^cot*, *meḥillah*, and *parwar*.

Particularly in regard to technical halakic terminology we are
even more struck by the gap between the *Temple Scroll* and the sectarian texts. Yadin has assembled lists of forms typifying mishnaic and sectarian usage. The list of mishnaic forms is much
longer. Nevertheless, Yadin concludes that the few sectarian
usages prove that the author was a member of the sect.[18] For the
Rabbinic cases, he cites terms that are central to both mishnaic
Hebrew and the language of our text. He even cites several cases
where the phraseology of passages in the *Temple Scroll* is almost

exactly the same as that found in tannaitic sources. For Qumran
Hebrew he cites only cases that are unimportant to both corpuses.
Besides, there is a complete absence from the scroll of what we
would consider the basic terms and expressions of Qumran literature, precisely because most of these are connected with sectarian
concerns and animus, which are completely lacking in our text.

What we have said here is even more telling in light of the
work of C. Rabin.[19] He has shown that the Qumran sectarian texts
prefer archaic biblical legal terminology where later mishnaic
texts have replaced the biblical terms with neologisms or with
other terms not necessarily mentioned in the biblical texts. It
is therefore most surprising to find this supposed sectarian writing, composed at least by the Hasmonean period, using the terms so
common in mishnaic Hebrew.

With regard to syntax there is little to say. The author has
really molded his work out of biblical passages. (We will discuss
the literary character of the text below.) Nevertheless, where he
wrote his own passages, a rare phenomenon, he did so in quasi-
biblical style. It has become common to claim that Qumran sectarian texts are written in archaizing biblical style, but this is
false. The loose syntax, the tendency to connect long strings of
clauses, and the use of '*ăšer* to introduce laws, all peculiarities of Qumran Hebrew, are absent from the scroll. Our author
succeeded in writing in biblical style, whereas the Qumranites, I
think, did not really try to do so.

What conclusions can be drawn from this data? On the one
hand, the *Temple Scroll* shares many features of Qumran orthography.
On the other hand, certain typical and extremely significant features of the Qumran linguistic topography are absent. In view of
the dating of its manuscripts, it seems most likely that the
Temple Scroll lies somewhere between the orthography of the Dead
Sea Scrolls and that of massoretic Hebrew.

We have also seen that the *Temple Scroll* contains many linguistic elements similar to what is found in the later tannaitic
texts. We will probably have to conclude that the text of the
Temple Scroll originated in a group whose basic language characteristics were close to that of the Qumran sect but which had also
imbibed teachings attested later in Rabbinic literature. This
conclusion brings into question, then, the view that the *Temple
Scroll* originated in and represents the teachings of the group we
have come to know as the Dead Sea sect.

Literary Character

The literary character of the text may be analyzed from two points of view, what we might call the micro- and macro-structures. By microstructure we mean the way in which individual passages are put together. By macrostructure we mean the way in which the entire composition has been formed.

In regard to the individual sections of the text, the author has followed a simple technique. He has taken the material on the subject scattered throughout the Pentateuch (and occasionally elsewhere in the Bible) and gathered it together. In doing so, he has created a unified version of each law.[20] Yadin has correctly observed time and again in his notes that the author often depends on a reading known to us from the ancient versions and different from that of the massoretic text. In weaving together the various Pentateuchal verses on a subject, the author often does so in such a way as to emphasize aspects he deems important. Sometimes he inserts his own explanations as well.[21] Yadin, however, has gone too far in finding alleged polemics in the text. Often, when the author simply copies from the verses of the Pentateuch, Yadin finds a polemic to prove that our text is sectarian. A clear example is the calendar controversy regarding the counting of the Omer, where Yadin assumes a polemical view and then uses his interpretation to prove all kinds of other things.[22]

The basic literary characteristic of the microstructure is the weaving together of the Pentateuchal verses on a given theme with some additional verses which, in the interpretation of the author, have a bearing on the subject, even if they seem literally to be irrelevant. This is an early form of midrashic exegesis.

Yehezkel Kaufmann has discussed in detail the midrashic exegesis found in Ezra and Nehemiah.[23] It is clear that the earliest attempts at *midrash* were intended to solve the problems of contradiction and repetition in the various portions of the Torah that modern scholars call "documents" or "sources." The problem came to the fore at the beginning of the Second Temple period as a result of the canonization of the Torah that had taken place in the exilic period. Indeed, such a form of *midrash* has been found in many of the laws of the *Zadokite Fragments*, as well as in other texts from the Qumran corpus.[24] It must be noted that these texts do not explicitly (for the most part) cite the texts on which the *midrash* is built. Rather, they weave the texts together into a unified whole. Only the detailed analysis of the scholar can unravel the pieces and allow us to explain which verses served as the bases of the law. Indeed, a similar approach can be traced in

the Samaritan Pentateuch, where there is a tendency to supplement
material from one Pentateuchal source with that in the parallel
sources.

A later stage in the historical development of this phenomenon
comes in a text such as the *midrash* in the *Passover Haggadah*. This
text cites Deut 26:5-9 word for word, supplementing it with its own
explanations, which are then proven by citing the appropriate
material from Exodus. Here we find the addition of explanations.
Further, the biblical sources are no longer implicit but are now
explicit. While it might be said that the *Passover Haggadah* is
aggadic while the other material we are discussing is halakic, the
same tendencies are observed in the halakic *midrashim* of the Rabbis.

But where in this scheme does the *Temple Scroll* fit? Certainly it stands apart. It would be difficult to say that it is closer
to the traditions of the later Rabbinic texts than to what we know
of the Qumran sect. We can say with certainty that its approach
does not accord with what we can document as the sectarian exegetical approach during the period in which the *Temple Scroll* was probably composed.

The inescapable conclusion, then, is simply that one cannot
say with impunity that the text of the *Temple Scroll* in its microstructure accords with the sectarian halakic literature of the
Qumran sect. In fact, it is only in Rabbinic literature that we
encounter the regular citation of biblical proof texts, and one
might maintain that in this respect our text is a forerunner of
Rabbinic *midrash*, although this kind of speculation is probably
premature.

It is significant that our author has chosen to make use of
texts from the Prophets as well as the Torah. Qumran *halakah*
often is derived from texts in the Prophets and Writings. However,
the *tannaim* avoided such derivations, even where this led them to
cite less relevant passages from the Pentateuch. It is possible
that in this respect the Rabbis were influenced by what they saw
as the Christian misuse of the Prophets. In order to avoid all
misunderstandings in regard to the Prophetic role in Jewish law,
they went out of their way to limit their halakic *midrashim* almost
completely to the Torah.

The *Temple Scroll* is based primarily on the Torah. Because
of the subject matter, however, the author makes use of descriptions of the Solomonic Temple in Kings and Chronicles, as well as
of the vision of the Temple found in Ezekiel. The use of the
Ezekiel material is especially interesting in light of the Talmudic
discomfort with the way in which Ezekiel's plan and cultic

regulations seemed to contradict those of the Pentateuch.[25]

While what we have just said might lead to the conclusion that in regard to the use of scriptural material our text is similar to the Qumran corpus, we must note that the early halakic *midrashim* discussed by Kaufmann also make use of the Prophets. It is possible, then, as we have said, that the avoidance of the use of Prophetic material for legal derivation took place only in the Christian period and hence that all groups would have drawn freely on the entire Bible (leaving aside the issue of canonization) in the Second Commonwealth period.

Yadin has stressed that, like the book of Deuteronomy, much in this text has been rephrased into the first person, as if to say that it was the direct word of God. Priestly material is by and large left as is, while Deuteronomic material is recast into the first person in order to eliminate the intermediation of Moses.[26] Levine has already noted[27] in this connection that the name of Moses is also absent from the midrashic sections of the *Passover Haggadah*. This is certainly curious in a text that retells the story of the Exodus from Egypt. The implied attitude of the author(s) of our scroll toward Moses and his prophetic status will have to be analyzed as part of future study of the *Temple Scroll*.

The macrostructure of the text is clearly deserving of a special study. Yadin has paved the way with detailed tables and listings of the contents, which certainly make it easier to approach this topic.[28] The basic problem here is to understand the order in which the material is presented. At first glance the order seems erratic, but some possible theories of organization can be suggested for detailed investigation. We will take advantage of this opportunity to summarize the contents of the scroll in the order in which the author presents them. We note that there was one column which was not preserved at the beginning.

```
Covenant between God and Israel
Command to build Temple
Measurements of Temple and some chambers
Kaporet, kerubim, paroket, shewbread table, menorah, curtains
Obligation of festival sacrifices
Altar for burnt offerings
Specific discussion of Sabbath and festival offerings,
    first fruits, milu'im and wood offerings
Offering of limbs, 'azkarah and salting
Continuation of festival offerings
Structures in the inner courtyard--staircase, lavatory,
    clothes closet, slaughterhouse
Measurements of inner courtyard
Command to build middle courtyard
Gates of middle courtyard, who may and who may not enter
Outer courtyard, its measures and gates
Structures of outer courtyard, sukkot and description of
    sukkot offerings
```

Eating of tithes
Structures of outer courtyard
Changing of *mišmarot*
Impure who may not enter sanctuary
Methods of purification
Structures to keep impure animals out of holy precincts
Placing of latrines and houses for impure
Holiness of sanctuary
Kosher and non-kosher animals
Laws of impurity
Cultic regulations
Slaughter for sacrifice and ordinary use
Vows, false prophet, enticer, foreign worship
Laws of king and army
Priestly and Levitical gifts
Prophecy--true and false
Witnesses
Destruction of native population
Laws of war, finding of corpse and captive slave girl
Various Deuteronomic prohibitions
Rape, forbidden marriage and sexual unions

The simplest observation that can be made is that the text
begins with Exodus (the covenant and command to build a sanctuary)
and ends with Deuteronomy. It seems that the organization may
have begun with the order of the Torah itself. The author deviated
from the Torah's order whenever associative principles dictated it.
For this reason he began to discuss the structure and equipment of
the Temple according to the order of the Torah, but at each point
he digressed to discuss the relevant offerings that utilized those
structures or equipment,[29] then returning to the scriptural order.
Further, he deals in general with cult and ritual first, and then
moves on to the various prescriptions culled from Deut. 18-22,
curiously appended to this work of cultic significance.

The question of the organization of the scroll is certainly
deserving of detailed study, yet certain conclusions can already
be drawn. The author apparently worked through the Pentateuch in
order, reorganizing and writing as he went along. While he tends
toward scriptural order, he maintains in the macrostructure, as he
did in the microstructure, the desire to associate material that
somehow is related by subject. This is especially true in his
tendency to organize sacrificial law around his descriptions of
the relevant Temple furnishings and equipment needed for the per-
formance of the rituals.

Our author seems to be torn between the midrashic and "mishnaic" (abstract) modes of organization. He tends to follow the
order of the Bible while also using an associative technique to
gather relevant material together. In this respect, the *Temple
Scroll* differs from the Qumran sectarian works contemporaneous
with it. The Qumran texts have gone much further in providing
the legal material with a coherent subject organization, as can be

seen in the *Zadokite Fragments* and in the *Manual of Discipline*.
The later tannaitic Mishnah and Tosefta collections as well are
organized primarily by subject.

The *Temple Scroll* is certainly a literary composition. By
this we mean that it is not the product of an oral tradition such
as lies behind the great collections of tannaitic literature.
Some will seek to argue that since Rabbinic tradition emphasizes
the concept of oral Law, the text before us must be sectarian.
Here there is a methodological flaw. The evidence for the Rabbinic
prohibition on writing *halakot* is much later than our text. We do
not really know how Pharisaic or proto-Pharisaic traditions were
transmitted.[30] We cannot assume that the prohibition on the writing down of legal teachings was already in existence at this time.
Further, since the author of this text, according to Yadin, sought
to emphasize that his interpretations and doctrines were in fact
part of the revelation of God, he might have regarded his text as
written Torah, even if he knew the concept of the oral Law and the
attendant prohibition on writing *halakot*.

What results emerge from our study of the linguistic and literary character of the *Temple Scroll*? First, we may say with no
reservations that the *Temple Scroll* does not correspond to what we
would have expected from a Qumran sectarian text composed in the
Hasmonean period. Neither its linguistic topography nor its literary structure justify Yadin's assumption that this scroll represents a text composed by the so-called Dead Sea sect.

The composers of this text were much closer to what later became the Pharisaic or tannaitic tradition than were the authors of
the sectarian texts previously known. Yet the linguistic structure
of the *Temple Scroll* might indicate some relationship to the Qumran
group or to allied circles. This would serve to explain how this
text got into the Qumran library. Perhaps we might even speculate
that the text was composed by a group that was ideologically
aligned between Qumran sectarianism and the Pharisaic tradition,
tending toward Pharisaism. To be sure, the authors, in light of
the limited evidence available, cannot be said to be the Pharisees
because of halakic differences between this text and some of the
views ascribed to the Pharisees.

Of course, we have only discussed here the linguistic and
literary evidence regarding the *Temple Scroll*. Thorough study of
the *halakah* of this text remains to be carried out before definitive conclusions can be made. It seems to us, though, that such
research will confirm the general direction in which the literary
and linguistic data have pointed.

Perhaps the content of our text would dictate that we look for its authors among the priestly groups of the Second Commonwealth. Our observations do not preclude this. They only show that whoever authored this text must have been in close contact with what was to be termed the Pharisaic approach. Further investigation of the *Sitz im Leben* of the *Temple Scroll* will no doubt revolve around its relationship to the priesthood and Temple in the pre-Herodian period.

Despite the excellent job Yadin has done both in the technical aspects and in tackling the many important questions, we cannot accept his primary assumption of authorship by the Qumran sect. Each of us must confront the text with a fresh point of view so that ultimately scholarly consensus will be able to reach a conclusion about the fundamental questions of who wrote the *Temple Scroll* and why. Finally, we hope to have shown how philological and literary considerations can be and must be brought to bear in our search to determine the affinities between the various Jewish groups in late antiquity.

NOTES

THE *TEMPLE SCROLL*

[1]See B. Levine, "*Peraqim Be-Toledot Ha-^{C}Ibrit Ha-Medubberet*," *Eretz Israel* 14 (1978), 266-270, and "Rabbinic Hebrew" in the forthcoming *Cambridge History of Judaism*.

[2]See E. Qimron, *Diqduq Ha-Lashon Ha-^{C}Ibrit shel Megillot Midbar Yehudah* (Jerusalem: Hebrew University Dissertation, 1976) which is an excellent study on Qumran Hebrew.

[3]An excellent summary of the problem and bibliography is found in M. D. Herr, "Midreshei Halakhah," *EJ* 11, 1521-3. The terminology is discussed by H. Albeck, *Mabo' La-Talmudim* (Tel Aviv: Dvir, 1969), 84-102.

[4]*Megillat Ha-Miqdash*, 3 vols. (Jerusalem: Israel Exploration Society, 1977).

[5]Yadin I, 295-307. For the scribal techniques, see 8-21. Fragments of other MSS. are discussed on 7.

[6]Notable examples are the libraries of Ashurbanipal, Alexandria, and Pergamum.

[7]See M. Martin, *The Scribal Character of the Dead Sea Scrolls* (Louvain: Université de Louvain, 1958) I, 37-203.

[8]F. M. Cross, *The Ancient Library of Qumran* (Garden City, N.Y.: Doubleday, 1961), 66f., J. Poole, R. Reed, "The Preparation of Leather and Parchment by the Dead Sea Scrolls Community," *Technology and Culture* 3 (1962), 1-26, B. M. Metzger, "The Furniture in the Scriptorium at Qumran," *RQ* 1 (1958-9), 509-516, "When did Scribes Begin to Use Writing Desks?," *Akten des XI Internationalen Byzantinischen-Kongresses* 1958 (1960), 355-62, G. R. Driver, "Myths of Qumran," *Annual of the Leeds University Oriental Society* 6 (1966-8), 23-27, K. W. Clark, "The Posture of the Ancient Scribe," *BA* 26 (1963), 63-72.

[9]The latter view seems most logical and is argued forcefully by R. de Vaux, *Discoveries in the Judaean Desert* VI, 21f. and 22 n. 1.

[10]Yadin I, 141 (my translation).

[11]Yadin I, 141f.

[12]See my *Halakhah at Qumran* (Leiden: E. J. Brill, 1975), 129 and my Response to B. M. Bokser, "Philo's Description of Jewish Practices," *Center for Hermeneutical Studies* Colloquy 30 (1977), 21 and ns. 14-16. (This response will appear in expanded form under the title "Communal Meals at Qumran" in a forthcoming *RQ*.) My statement in no. 15 regarding the nature of the *Temple Scroll* must now be modified in light of the publication of the text and the present study.

[13]Yadin I, 300-304.

[14]Yadin I, 21-34. Cf. E. Qimron, "*Leshonah shel Megillat Ha-Miqdash*," *Leshonenu* 42 (1978), 83-98.

[15]Yadin I, 29 (my translation).

[16]Yadin I, 30.

[17]Yadin I, 31-34.

[18]Yadin I, 33.

[19]*Qumran Studies* (Oxford: University Press, 1957), 108-111.

[20]Yadin I, 62-65.

[21]Yadin I, 65-69.

[22]See the forthcoming review article of the Hebrew edition of the *Temple Scroll* by B. Levine to appear in *BASOR*.

[23]*Toledot Ha-'Emunah Ha-Yisra'elit* (Jerusalem: Mossad Bialik, Tel Aviv: Dvir, 1966/7) IV, 291-293, 327-338. See also an as yet unpublished section of my Brandeis University dissertation, *Halakhah at Qumran* (Waltham, Mass., 1974), 159-180.

[24]This is shown time and again in our study of the Sabbath laws in *Halakhah at Qumran* (Leiden: E. J. Brill, 1975), 84-133. A study in progress regarding the laws of courts, testimony, and court procedure will confirm this same conclusion. See also my study "The Qumran Law of Testimony," *RQ* 8 (1975), 603-612 and "Addenda and Corrigenda," *RQ* 9 (1977), 261f.

[25]See M. Greenberg, "Ezekiel," *EJ* 6, 1094 and S. Zeitlin, "An Historical Study of the Canonization of the Hebrew Scriptures," *PAAJR* 3 (1933), 122-128, reprinted in S. Leiman, Ed., *The Canon and Masorah of the Hebrew Bible* (New York: KTAV, 1974), 165-171.

[26]Yadin I, 61f.

[27]Cf. Levine's forthcoming study in *BASOR* where he deals at length with this matter.

[28]Yadin I, 34-60.

[29]So also J. Milgrom, "The *Temple Scroll*," *BA* 41 (1978), 108.

[30]J. Neusner has found the possibility of written traditions in pre-70 Pharisaism, although the caution with which he presented his material must be emphasized. See "The Written Tradition in the Pre-Rabbinic Period," *JSJ* 4 (1973), 56-65.

ATONEMENT AND SACRIFICE IN THE QUMRAN COMMUNITY

Hermann Lichtenberger

University of Tübingen

I

Scholars often have assumed the theological unity of the Qumran texts and have understood it in a relatively uncomplicated way.[1] Recently, however, research on the literary character of several documents and on the tradition-history of the Qumran texts has provided more insight into both the uniqueness of each individual manuscript and the theological development within the Qumran community itself.[2] The unhistorical assertion that a group that existed for 200 years possessed a static theology fails to take seriously both the theological development within, and the external influences exerted upon, this group.

This theological development can be illustrated, at least in part, by the various statements in the Qumran literature that describe the concept of atonement. There are tensions that are explicable only in relationship to the theological thinking of this community. If we look at the concept of atonement in three manuscripts of the early period of the community: the Hymns,[3] the War Scroll,[4] and the Manual of Discipline,[5] we find that the root *kpr* is used differently in these texts in connection with the concept of atonement. It is used in a non-cultic sense in the Hymns,[6] exclusively in a cultic context in the War Scroll,[7] and has both a cultic and a non-cultic meaning in the Manual of Discipline.[8] To be sure, this shift from cultic to non-cultic meanings does not encompass the various facets of the concept in the documents.

This paper aims to contribute to the discussion of this issue by examining the cultic understanding of atonement in the literature of the Qumran community. I shall try to clarify the similarities and differences among several versions of the concept as well as to suggest why these similarities and differences developed.

II

The cultic statements about atonement relate to the concepts of temple and sacrifice and will be discussed here in regard to their context in the Qumran community.

The various manuscripts provide the following differentiated picture of the temple:

1.   The temple in Jerusalem is described both neutrally and

polemically.[9] The description of the desecration of the Jerusalem temple by its priests, for example, is polemic.

2. The Qumran community, however, expected to inherit the temple in Jerusalem at some future date (1QM 2,3[10]; 7,11). This same idea also is clearly expressed in the *Pesher* to Psalm 37 (4Q171, 1, 3-4, III, 10f.): *The wicked borrows and does not repay, but the righteous is generous and gives. Truly, those whom He [blesses shall possess] the land, but those whom he curses [shall be cut off]* (Ps. 37:21-22) -- Interpreted, this concerns the congregation of the Poor, who [shall possess] the portion of all . . . They shall possess the High Mountain of Israel [for ever], and shall enjoy [everlasting] delights in His Sanctuary" (DSSE, 244-5).

3. The expectation of a new eschatological sanctuary (*hbyt 'šr [b']hryt hymym*, see 4QFlor 1,2ff.[11]) is also clearly expressed in the descriptions of the new Jerusalem and its cult.

4. The Qumran community, however, could speak of the worship in the heavenly sanctuary (4QS1).

The rejection of the Jerusalem cult probably forms part of the background for these statements. The problem, however, becomes more complicated when we consider the Damascus Document. On the basis of 9,13f., 11,17ff., and 16,13ff. it might be concluded that the community of CD participated in some way in the Jerusalem cult. This seems to be substantiated by Josephus, who reports in *Antiquities* 18.19:

> They send votive gifts to the Temple, and complete their
> sacrifices employing a different ritual of purification.
> For this reason they are prevented from using those pre-
> cincts of the Temple that are frequented by the common
> people and complete their sacrifices by themselves.[13]

J. M. Baumgarten concludes:

> It is true that the Qumran sect was lead by its separa-
> tist orientation to stress the value of substitute
> sacrifices, but it never abandoned the belief in the
> sanctity of Jerusalem and the centrality of the Temple.
> The hypothesis that they brought offerings there when
> religious and political circumstances were favorable
> is compatible with the presently available evidence.[14]

On the other hand, Philo reports that the Essenes showed themselves especially devout in the service of God not by offering sacrifices of animals but by resolving to sanctify their minds (*Quod omnis probus liber sit* 75). G. Klinzing[15] suggests that the contradiction between Philo and Josephus may perhaps be explained as follows:

> The common paradigm asserted that the Essenes did not
> sacrifice in the temple and stayed clear of it because

of different ideas about purity. Philo thus concluded correctly that the Essenes did not sacrifice at all, and he substituted a reason more acceptable to him and his readers for that supplied by the paradigm. Josephus rendered the source more faithfully, but he concluded incorrectly that the Essenes practiced a special form of the sacrificial cult.

The problem of the CD-texts perhaps may be better explained if we refer the laws about the temple and sacrifice either to older traditions or to the expected participation in the restored Jerusalem cult in the future.[16] The problems still remain and should not be harmonized, but these views are not as contradictory as might at first glance appear. Despite the possibility that the present Jerusalem cult was rejected, a basic respect for both temple and sacrifice is common to all these statements.

Let us now turn our attention to the central understanding of atonement in relationship to community and temple as it appears in the Manual of Discipline.

At the outset, we should look at an important passage from that document, 1QS 9,4-5[18]:

> They shall atone for guilty rebellion and for sins of faithlessness that they may obtain favor (rṣwn) for the Land without the flesh of burnt-offerings and without the fat of sacrifice (mbśr ᶜwlwt wmḥlby zbḥ). And the right offering of lips shall be as fragrance of righteousness, and perfection of the way as a pleasing free-will offering (wtrwmt śptym lmśpṭ knyḥwt ṣdq wtmym drk kndbt mnḥt rṣwn).

This passage should be examined in some detail so that some of its problematic elements can be treated.

The interpretation of the preposition min in the phrase mbśr ᶜwlwt wmḥlby zbḥ is problematic here. The following three possibilities have been suggested:

a. Min can be interpreted as "by means of." This understanding, based on the organization of the passage, is reflected in the translation of Wernberg-Møller:

> They shall atone for iniquitous guilt and for sinful faithlessness, and <pay off> (sin) for the earth by means of the flesh of burnt-offerings and from the fat pieces of the sacrifices of right offerings of lips as a proper sweetness, and a perfect way of life as a pleasing freewill offering.

He comments:

> The sacrificial language is retained, the attitude is thoroughly spiritual and there is hardly any doubt that the religious circles behind 1QS did not practice sacrificial cult.[19]

But this interpretation ignores the parallelism of the clauses:

> *wtrwmt śptym lmšpṭ knḥwt ṣdq*
> *w tmym drk kndbt rṣwn.*

        b.   *Min* also can be understood comparatively, but the content of the passage would tend to argue against this interpretation. The Qumran community was not interested in devaluing the concept of sacrifice, but rather in effectively replacing it in the present time, a time devoid of legitimate sacrifice for them.

        c.   The privative[20] use of the preposition appears to me to be the most appropriate explanation. G. Klinzing[21] cites Hos. 6:6 in this context. Of course, in our passage the protest is not prophetic,[23] but priestly. "According to the will of God, something else had to take the place of blood sacrifice. God's pleasure should be gained without sacrifice."[23]

The first part of the passage speaks of the replacement of blood sacrifice, and afterward the proposition is changed to *k*:

> And the right offering of lips shall be as (*k*) a
> fragrance of righteousness, and perfection of the
> way as (*k*) a pleasing free-will offering.

Although the community does not perform sacrifices, it makes atonement by praising God (*trwmt śptym*) and the perfect way of life (*tmym drk*).

This new atonement is founded on the "holy spirit of eternal truth (*rwḥ qdš l'mt*)" (1QS 9,3). The holy spirit not only enables the individual to live a perfect life, it also provides the foundation for the community and its atoning activity. "The community itself has an atoning function."[24] This view of the community is developed in 1QS 9,5-6, which speaks of the establishment within the community of "a house of holiness for Aaron to be united as a holy of holies (*byt qwdš l'hrwn lhwḥd qwdš qwdšym*)" and "a house of community for Israel, who walk in perfection (*wbyt yḥd lyśr'l hhwlkym btmym*)." It is not necessary at this point to delve into the details of the tradition and redaction of this passage in relation to 1QS 5,4-7 and 8,4-8, 8-10.[25] What is important for us is that the temple that brings atonement through the holy spirit and be means of praise to God and the perfect life consists of both priests and laymen. The parallelism of the passages mentioned above emphasizes the connection of atonement with praise to God and the perfect life in the theology of the Qumran community. It also indicates that the community acquired a juridical and retributive function (1QS 8,6f.).

The main passage outlining the relationship among divine spirit, perfect life, and atonement is 1QS 2,25-3,13.[26] It states

that whoever refuses to accept the covenantal obligation to observe
the Torah perfectly cannot become a member of the community because
"contaminations are at his conversion." He cannot be justified so
long as he remains "stubborn of heart." He experiences evil
instead of the salvation expected in the community (3,3: *wḥwšk*
ybyṭ ldrky 'wr) because he who does not enter into God's covenant
"shall not be made guiltless by atonement, nor be purified by the
waters of purification, nor sanctify himself in seas and rivers,
nor be purified in cleansing waters." He remains impure "all the
days of his rejection of the precepts of God" because of "his
refusal to discipline himself in the community of his counsel."
Two points should be emphasized here. First, the rejection of
divine rule is the reason that purification and sanctification are
not received. Second, "discipline" or submission to the divine
rule must be accepted inside the community.

The attainment of atonement and purity, then, is described in
a group of sentences that basically state that God is active in
the community through the spirit: "Through the spirit of true
counsel. . .all his sins will find atonement so that he may behold
the light of life." In other words, he who refuses to follow God's
commands as they are understood by the community obtains neither
atonement nor purification. Atoning rites do not function *ex
opere operato*, for they demand total submission to God's will:
"Then he will be accepted through pleasing atonement before God,
and it shall be to him a covenant of eternal community"
(1QS 3,11f.).[27]

Atonement is not only given to the individual; the entire
community may exercise an atoning function. Only those elected by
God, that is, the completely converted, those living a perfect
life, those who have experienced atonement for themselves, can
bring about atonement within the community for the land.

Purity, sanctification, and atonement depend on the fulfillment of God's will through the perfect life.[28] The temple, represented by the community itself, is founded on the holy spirit,
which enables man to fulfill God's will.

Each and every individual in the Qumran community, whether
priest or layman, was obligated to perform this "temple service,"
and as a sort of full-time "priest on duty," was to adhere to the
strict purification codes. This priestly service was understood
in the Qumran sect as a service in community with the angels.
Community with the angels was construed in a functional way: as
service and praise to God. This praise to God is the "offering of
lips." It is oriented toward praising God "in his mercy" for his

forgiveness of sin.

> In His compassion He draws me near
> and in His mercy He brings my judgment.
> In the righteousness of His truth He judges me.
> And in His great goodness He pardons all my sins.
>
> And in His righteousness He pronounces me clean
> of impurity of man and of sin of mankind,
> in order that I should praise God for His righteousness
> and the Most High for His glory (1QS 11, 14f).

This is also clearly illustrated by the *Hymns* to be the ability to
praise God. It is precisely for this reason that man only then
attains his true destiny. Praise replaces sacrifice and is pleasing to God. The requirement of the exemplary life and cultic
purity is the precondition for the presence of the angels in the
community.

III

Let us now turn our attention to the Temple Scroll.[29] A completely different world is portrayed here. Indeed, at first glance
there seems to be no similarity at all between it and the materials
we have examined above. There is a real temple in the Temple
Scroll, and the priests perform real sacrifices. The scroll contains the minute details of these sacrifices, for both the daily
and special festival offerings. The ritual for the Day of Atonement is described in detail. The rituals described here are more
elaborate than those described in the Pentateuch, and new festival
days, together with their respective sacrifices, have been added.
Everything we have seen above in the Manual of Discipline and the
other Qumran manuscripts is directly contradicted by the Temple
Scroll. Here the community is not the temple; a real temple is
described in terms of its dimensions and the details of its construction. Atonement is effected by sacrifice, not by praise to
God and the perfect life.

It seems appropriate now to ask how these two fundamental but
very different theological conceptions relate to one another. Let
us first outline what the two conceptions have in common. First,
in both, atonement depends on sacrifice and temple. Temple and
sacrifice, however, are defined differently in each. Second, both
conceptions exhibit a respect for sacrifice. The Manual of Discipline does not attempt to eliminate sacrifice, but rather to replace it. The perfect life and praise to God serve as sacrifice.
Third, both share a similar view of the role of the priests. In
the Temple Scroll, naturally, the priests are portrayed in terms of
their service at the temple and in the rites of sacrifice, but they
also are depicted as royal counsel (57,12ff.). In 1QS, despite the

concurrence of priests and laymen and the "democratization" of the
community, the role of laymen is subordinate to that of priests.

But is there not a fundamental mistake here? Should we compare the Temple Scroll to the other Dead Sea Scrolls? Or is the
Temple Scroll perhaps the document of another "unknown Jewish sect"?
These are difficult questions and hardly can be definitively
answered now, in the immediate aftermath of Y. Yadin's magnificent
edition, commentary, and introduction, when scholarly work on the
Temple Scroll has just begun.[30] This work must take into account
all the philological, theological, and historical aspects of the
scroll. My purpose here is to suggest that, despite the obvious
contradiction between the concepts of temple and atonement in the
Qumran texts and those in the Temple Scroll, there is a fundamental
relationship between the historical realities of the Qumran "present" and the future expectation expressed in the Temple Scroll.
Strictly speaking, I neither will nor can answer the question of
whether or not the Temple Scroll is Essene in origin.[31] But the
fact remains that the Temple Scroll is part of the library of the
Qumran community, and the manuscripts and fragments date from the
period in which the Qumran community existed. To be sure, this is
true for other works as well, but, as with the Temple Scroll, the
question of their relationship to the (Essene) Qumran texts must
be raised.

Let us now return to the question of whether or not the group
by or for whom the Temple Scroll was written performed sacrifices
and sought atonement in the manner described there. This question
can be answered only by taking a closer look at the essence and
significance of the temple that is portrayed in the Temple Scroll.
The temple of the Temple Scroll is an idealized temple, the temple
as it should have been, as it was ordained by God. The scroll
depicts the cult that should have been celebrated. How does this
sort of Temple Torah come to be written? Yadin[33] suggests that a
special Temple Torah was necessary for two reasons. First, the
Pentateuch contains no special directions for the construction of
the temple, as it does for the construction of the tabernacle.
Second, I Chron. 28:11ff. expressly states that the plan for the
temple was *all. . .drafted in the hand of the Lord.* "This missing
Torah is provided here [in the Temple Scroll], according to the belief of the author."[34] Strictly speaking, this ideal temple, which
harmonizes Solomon's temple with the post-exilic one, which contains a few similarities to the temple of Ezekiel, and which exhibits "a basic difference between the plan of the courts and its
installations and those of Herod's, as described by Josephus and

the Mishnah,"[35] never existed exactly as it is described in the
Temple Scroll.[36]

For the people of the Qumran community, then, this completes
the reasons for their rejection of the temple in Jerusalem. That
temple had been desecrated by evil priests who followed a false
calendar; the inhabitants of the Holy City did not adhere to the
rules of purity. As J. Neusner[37] has stated, "The Qumran community
believed that the presence of God had left Jerusalem and had come
to the Dead Sea." In terms of the Temple Scroll, one may perhaps
say that God was never present in this temple. The temple of the
Temple Scroll is believed to be the only place where God allows his
glory to dwell. Atonement can be obtained only within its cult.
The atoning function of the sacrifice is emphasized, often in connection with forgiveness. The rite for the Day of Atonement
(26.9f.) states about the sacrificial goat, "And he atones for all
the people of the assembly through it [the goat]; and they will be
forgiven ($wykpr$ bw $^c l$ kwl $^c m$ $hqhl$ $wnslh$ $lhmh$). Atonement formulae
were also used for the new wine and the new oil to purify them for
cultic usage (21,8; 22,15.).[38] The temple of the Temple Scroll itself, however, is to be replaced by an eschatological temple.

An important passage from the Temple Scroll illustrates and
clarifies this relationship between the Temple of the Temple Scroll
and the eschatological temple:

> And I will consecrate my temple by my glory, the
> temple in which I will make my glory dwell, until
> the Day of Blessing, on which I will create my
> temple and establish it for myself for all time,
> like the covenant I have made with Jacob at Bethel
> (29,7-10).[39]

In other words, God desires his *kabod*, his glory, to dwell in the
temple described in the Temple Scroll, and God himself will create
(br') a temple on the Day of Blessing, that is, at the end of time,
which, like the covenant with Jacob at Bethel, will exist for eter-
nity. We will return to this last point shortly because it illustrates the relationship with theological statements of the Qumran
community in a very special way.

Against the background of the perceived illegitimacy of the
Jerusalem temple and the nonexistence of the true temple of the
Temple Scroll, the presence and importance of the Temple Scroll
within the Qumran community suggests that this strictly religious
group understood itself as the temple in which God dwells and in
which atonement is achieved. We do not know when the community
expected God to create this new eschatological temple. It can be

assumed that the community's desert existence was expected to ter-
minate when it was replaced by the temple created by God.

What, then, is the relationship between present and future?
Let us return to the passage from the Temple Scroll, recalling the
sect's understanding of its existence as community with the angels.

> . . . until the Day of Blessing, on which I will create
> my temple and establish it for myself for all time,
> like the covenant I have made with Jacob at Bethel.

O. Betz has suggested that the Temple Scroll understood the ascending and descending angels mentioned in Gen. 28:12 as community with
the angels. If this is correct, then for the Qumran community the
present worship, with its praise to God in community with the
angels (see Jub. 31:14), is nothing less than the anticipation of
the eschatological worship at the Day of Blessing.

J. Maier[40] stresses the importance of Jub. 32, where Levi is
ordained priest in Bethel:

> And Levi discharged the priestly office at Bethel
> before Jacob his father in preference to his ten
> brothers, and he was priest there, and Jacob gave
> his vow: thus he tithed again the tithe to the
> Lord and sanctified it, and it became holy unto him
> (Jub. 32:9, trans. R. H. Charles).

The connection of the priestly service with Bethel (Jub. 31:14)
provides the link between the here-and-now of the Qumran community
and the eschatological expectation of the true temple and its
service.

The Qumran community, in the time of Belial's rule, theologi-
cally dealt with two complex problems--the existence of an illegitimate place of atonement and the nonexistence of the legitimate
place of atonement in which God would dwell--and solved them. It
did this by claiming to represent both temples and simultaneously
anticipating the eschatological temple. On the one hand, it
atoned by perfect life and praise to God in place of the present
but desecrated temple in Jerusalem and the non-present or not-yet-
present true temple of the Temple Scroll. On the other hand, it
participated here and now, through perfect life and praise to God,
in that community and service with the angels which is promised
for the Day of Blessing.

ATONEMENT AT QUMRAN

*My gratitude goes to Mrs. M. Clarkson, Tübingen, who translated a first draft of this paper from the German original. I also am pleased to thank Professor Dr. O. Betz, Professor Dr. M. Hengel, and Mr. B. Janowski of the University of Tübingen for discussing this paper with me in its various stages. Finally, I am grateful to Professor Jacob Neusner for the opportunity to read an earlier version of this paper at the Fourth Max Richter Conversation on Ancient Judaism, Providence, June 1978.

[1]Consider, for instance, the assumption that the major manuscripts from Cave 1 were composed by the Teacher of Righteousness.

[2]For pertinent bibliography, see my *Studien zum Menschenbild in Texten der Qumrangemeinde* (Göttingen, 1980). The work of J. Murphy-O'Connor is especially important; see *BA* 40 (September 1977): 100-124 for bibliography. Also see P. von der Osten-Sacken, *Gott und Belial* StUNT 6 (Göttingen, 1968).

[3]I accept the division of the Hymns into those composed by the Teacher of Righteousness ("Lehrerlieder") and those deriving from unknown members of the Qumran community ("Gemeindelieder"). This follows the hypothesis developed by G. Jeremias, *Der Lehrer der Gerechtigkeit*, StUNT 2 (Göttingen, 1963); also, J. Becker, *Das Heil Gottes*, StUNT 3 (Göttingen, 1964); H.-W. Kuhn, *Enderwartung und gegenwärtiges Heil*, StUNT 4 (Göttingen, 1966); P. Schulz, *Der Autoritätsanspruch des Lehrers der Gerechtigkeit* (Meisenheim am Glan, 1974). The assumption that the Teacher of Righteousness was the author of part of the Hymns fixes the date of their composition to the time after 150 B.C.

[4]As to the date of the War Scroll, the Hasmonean manuscript from 4Q (4QM^c) shows that an early date of the War Scroll is highly probable; cf. M. Baillet, "Le volume VII de 'Discoveries in the Judaean Desert'. Présentation," in M. Delcor, ed., *Qumrân. Sa piété, sa théologie et son milieu* (Paris-Leuven, 1978), p. 79. As new studies have proved, there is a process of redaction that uses traditions from pre-Qumran times; cf. von der Osten-Sacken, op. cit., passim. Also see E. P. Sanders, *Paul and Palestinian Judaism* (London, 1977), p. 251: "It is likely that the War Scroll has an older history, and may not have been originally a sectarian document."

[5]Because the manuscript 1QS is to be dated at about 100 B.C., the composition of the text seems to be close to the foundations of the Qumran community.

[6]1QH 4,37; 17,12; cf. f2,13; cf. P. Garnet, *Salvation and Atonement in the Qumran Scrolls*, WUNT, 2. Reihe, Bd. 3, p. 55f.

[7]1QM 2,5; cf. G. Klinzing, *Die Umdeutung des Kultus in der Qumrangemeinde und im NT*, StUNT 7 (Göttingen, 1971), p. 34f.; Garnet, op. cit., pp. 100-102.

[8]Cultic meaning: 1QS 2,8; 3,6.8; 5,6; 8,6.10; 9,4; cf. Garnet, op. cit., pp. 57-73. Uncultic meaning: 1QS 11,14; cf. Garnet, op. cit., pp. 73-80.

[9] For this survey, see Klinzing, op. cit., pp. 22f.

[10] Concerning this problem, see B. Gärtner, *The Temple and the Community in Qumran and the New Testament*, SNTSMS 1 (Cambridge, 1965), pp. 8f.

[11] On this text, cf. Gärtner, op. cit., pp. 40ff.

[12] Cf. L. Ginsberg, *An Unknown Jewish Sect* (New York, 1976), pp. 70f. The reasons may be as Ginsberg states there: ". . . it appears that the followers of this sect did not possess a sanctuary where they could sacrifice, and for that reason many of them sent their sacrifices to the Temple in Jerusalem, and these persons are here reminded that their prayer is just as acceptable to God as sacrificial offerings."

[13] The translation is from J. M. Baumgarten, "The Essenes and the Temple: A Reappraisal," in his *Studies in Qumran Law*, SJLA 24 (Leiden, 1977), p. 62; cf. J. Strugnell, "Flavius Josephus and the Essenes: Antiquities XVIII. 18-22" *JBL* 77 (1958), pp. 113-115.

[14] Baumgarten, op. cit., p. 74.

[15] Klinzing, op. cit., pp. 48f.: "Die gemeinsame Vorlage berichtete, dass die Essener nicht im Tempel opferten und sich von ihm fernhielten wegen unterschiedlicher Reinheitsvorstellungen. Philo nun folgerte zutreffend, dass die Essener überhaupt nicht opferten und ersetzte die in der Vorlage gegebene Begründung durch eine ihm und seinen Lesern gemässere. Josephus gab die Quelle getreuer wieder, folgerte aber unzutreffend, die Essener hätten einen eigenen Opferkult ausgeübt."

[16] L. H. Schiffman, *The Halakhah at Qumran*, SJLA 16 (Leiden, 1975), p. 129.

[17] This has already been stressed by Ginsberg, op. cit., p. 70.

[18] For the interpretation of this paragraph, cf. in addition to the commentaries to 1QS: J. Carmignac, "L'utilité ou l'inutilité des sacrifices sanglants dans la 'Règle de la Communauté' de Qumrân," *RB* 63 (1956), pp. 524-532; Klinzing, op. cit., pp. 38ff.; Baumgarten, op. cit., pp. 67f.; Sanders, op. cit., pp. 299f. It is to be regretted that the book by Garnet (above, n. 6) was written without noticing the fundamental insights gained by Klinzing.

[19] P. Wernberg-Møller, *The Manual of Discipline* (Leiden, 1957), p. 35 and p. 133, n. 9; similarly, Carmignac, art. cit., p. 526: "à partir de."

[20] Klinzing, op. cit., pp. 39f., contradicted by Baumgarten, op. cit., pp. 67f.

[21] Klinzing, op. cit., pp. 39f.

[22] For the prophetic tradition of criticism of the cult, see Gärtner, op. cit., p. 46.

[23] Klinzing, op. cit., pp. 40f.: "Nach dem Willen Gottes musste jetzt an die Stelle der blutigen Opfer etwas anderes treten. Ohne Opfer sollte das göttliche Wohlgefallen erworben werden."

[24] Sanders, op. cit., p. 300.

[25] Klinzing, op. cit., pp. 50-74.

[26]Klinzing, op. cit., pp. 99-102; J. Neusner, *The Idea of Purity in Ancient Judaism*, SJLA 1 (Leiden, 1973), pp. 52f.; Gärnet, op. cit., pp. 57-60; Sanders, op. cit., p. 304.

[27]Concerning the "echo of Num. 25:13" cf. Garnet, op. cit., pp. 59f.

[28]O. Betz, "Rechtfertigung und Heiligung," in *Rechtfertigung, Realismus, Universalismus in biblischer Sicht*, FS A. Köberle (Darmstadt, 1978), pp. 30-44.

[29]Y. Yadin, *Megillat ham-Miqdaš. The Temple Scroll* (Hebrew Edition) (Jerusalem, 1977), Vol. I-IIIA.

[30]The first German translation and commentary was published by J. Maier, *Die Tempelrolle vom Toten Meer*, UTB 829 (München-Basel, 1978).

[31]This important question received considerable attention at the Richter Conversation in the discussions following this and Professor Schiffman's paper (above, pp. 143-158). Professor B. A. Levine, New York University, argued that the calendar reckoning of the Temple Scroll is non-Essene.

[32]Cf. Maier, op. cit., pp. 69ff.

[33]Yadin, op. cit., Vol. I, p. 70.

[34]Cited according to the summary of a paper read by Professor Yadin at the 1976 "Journées bibliques de Louvain." The French translation appears in Delcor, ed., op. cit., pp. 115-119.

[35]See note 34.

[36]In the discussion at the Richter Conversation, Professor Morton Smith, Columbia University, cautioned against hasty conclusions made on the basis of the comparison of the measurements of the temple in the Temple Scroll to those of the Jerusalem Temple. There may be, as archaeological evidence shows in other cases, considerable differences between pictures or plans and the reality they show.

[37]Neusner, op. cit., p. 50; cf. Gärtner, op. cit., p. 16.

[38]For the use of *kipper*, cf. Yadin, op. cit., Vol. II, p. 286.

[39]Cited according to Yadin's translation in the Louvain paper, above, n. 34. Cf. Yadin, op. cit., Vol. I, pp. 141f., Vol. II, p. 92, and especially the references to the Book of Jubilees.

[40]Maier, op. cit., p. 90.

SCRIPTURE AND TRADITION IN JUDAISM
with special reference to the Mishnah

Jacob Neusner

Brown University

Since we shall shortly celebrate the completion of twenty years from the publication of Geza Vermes' landmark work, *Scripture and Tradition in Judaism*,[1] it is appropriate to borrow his title and take up part of his thoughtful program for this analysis of the role of Scripture in the community represented by the Mishnah, the nature of Scriptural authority in the Mishnah's frame of reference, the relationship between Scripture and the authority of the Mishnah, and the extent to which the structures envisaged by the Mishnah are based upon, or dictated by, Scripture. These four questions cut to the core of the matter of the interplay between Scripture and tradition in Judaism. They force us to take seriously the centrality of Scripture in the formation of tradition--that is, of everything beyond what is not stated in Scripture yet what is deemed authoritative--in the diverse sorts of Judaism known to us from ancient to modern times. For, as everyone knows, one may write the history of Judaism or of Christianity by telling the story of the place and disposition of Scripture in succeeding ages and diverse circles and versions of the two great Scriptural religious traditions. I hasten to add, the remarkable diversity of the versions of Judaism and of Christianity, diversity which renders those encompassing categories (the -ism, the -ity) a mere convenience, warns us never to speak of a single defintion for the nature of Scriptural authority. There can be no single answer, governing the whole of time, for the four questions raised just now.

Let us begin by ridding ourselves of banal but necessary and true observations. First, Scripture is the ultimate authority in Judaism, in all its versions. Second, people do whatever they want with Scripture. Third, while we may speak of the contents, the laws and stories, of Scripture, we also must discuss Scripture as an entity, as a category unto itself. It follows that when we have said that all forms of Judaism appeal to Scripture as the basis of their authority, that all contents of all versions of Judaism may be shown to derive from Scripture through some technology of exegesis or other, when we have rehearsed the standard exegetical apologetic formulated for each and every version of Judaism through the ages, we have said nothing of consequence.

173

The important question is different. It is how we can use the relationship to the Scripture of a community of Judaism to characterize that community, to describe it and interpret its world view. In all, the taxonomy of relationships of diverse communities of Judaism to the single Scripture, the repertoire of verses selected for special attention, the attitudes and doctrines of Scriptural authority and of the origin of non-scriptural laws and theology to Scripture--these kinds of data serve to differentiate one version of Judaism from some other. ` They help us to compare one to another and make sense of each. The point is that when we come to a fact so ubiquitous as the obvious one that Scripture forms the court of ultimate appeal, but that people write the opinions of the court pretty much as lawyers in uncontested cases would want to write them, we uncover a significant point of differentiation and analysis. We have to distinguish and categorize, differentiate and seek a taxonomy for, one type of Judaism as against some other type. It is on the common plane of Scripture that this work can be done.

I

SCRIPTURES AND TRADITIONS

The issue of Scripture and tradition is to be addressed to every sort of Judaism. How is the issue to be phrased? Of what sort of tradition do we speak. Stated most simply, the definition of *tradition* in the biblically-based religions is any canonical truth or normative rite which is believed to be authoritative but which is not directly or explicitly expressed in Scripture. If, then, we say tradition is everything not in Scripture, and our work is to situate tradition in relationship to Scripture, we forthwith must ask for a clearer picture of what we mean by tradition. In this regard, we should return to the simple observation that there are biblical teachings and there is the Bible as a book, a symbol, a sacred thing. So too there are traditions which are practices, stories, comments on what has gone before. And then there is Tradition, which is given an existence unto itself. This latter sense, The Tradition, may be imputed to a particular book, as in the case of the Mishnah. The Tradition may refer also to a corpus of otherwise discrete teachings. This is illustrated by the conception of "oral Torah," which circulated in the history of Judaism and served both as a categorization of the Mishnah and also as a category for holy laws not found in the Scripture or in the Mishnah but assigned the authority of both.

When Vermes speaks of "tradition," he means various stories
told about biblical figures or themes. These are meanings imputed
to the Scripture's materials by later exegetes. The study of
traditions is the study of the history of various ideas--*midrashic*
ideas. It is an effort to consider the history of those ideas in
their original and later settings, to determine the bases of the
history. It is traditions which are to be classified and dated.
So in this context, which, of course, is completely legitimate,
tradition is best replaced by traditions. The comparison of
stories tells us the story of Scripture and later traditions pre-
cipitated by Scripture.

Vermes two decades ago carried the matter to a sophisticated
level, never surpassed, by raising the questions of the origin and
development of exegetical symbolism, the structure and purpose of
the rewriting of the Bible, the historical bond between the Bible
and its interpretation, and the impact of theology on exegesis and
vice versa. The result of this sort of history of ideas is to
tell us when a given set of ideas circulated. Traditions-history
tells us the state of "tradition" *vis à vis* Scripture at various
points in the history of Judaism. The means by which this altogether laudable result is to be attained are to ignore the lines
of particular documents. Those who work on what is called "comparative midrash," that is to say, the comparison and history of
traditions *vis à vis* Scripture, shake out the contents of the
various books of ancient Judaism and Christianity. They create a
jumble of puzzle pieces, reconstructing the original puzzle, the
puzzle broken by the framers of documents as much as by the
scholars who disintegrate the documents into their smallest cog-
nitive components, that is, complete thoughts.

Renée Bloch[2] thus proposed to classify and date traditions
through the established historical and philological criteria, and
yet through two others. First, external, second, internal, comparison would make possible the reconstruction of the whole out of
the scattered parts.[3] Vermes describes this process with the
usual clarity:

> In her view, external comparison consists in confronting
> Rabbinic writings recording undated traditions with
> non-Rabbinic Jewish texts which are at least approximately
> dated.[4]

The result will be that we can show that a story ("a tradition")
found in a late rabbinic document circulated much earlier than the
point at which that late document came to closure. As to the
other:

> Internal comparison...follows the development of a
> tradition within the boundaries of Rabbinic literature
> itself....[5]

The valuable result is the tracing of the history of traditions,
as they surface in one place, then in another. Certainly the most
successful and persuasive results are those of Vermes, typified
(but only typified, not exhausted by any means) in the brilliant
papers on Lebanon, the life of Abraham, the story of Balaam, and
the other topics in the book celebrated just now.

The advantage of this radical procedure, of treating stories
or ideas independent of their documentary, redactional setting, is
to allow the story or idea itself to come under careful analysis.
Its unfolding may be traced over a long span and across many frontiers. But violating the frontiers constituted by the work of
redaction, we no longer are able to raise the questions of political and social description and concrete historical, institutional
analysis that begin when we ask, To whom was this story important?
For telling a story may or may not be an act of politics, a work
of social relevance. But redaction, the formation of a book, the
declaration of a canon, and the decision to preserve and revere a
book and what is in it--these invariably are an act of politics
and a statement of a group, a socially and institutionally consequential deed. That is why traditions-history by itself makes
extremely parlous the social history of ideas and motifs. Even
when we know with some measure of certainty at what *time* a particular conception circulated, we do not then know *who* held that idea.

The exclusion of said idea, story or motif, from its particular redactional setting furthermore means that the story is not
going to be interpreted as part of a whole and cogent system. On
the contrary, the traditions must be considered independent of the
documentary systems to which, at various times and for various
purposes, the tales and ideas proved useful and expressive.
Traditions-history produces historical results essentially useless
for social description.

The relationship between Scripture and tradition depicted by
traditions-history is intellectual, therefore formal and abstract.
Nothing is explained; everything is merely described. The pres-
sing issues of social and institutional description involved in
answering the questions with which we began are reduced to a set
of descriptions of the transfer of motifs and the development and
circulation of themes. Or we may be told, in stupefying description lacking all analysis, what irritant in Scripture triggered
the formation of a particular pearl of midrash. That is yet

another exercise in empty formalism. People made books and preserved and revered them for social purposes. The contents of books, removed from the limns of their covers, float out of reach when who told a story and why are questions deemed not to be asked. It is as if in archaeology the site was ignored, the objects displayed in a museum with other objects from somewhere else--and yet we wish to know something about material culture and the concrete context of that material culture.

That is why, when we stand back and reconsider the four questions with which we began, we cannot make progress. On the basis of the meaning legitimately assigned by Vermes and others to the word "tradition," we are not able to answer those social and political questions of tradition. Such questions assume and require a different understanding of the same word. That fact will constitute a step forward in the phrasing of the questions of Scripture and tradition, Scriptural authority, and related issues.

"Traditions," in the sense of stories or tales or interpretations of Scriptural figures or motifs, travel from one group to another. Let us dwell on the implications of fact, which Vermes and other scholars of traditions-history in Judaism have amply demonstrated and explained. We sometimes notice that a story may occur in a Hellenistic Jewish framework redacted early, and in a rabbinic text redacted much later. Then if the story is early, it cannot be rabbinic (all the more so: Pharisaic). If it is rabbinic (Pharisaic), then it cannot be early. Occurrence in a Hellenistic provenance tells us that the point and purpose of story, whatever its origins, cannot be deemed quintessentially rabbinic. The tradition thus cannot tell us about the conceptions of Scripture held in the formative circles of rabbinism, that is, among the people who gave to rabbinic Judaism its distinctive modes of reading Scripture and its particular conceptions of the place and meaning of Scripture. On the contrary, the historical question to be asked in the context of discovery that a story is early is what the later *entry* into the rabbinic system of such a quintessentially non-rabbinic story tells us about the later history of the rabbinic system itself. We must reckon with the point at which the story was found authoritative. We then may speculate on those traits of the story that were found attractive, therefore self-evidently authoritative. Consequently, we learn much about the unfolding and development not only of the kind of Judaism that made up the story but also of the kind of Judaism that received the story and discerned its authenticity to its already-defined world view and way of life.

So the history of traditions shown to be early and, let us say, Essenic, or located in pseudepigraphic apocalypse, or originally found in the writings of Pseudo-Philo, or Philo, or Hellenistic Jewish philosophy or historiography, in patristic writings or in Targumim--the history of such traditions tells us that we can not speak about the place of those stories in rabbinical circles that made them up. For they were made up elsewhere. It follows that the stories tell us nothing about the authority and role of Scripture in those adoptive circles. What we know is that simple banality with which we began: Scripture was important and authoritative. No important insight follows. The reason is that there are no points of differentiation, therefore no important questions or generative and encompassing tensions to be discerned.

In this setting I need hardly dwell on the fact that we are equally paralyzed before the other questions critical to an understanding of Scripture and tradition in Judaism. We cannot speak of the character of Scriptural authority in the traditions when they are viewed as discrete stories. We cannot describe the relationship between Scripture and authoritative structures of the adoptive community. The reason, to repeat, is that, by breaking up tradition into traditions, we no longer are able to speak of a community that receives whole and integrated a given corpus of traditions and deems the whole to constitute its tradition. To be concrete, we cannot describe a community that shaped its life around the authority of the Targumim. All the more so are we unable to trace the principal characteristics, whether social or doctrinal, of a community behind, e.g., the understanding of the word Lebanon as the Temple, as Vermes brilliantly traces it.

This does not mean that there is no historical insight in the historical successes of Vermes and others in comparative midrash. Vermes furnishes rich historical insight. We learn how earthshaking events came to full expression through Scriptural exegesis. The fact that, in the aftermath of the destruction of the second Temple, the word *Lebanon* took on weighty meanings associated with the destruction, surely is a major insight into the formation of the tradition on the word *Lebanon*. But it then is the tradition which is the object of study; its history is what we learn. So when "tradition" means "traditions," then history is the history of traditions. The history of traditions tells us about ideas held in the sectors of Jewish world in which the history of the traditions took shape. But these are not cogent or even identifiably concrete groups.

Before proceeding, I want to dismiss the notion that knowing the technology of tradition-making, that is, the *how* of exegesis, we learn anything compelling or suggestive about the history of traditions. One of the many strengths in Vermes's work is his reticence to "explain" merely on the basis of some trait of a verse subject to exegesis how an exegete reached a particular con- clusion. Those who conceive that, by showing the formal bases of a meaning imputed to a Scripture, they have accounted for the for- mation of that meaning, seem to me to stand altogether too much within the tradition of formal exegesis to make a contribution to historical study. When we can discern a formal trait that trig- gered a substantive comment, we answer the question of the role of Scripture in a purely formal way. Scripture then becomes a set of discrete grammatical and syntactical problems. And so it was--but only after the decision had been reached to accord to those prob- lems the generative focus that allows them to yield their insight into how conclusions were reached. The authority of Scripture is prior to the exegesis of its formal, as much as of substantive, traits. If we can explain what in Scripture stands behind a par- ticular tradition, if we can point to the '*et* or *raq* or the '*ak* that supposedly served to exclude or to include, we gain nothing but a renewed expression of the simple banality: Scripture is important and authoritative. We do not know why, how, or for whom, any more than we did before we discovered the '*et* or the '*ak* and concluded that, indeed, ^cAqiba and Nahum of Gimzu were "right."

One of the marks of scholarly greatness is reticence, the presence of informed silence. In this regard Vermes is a model for us all. He is not a participant in the formal mode of exegesis recommended at certain points in the history of Judaism. He is a scholar of what was done within that mode, as of what was done with much else. He never asks us to believe, therefore, that the given "tradition" is natural, right, authentic, or, therefore, norma- tive,"[6] because it states what Scripture "really" says and means. That apologic is not part of his repertoire, or, in consequence, part of the repertoire of the present, flourishing generation of traditions-historians.

II
SCRIPTURE AND TRADITION

Let me review the argument before proceeding to take up the questions with which I started, now in the context that I believe does permit suitable differentiation and therefore development of suitable responses. I pointed out that when by "tradition" we mean "traditions about matters relevant to Scripture, but not

located in Scripture" or "traditions about the meaning of specific
Scriptural verses," we undertake a rich inquiry into the history
of ideas. When successful, that inquiry shows us how historical
events contributed to the shaping of ideas ("traditions"). It is
possible to classify and date traditions. These facts allow us
insight into the relationship of various verses or motifs of Scripture to traditions. But they leave in an undifferentiated and one-
dimensional framework that matter, with which we began, of the
authority and impact of Scripture. We reach an impasse. Important
questions about Scripture and tradition in Judaism cannot be
confronted.

The reason is not difficult to see. When we speak of Scripture and tradition in the comparative-*midrashic* context of traditions-history, we really mean, as I just now said, various Scriptures and various traditions. That meaning is valid, fructifying,
legitimate. But when we ask about Scriptures and traditions, our
answers cannot then be used for the present inquiry, which now
appears as separate and distinct.

That is to say, when we treat Scripture as a single thing, we
must also find its counterpart in tradition. That too must be
appropriately single, not merely a collection of things. Our
questions on the nature of Scriptural authority, the relationship
between Scripture and the authority of tradition, the extent to
which structures are based on or dictated by Scripture, the role
of Scripture in the community of Judaism—these questions require
that the answers be framed in a way closely congruent to the categories introduced by the questions themselves. If the subject is
Scripture, the simile cannot speak of traditions. We must rather
take up the matter of tradition, viewed as an entity with its own
being, as much as Scripture is viewed as an entity with its own
being.

Introducing the language of "entity" and "own being" does not
answer any questions. But it defines the terms of an answer.
These terms are to be discovered in the character of Scripture itself. We look for something like *Scripture*, seeking a meaning for
tradition that is like the meaning we impute to *Scripture*. Scripture is treated as generative of an analogy, so we want to locate
an appropriately responsive analogy. Now if Scripture is the base
of the analogy, then what is like Scripture, the simile, in a
simple way must be like Scripture, in a way that begs no questions.
The obvious solution to the problem of locating an appropriate
analogy is to regard the entity, Scripture, as a species of the
genus, book. What makes Scripture into a distinctive entity is

the fact that it is a closed canon and autonomous corpus of authoritative writings. I cannot think of a more fundamental and unex-
ceptionable statement of what sort of entity Scripture is.

Then what sort of tradition is it which, to begin with, also
constitutes a closed canon and autonomous corpus of writings? In
the history of Christianity and Judaism, there are many such collections. But these would not be deemed analogous to Scripture
unless, like Scripture, they are regarded as a canon and holy too.
Scripture is a holy book. So if in the history of Judaism we look
for our analogy among other holy books, we are on the right path.
There are not a few such holy books. There in fact are a great
many. To each of the holy books, books deemed *torah* and part of
the Torah of Moses "our rabbi," must be asked those same questions
with which we began: what is the role of Scripture in the community which produced and which reveres this holy book? the
character of Scriptural authority in this holy book? the relationship between Scripture and authoritative structures of the community behind this holy book ("which reveres this holy book"),
including disciplinary and doctrinal statements, decisions, and
interpretations? and, finally, to what extent are community structures (repeating the just-stated qualifications) based upon or
dictated by Scripture?

As I said, the history of Judaism yields many holy books,
revered by communities large or small. In choosing the Mishnah I
take up a book which from its time onward was received as a holy
book. More important: we can isolate in the Talmudic and later
rabbinic literature that community of Judaism which revered the
Mishnah, and which therefore reveals authoritative structures and
doctrines and decisions flowing from the Mishnah. By contrast, it
is exceedingly difficult to point to that community which revered
the holy book constituted by the Targumim, or, therefore, to ask
about the authoritative structures and doctrines of "the Targumic
community." We have the advantage, moreover, of seeing how the
Mishnah was brought into relationship with Scripture. So in due
course we confront the several questions that, all together, correctly phrase the critical issue of the relationship of Scripture
to tradition in Judaism. So the Mishnah is a suitable choice,
among many appropriate candidates, for specification as "tradition"
in the sense of "the Tradition." Why? First, because it does
address a particular community at a specific time. Second, because
the very critical question at the center of this discourse in fact
confronted the very framers of the Mishnah and their immediate
successors. The question now is appropriate to the data.

III

SCRIPTURE AND THE MISHNAH

Having spent so long on defining the question and locating the appropriate evidence to be used in answering the question, we now benefit from our laborious exercise. For stating the facts and answering the questions become entirely straightforward exercises, requiring no speculation, producing no confusion.

First, what is the role of Scripture in the Mishnah? The answer is that, on the surface, Scripture plays little role. The Mishnah rarely cites a verse of Scripture rarely refers to Scripture as an entity, rarely links its own ideas to those of Scripture, and rarely lays claim to originate in what Scripture has said, even by indirect or remote allusion to a Scriptural verse or teaching. So, superficially, the Mishnah is tradition totally indifferent to Scripture. That impression, moreover, is re-enforced by the traits of the language of the Mishnah. The framers of Mishnaic discourse never attempt to imitate the language of Scripture, as do those of the Essene writings at Qumran. The very redactional structure of Scripture, found so serviceable to the writer of the Temple scroll, is of no interest whatever to the organizers of the Mishnah and its tractates, except in a few cases (Yoma, Pesahim).

I wish now to dwell on these facts. Formally, redactionally, and linguistically the Mishnah stands in splendid isolation from Scripture. This is something that had to be confronted as soon as the Mishnah came to closure and was presented as authoritative to the Jewish community of the Holy Land and of Babylonia. It is not possible to point to many parallels, that is, cases of anonymous books, received as holy, in which the forms and formulations (specific verses) of Scripture play so slight a role. People commonly imitate the Scripture's language. They cite concrete verses. They claim (at the very least) that direct revelation has come to them, so that what they say stands on an equal plane with Scripture. The internal evidence of the Mishnah's sixty-two usable tractates (excluding Abot), by contrast, in no way suggests that anyone pretended to talk like Moses, write like Moses, claimed to cite and correctly interpret things that Moses had said, or even alleged to have had a revelation like that of Moses and so to stand on the mountain with Moses. There is none of this. So the claim of Scriptural authority for the Mishnah's doctrines and institutions is difficult to locate within the internal evidence of the Mishnah itself.

We cannot be surprised that, in consequence of this amazing

position of autonomous authority implicit in the character of
Mishnaic discourse, the Mishnah should have demanded in its own
behalf some sort of apologetic. Nor are we surprised that the
Mishnah attracted its share of quite hostile criticism. The issue
then, in the third century, was precisely the issue phrased when
we ask about the authority of tradition in Judaism: Why should we
listen to this mostly anonymous document, which makes statements
on the nature of institutions and social conduct, statements we
obviously are expected to keep? Who are Meir, Yosé, Judah, Simeon,
and Eleazar--people who lived fifty or a hundred years ago--that
we should listen to what they have to say? God revealed the Torah.
Is this too part of the Torah? If so, how? What, in other words,
is the relationship of the Mishnah to Scripture, and how does the
Mishnah claim authority over us such as we accord to the revelation
to Moses by God at Mount Sinai?

There are two important responses to the question of the place
of Scripture in the Mishnaic tradition.

First and the more radical: the Mishnah constitutes *torah*.
It too is a statement of revelation "to Moses at Sinai." But this
part of revelation has come down in a form different from the
well-known written part, the Scripture. This tradition truly
deserves the name "tradition," because for a long time it was
handed down orally, not in writing, until given the written formulation now before us in the Mishnah. This sort of apologetic for
the Mishnah appears, to begin with, in Abot, with its stunning
opening chapter, linking Moses on Sinai through the ages to the
earliest-named authorities of the Mishnah itself, the five pairs,
on down to Shammai and Hillel. Since some of the named authorities
in the chain of tradition appear throughout the materials of the
Mishnah, the claim is that what these people say comes to them
from Sinai through the processes of *qabbalah* and *massoret*--handing
down, traditioning.

So the reason that the Mishnah does not cite Scripture is that
it does not have to. It stands on the same plane as Scripture.
It enjoys the same authority as Scripture. This radical position
is still more extreme than that taken by pseudepigraphic writers,
who imitate the style of Scripture and sign the names of prophets
or others who received revelations, or who claim to speak within
that same gift of revelation as Moses. It is one thing to say
one's holy book is Scripture because it is like Scripture, or to
claim that the author of the holy book has a revelation independent of that of Moses. These two positions, it seems to me, still
concede to the Torah of Moses the analogical priority over their

own holy books. The Mishnah's apologists make no such concession when they allege that the Mishnah is part of the Torah of Moses. They appeal to the highest possible authority in the Israelite framework, claiming the most one can claim in behalf of the book which, in fact, bears the names of men who lived fifty years before the apologists themselves. That seems to me remarkable courage.

Then there is this matter of the Mishnah's not citing Scripture. When we consider the rich corpus of allusions to Scripture in other holy books, both those hearing the names of authors and those presented anonymously, we realize that the Mishnah claims its authority to be co-equal with that of Scripture. Many other holy books are made to lay claim to authority only because they depend upon the authority of Scripture and state the true meaning of Scripture. That fact brings us to the second answer to the question of the place of Scripture in the Mishnaic tradition, the position that the Mishnah is contingent upon Scripture. It is the result of exegesis of Scripture.

The two Talmuds and the legal-exegetical writings produced in the two hundred years after the closure of the Mishnah take the position that the Mishnah is wholly dependent upon Scripture. Whatever is of worth in the Mishnah can be shown to derive directly from Scripture. So the Mishnah--tradition--is deemed distinct from, and subordinate to, Scripture. This position is expressed in an obvious way. Once the Talmuds cite a Mishnah-pericope, they commonly ask, "What is the source of these words?" And the answer invariably is, "As it is said in Scripture." This constitutes not only a powerful defense for the revealed truth of the Mishnah. It also bespeaks a profound criticism of the character of the Mishnah. For when the exegetes find themselves constrained to add, they admit the need to improve and correct an existing flaw.

That the search for the Scriptural bases for the Mishnah's laws constitutes both an apologetic and a criticism is shown in the character of a correlative response to the Mishnah, namely, the Sifra and its exegesis of Leviticus.[7] This rhetorical exegesis follows a standard syntactical-redactional form. Scripture will be cited. Then a statement will be made about its meaning, or a statement of law correlative to that Scripture will be given. Finally the author of Sifra invariably states, Now is this not (merely) logical? And the point of that statement will be, Can this position not be gained through the working of mere logic, based upon facts supplied (to be sure) by Scripture? The polemical power of Sifra lies in its repetitive demonstration that the stated position, commonly, though not always, a verbatim or near-verbatim citation of a Mishnah-pericope, is not only *not* the product of logic, but is, and can only be, the product of an exegesis of Scripture.

What is still more to the point, that exegesis is formal in its character. That is, it is based upon some established mode of exegesis of the formal traits of Scriptural grammar and syntax, assigned to the remote antiquity represented by the names of Ishmael or ^cAqiba. So the polemic of Sifra is against the positions that, first, what the Mishnah says (in the Mishnah's own words) is merely logical; and, second, that the position taken by the Mishnah can have been reached, in any way other than through grammatical-syntactical, hence formal, exegesis of Scripture. That other way, the way of reading the Scripture through philosophical logic or practical reason, is explicitly rejected time and again. Philosophical logic is inadequate. Formal exegesis is shown to be not only adequate but necessary and inexorable. It follows that Sifra undertakes to demonstrate precisely what the framers of the opening pericopae of the Talmuds' treatment of the Mishnah's successive units of thought also wish to show. The Mishnah is not autonomous. It is not independent. It is not correlative, separate but equal. It is contingent, secondary, derivative, resting wholly on the foundations of the (written) revelation of God to Moses at Mount Sinai. Therein, too, lies the authority of the Mishnah as tradition.

If, at this point in the argument, we should stand back and deal with our program of questions, we should offer the following answers.

First, tradition in the form of the Mishnah is deemed autonomous of Scripture and enjoys the same authority as that of Scripture. The reason is that Scripture and ("oral") tradition are merely two media for conveying a single corpus of revealed law and doctrine. Or, tradition in the form of the Mishnah is true because it is not autonomous of Scripture. Tradition is secondary and dependent upon Scripture.

The authority of the Mishnah is the authority of Moses. That authority comes to the Mishnah directly and in an unmediated way, because the Mishnah's words were said by God to Moses at Mount Sinai and faithfully transmitted through a process of oral formulation and oral transmission from that time until those words were written down by Judah the Patriarch at the end of the second century. Or, that authority comes to the Mishnah indirectly, in a way mediated through the written Scriptures.

What the Mishnah says is what the Scripture says, when

Scripture is rightly interpreted. The authority of tradition lies
in its correct interpretation of the Scripture. Tradition bears
no autonomous authority. It is not an independent entity, and
correlative with Scripture. A technology of exegesis of grammar
and syntax is needed to build the bridge between tradition as contained in the Mishnah and Scripture, the original utensil shaped
by God and revealed to Moses to convey the truth of revelation to
the community of Israel. Or matters are otherwise. I hardly need
to make them explicit.

These same either-or, yes-and-no, answers of course are to be
formulated to deal with the matters of the relationship between
Scripture and the authoritative structures of the community, both
discipline and doctrine, and the extent to which community structures are based upon or dictated by Scripture. If we regard the
Mishnah as independent revelation, "oral Torah" in the strict
sense, then we must deem tradition to be a kind of Torah. If we
regard the Mishnah as contingent, then tradition stands in a very
close and comfortable bond with Scripture: Scripture's companion,
complement, necessary consequence. So the Mishnah may be deemed
(to invoke the appropriate metaphor), depending upon the position
you take, to be the daughter of Scripture or the wife.

IV

THE FACTS OF THE MATTER

Matters are not to be left with a mere description of opinions about a second-century holy book held by contentious third-
century philosopher-theologian-exegetes. Our generation has
access to an independent stance. We can ask the question all over
again, wholly free of the phrasing of the question from the third
century to our own day. For we may state the facts of the matter.
We know what the relationship between the Mishnah and Scripture
really is.

There are two sides to the question. First, we must speak of
the principal components of the Mishnah, bearers of its doctrines
and ideas. Second, we must evaluate the claim of the Mishnah itself, asking not about its relationship to Scripture in general,
but its relationship to particular components of Scripture. So
we conclude with that point with which we began, only we do so by
turning the question around. From asking about Scripture and the
Mishnah, we turn at the end to discuss the Mishnah and Scripture:
what statement does the Mishnah make about Scripture?

The components of the Mishnah are formed of its six divisions,
themselves divided into tractates. My studies[8] of the relationship

of each of the sixty-two usable tractates (omitting Abot, which
has no internal relationship to Scripture, but a rich external one
in its frequent citations of Scripture) lead to the following
simple generalizations.

1. First, there are tractates which simply repeat in their
own words precisely what Scripture has to say, and at best serve
to amplify and complete the basic ideas of Scripture. For example,
all of the cultic tractates of the second division, the one on
Appointed Times, which tell what one is supposed to do in the
Temple on the various special days of the year, and the bulk of
the cultic tractates of the fifth division, which deals with Holy
Things, simply restate facts of Scripture. For another example,
all of those tractates of the sixth division, on Purities, which
specify sources of uncleanness, depend completely on information
supplied by Scripture. I have demonstrated in detail that every
important statement in Niddah, on menstrual uncleanness, and the
most fundamental notions of Zabim, on the uncleanness of the person with flux referred to in Leviticus, Chapter Fifteen, as well
as every detail in Negaim, on the uncleanness of the person or
house suffering the uncleanness described in Leviticus Chapters
Thirteen and Fourteen--all of these tractates serve only to restate the basic facts of Scripture and to complement those facts
with other important but derivative ones.

2. There are, second, tractates which take up facts of
Scripture but work them out in a way in which those Scriptural
facts cannot have led us to predict. A supposition in said tractates concerning what is important *about* the facts, a generative
issue utterly remote from the suppositions or points of interest
of Scripture, will explain why the Mishnah-tractates under discussion in confronting those Scripturally-provided facts say the
original things they say. For one example, Scripture (Num. 19:1ff.)
takes for granted that the red cow will be burned in a state of
uncleanness, because it is burned outside of the camp-Temple. The
priestly writers cannot have imagined that a state of cultic
cleanness was to be attained outside of the cult. The absolute
datum of tractate Parah, by contrast, is that cultic cleanness not
only can be attained outside of the 'tent of meeting.' The red
cow was to be burned in a state of cleanness even exceeding that
cultic cleanness required in the Temple itself. The problematic
that generates the intellectual agendum of Parah, therefore, is
how to work out the conduct of the rite of burning the cow in
relationship to the Temple: is it to be done in exactly the same
way, or in exactly the opposite way? This mode of contrastive and

analogical thinking--something is either like something else, therefore it follows its rule, or something is different from something else, therefore follows the exact opposite of its rule-- helps us to understand the generative problematic of such tractates as Erubin and Besah, to mention only two.

3.   And third, there are, predictably, many tractates that either take up problems in no way suggested by Scripture, or begin from facts at best merely relevant to facts of Scripture. In the former category are Tohorot, on the cleanness of foods, with its companion, Uqsin; Demai, on doubtfully tithed produce; Tamid, on the conduct of the daily whole-offering; Baba Batra, on rules of real estate transactions and certain other commercial and property relationships; and so on. In the latter category are Ohalot, which spins out its strange problems within the theory that a tent and a utensil are to be compared to one another (!), Kelim, on the susceptibility to uncleanness of various sorts of utensils, Miqvaot, on the sorts of water which effect purification from un- cleanness, and many others. These tractates amply draw on facts of Scripture. But the problems confronted in these tractates in no way respond to problems important to Scripture. What we have here is a prior program of inquiry, which will make ample provi- sion for facts of Scripture in an inquiry to begin with generated essentially outside of the framework of Scripture.

So there we have it: some tractates merely repeat what we find in Scripture; some are totally independent of Scripture; and some fall in-between. Clearly, we are no closer to a definitive answer to the question of Scripture and tradition than we were when we described the state of thought on the very same questions in the third and fourth centuries. We find everything and its opposite.

But to offer a final answer, we have to take that fact seri- ously. The Mishnah in no way is so remote from Scripture as its formal omission of citations of verses of Scripture suggests. In no way, however, can it be described as contingent upon, and secondary to, Scripture, as its third-century apologists claimed. But the right answer is not that it is somewhere in-between. Scripture confronts the framers of the Mishnah as revelation, not merely a source of facts. But the framers of the Mishnah have their own world with which to deal. They make statements within the framework, and to the fellowship, of their own age and genera- tion. They are bound, therefore, to come to Scripture with a set of questions generated other than in Scripture. They bring their own ideas about what is going to be important to Scripture. That is perfectly natural.

The philosophers of the Mishnah concede to Scripture the highest authority. At the same time what they will choose to hear, among the authoritative statements of Scripture, will in the end form a statement of its own. To state matters simply: all of Scripture is authoritative. But only some of Scripture is deemed relevant. And what happens is that the framers and philosophers of the tradition of the Mishnah come to Scripture when they have reason to. That is to say, they bring to Scripture a program of questions and inquiries framed essentially among themselves. So they were highly selective. Their program itself constitutes a statement *upon* the meaning of Scripture. They and their apologists of one sort hasten to add, their program consists of a statement *of* the meaning of Scripture. I think that often is true. But it always is beside the point.

In part, we must affirm the truth of that claim. When the framers of the Mishnah speak about the priestly passages of the Mosaic law codes, with deep insight they perceive profound layers of meaning embedded ("to begin with") in those codes. What they have done with the Priestly Code (P), moreover, they also have done, though I think less coherently, with the bulk of Deuteronomic laws and with some of those of the Covenant Code. But their exegetical triumph--exegetical, not merely eisegetical--lies in their handling of the complex corpus of materials of P. Theirs is a powerful statement on the meaning of Scripture, not merely a restatement of the meaning thereof.

True, others will have selected totally different passages of Scripture. Surely we must concede that, in reading those passages, they displayed that same perspicacity as did the framers of the Mishnaic tradition who interpreted the priestly code as they did. It is in the nature of Scripture itself that such should be the case. For, after all, Jeremiah and the framers of Deuteronomy are near contemporaries (though so too are the authors of important parts of Leviticus and Ezekiel). The same Scripture that gives us the prophets gives us the Pentateuch as well--and gives priority to the Pentateuchal codes as the revelation of God to Moses.

The authority of Scripture therefore is what we said in our rehearsal of the banal, but accurate view. Scripture is authoritative--once we have made our choice of which part of Scripture we shall read. Scripture generates important and authoritative structures of the community, including disciplinary and doctrinal statements, decisions, and interpretations--once we have determined

which part of Scripture we shall ask to provide those statements
and decisions. Community structures are wholly based on Scripture.
But Scripture is not wholly and exhaustively expressed in those
structures. Scripture has entirely dictated the character of formative structures of the Mishnah. But the Mishnah is not the
result of the dictation of close exegesis of Scripture, except
after the fact.

Let me close by giving a concrete example of that fact. We
recall that the Pharisees maintained Israelites should eat their
ordinary food, not meat or grain deriving from, and sanctified for,
the cult, in a state of cultic cleanness. They held that Israelites both should and can attain a state of cultic cleanness outside
of the Temple. Israelites can and should pretend to be priests by
eating their ordinary food at home as if they were priests engaged
in eating the priestly portions of Holy Things in the Temple.

Now when someone with the Pharisaic problematic in mind
opened Scripture, attention will have been drawn to the conception
that cleanness in respect to unclean bodily discharges must be
kept so that the tabernacle will be clean (Lev. 15:31): *Thus you
shall keep the people of Israel separate from their uncleanness,
lest they die in their uncleanness by defiling my tabernacle that
is in their midst.* But the menstruant, *Zab*, *Zabah*, and woman
after childbirth do not go to the Temple. The Priestly Code is
explicit that a rite of purification must be undertaken by the
last three named (Lev. 15:13-15 for the *Zab*, Lev. 15:28-30 for
the *Zabah*, and Lev. 12:6-8 for the woman after childbirth).
Accordingly, someone reading the Scripture will have asked himself,
How are the unclean people going to make the Temple unclean, when,
in point of fact, before they are able to enter its precincts,
they undergo the rite of purification Scripture itself specifies?
And, he will have answered, the people of Israel itself, *in whose
midst is the tabernacle*, is to be kept clean, so that the tabernacle which is in their midst will be in a clean setting. It will
follow that the rules of cleanness in general pertaining to the
Temple must apply as well to the people outside of the Temple.

The rules of menstrual uncleanness and comparable uncleanness
in the beginning, before the revision accomplished by the priestly
redactors of the fifth century B.C., had nothing to do with the
cult. Menstrual taboos are not associated with the cult even in
the very pericopae of the Priestly Code which refer to them. It
is only in the subscription that the Priestly Code naturally
insists upon an integral and necessary relationship between menstrual taboos and the cult, and this, as I said, is even

redactionally claimed only after the fact. We assume that everyone avoided having sexual relations with menstruating women, without regard to whether or not he intended to go to the Temple,
indeed to whether or not he even lived in the Land of Israel.
That fact then invites the conclusion, reached by the Pharisaism
known to us in the Gospels and in the rabbinical traditions attributed to authorities before 70 whom we assume to be Pharisees,
that the people must be kept clean for life in the land which is
holy, a conception explicit in the Priestly Code. Land, people,
Temple--all form an integrated and whole realm of being, to be kept
clean so as to serve as the locus of the sacred. Israel must be
clean because of the tabernacle in their midst. *Because the tabernacle is in their midst, Israel must be clean, even when not in
the tabernacle,* which is exactly what Lev. 15:31 says--to a
Pharisee.

NOTES

SCRIPTURE AND TRADITION IN JUDAISM

[1]Leiden, 1961: E. J. Brill. 2nd ed., 1973.

[2]Vermes, pp. 7ff. William Scott Green and others have translated the principal papers on comparative midrash by Renée Bloch. See William Scott Green, ed., *Approaches to Ancient Judaism: Theory and Practice* (Missoula, 1978: Scholars Press for Brown Judaic Studies), pp. 29-76. In that same book is published Jonathan Z. Smith, "Sacred Persistence: Towards a Redescription of Canon" (Green, ed., pp. 11-28), which should be understood as the platform upon which the remainder of this paper stands.

[3]This notion of "the whole" then refers to the story, and "the scattered parts" are the diverse versions of the story, thus the various books in which the tale makes an appearance. As I shall argue in a moment, this approach to the history of traditions in relationship to Scripture answers important questions about the intellectual and formal history of traditions, while rendering impertinent other important questions about the social history of traditions and of the institutions built upon them, in relationship to Scripture.

[4]Vermes, *loc. cit.*

[5]*Ibid.*

[6]For a discussion of the claim of normativity, see F. C. Porter's review of Moore's *Judaism*, cited at length in my *Judaism: The Evidence of the Mishnah* (in press at The University of Chicago Press).

[7]This is less blatant in Sifré for Numbers and Deuteronomy, though the same motif does surface.

[8]*A History of the Mishnaic Law of Purities* (Leiden, 1974-1977: E. J. Brill), I-XXII; *...of Holy Things* (Leiden, 1978-1979), I-IV; *...of Women* (Leiden, 1979-1980), I-V; *...Appointed Times* (Leiden, 1980-1981), I-V; and *...of Damages* (Leiden, 1981-1982), I-V.

INDEX OF BIBLICAL, RABBINIC, AND CLASSICAL SOURCES

GENERAL INDEX